CHANGING BEHAVIOUR

in Schools

CHANGING BEHAVIOUR

in Schools

Promoting Positive Relationships and Wellbeing

by

Sue Roffey

$SAGE

Los Angeles | London | New Delhi
Singapore | Washington DC

First published 2011

SAGE Publications Ltd
1 Oliver's Yard
55 City Road
London EC1Y 1SP

SAGE Publications Inc.
2455 Teller Road
Thousand Oaks, California 91320

SAGE Publications India Pvt Ltd
B 1/I 1 Mohan Cooperative Industrial Area
Mathura Road
New Delhi 110 044

SAGE Publications Asia-Pacific Pte Ltd
33 Pekin Street #02-01
Far East Square
Singapore 048763

Library of Congress Control Number: 2010925033

British Library Cataloguing in Publication data

A catalogue record for this book is available from
the British Library

ISBN 978-1-84920-077-6
ISBN 978-1-84920-078-3 (pbk)

Typeset by C&M Digitals (P) Ltd, Chennai, India
Printed and bound in Great Britain by TJ International, Padstow, Cornwall
Printed on paper from sustainable resources

This book is dedicated to the many unsung heroes in our schools who bring hope to the lives of vulnerable and challenging students.

CONTENTS

ACKNOWLEDGEMENTS

There are many students, teachers, colleagues and friends who have helped with this book in diverse ways. Fellow educators have provided case studies and anecdotes of good practice to illustrate and enrich the message that is here. Names and details have been changed. In particular I would like to acknowledge those dedicated individuals who have attended Circle Solutions trainer courses.

My thanks are due to the schools, students, teachers, colleagues and parents who have participated in the specific research studies that support the evidence base for good practice. Your stories have been inspirational.

I am immensely grateful to all those cited in the text whose work as practitioners and researchers has provided the evidence and foundation for the approaches advocated. If your name appears anywhere in the book please accept my thanks.

I would also like to acknowledge the tireless efforts of colleagues at Antidote in the UK, CASEL in the US and Wellbeing Australia.

Thanks to my dear friends and colleagues, Dominic Boddington and Elizabeth Gillies both of whom read drafts and gave helpful feedback.

Jude Bowen and Amy Jarrold at Sage were consistently supportive and efficient. It is a real pleasure to work with such high levels of friendly professionalism.

My partner David not only read the whole manuscript (many times!) but also formatted, checked references, helped with permissions, made tea and was constantly encouraging. I really couldn't have done it without him. My love as ever.

Finally, thanks to Emma for letting me use her desk for weeks last summer in London and to Ben for willingly sharing his car. You might not realise how much this helped get the book written but it did – another example of systems at work!

ABOUT THE AUTHOR

Sue Roffey spent many years teaching students with challenging behaviour in both mainstream and specialist provision. She is now an educational psychologist, consultant, writer and academic specialising in social, emotional and behavioural issues. An adjunct research fellow at the University of Western Sydney and an honorary lecturer at University College, London, Sue now divides her time between England and Australia.

Sue has been involved with Australian Government scoping studies on Student Wellbeing and Social and Emotional Learning. She also works for NAPCAN – the National Association for the Prevention of Child Abuse and Neglect in Australia and is a founder member of the Wellbeing Australia network.

Sue is a prolific writer of books, academic papers, media articles and teacher resources. She is in demand internationally to provide consultancy and professional development for educators on a range of related issues.

See www.sueroffey.com for more information and contact details.

PREFACE

Robert Barr is an academic, researching risk and resilience. He is also a grandfather. One morning as he was taking his young grandson to school a small child with ragged dress and dirty fingernails attached herself to him. He saw her desperate need for affection and suddenly realised that this child personalised the research he had worked with for so long. He knew that a deep yearning for love can turn into anger or even hate, and that the tragic story of one generation impose itself on the next.

The professor watched the little girl walk into her classroom to be greeted by a teacher who gave her a hug and a broad smile, saying how good it was to see her. She took her young pupil by the hand and told her about all the great things they would do together that day. The little girl glowed. He was reminded that although there are clear predictions for children at risk, the redeeming power of a good school with caring teachers and high expectations is not to be underestimated.

I knew that schools could make a difference, could transform the lives of children, could overcome the deficiencies of the home and the dysfunctions of the family ... (Barr, 1996, p. 382).

Behind closed doors some children and young people live with mothers who are addicted or depressed, fathers whose idea of manhood is to be a bully, and stepparents who come and go. Some grow up in homes where no-one knows much about child development, needs or appropriate expectations. There may be no regular routines or clear boundaries. Sometimes children run wild and inevitably get into trouble. When this happens they might be thrashed or ignored. They learn little about being considerate but a lot about surviving and looking after number one.

Children and young people with multiple negative experiences struggle with concentration and learning. It is hard to focus when your life is a mess. It is these students whose behaviour in school is most challenging. Without effective intervention they are the ones most likely to be excluded from school and eventually join the ranks of the socially excluded in society, thus perpetuating the cycle of risk and disadvantage.

Thousands of children and young people have teachers who *do* intervene in this negative spiral. The media make much of those individuals who fall through the cracks but rarely give credit to what happens every day in classrooms to rescue children and their futures; with schools and teachers who help students feel they matter, they belong and they can succeed – often despite educational policies that can undermine these efforts. For some students just holding the fort might be the best you can hope for, preventing things getting any worse. Few teachers get recognition, let alone accolades, for doing this valuable work.

Other children have less overwhelming experiences than those described above but nevertheless face situations that are far from easy. They deal with the confusion of loss and family breakdown or have families who are so busy making a living they don't have time to talk or play. Some children live in a milieu where they learn that personal interests are the only ones that matter. This leads to disconnection from others and a lack of authentic wellbeing.

Whatever a child brings with them to school is either exacerbated or modified by what happens there. Relying on reactive discipline policies and sanctions can make behaviour worse, not better (Mayer, 1995). We need to change behaviour by using co-ordinated and intelligent responses to promote the positive and respond effectively to challenges.

This book is based on research evidence illustrated by examples of good practice across the world. It challenges some traditional ways of going about things but offers an alternative framework for action. There is explicit detail of what this means in practice, both in terms of promoting pro-social behaviour, responding effectively to difficulties and exploring ways in which real change might occur. The core message is that positive relationships and school connectedness lead to both improved learning *and* better behaviour for all students. This is the crux of an effective learning environment.

This approach does not offer any quick fixes – because there are none. The evidence, however, suggests that this conceptual and action framework is:

- effective for teachers – who become more skilled and confident in their role and therefore have a more enjoyable time at work
- effective for distressed and difficult students who are offered positive experiences, opportunities to see themselves differently and develop a belief in themselves and who they can become
- effective for the whole school community where everyone benefits from a focus on the positive, valuing each individual and nurturing a sense of belonging.

This book has been written in the hope that every reader will begin to believe that they can make this difference, are inspired to try and will gain the confidence to be an effective, professional and caring educator, whatever the challenges!

The word 'teachers' refers to everyone who is involved in an educative role including teaching assistants, support personnel and early years practitioners. The word 'parents' refers to all who have parental responsibility to care for a child. The terms 'pupil' and 'student' are used interchangeably.

Sue Roffey

REFERENCES

Barr, R.D. (1996). Who is this child? *Phi Delta Kappan*, 77(5), 382.

Mayer, G.R. (1995). Preventing antisocial behavior in the schools. *Journal of Applied Behavior Analysis*, 28, 467–92.

INTRODUCTION

BEHAVIOUR IN PERSPECTIVE

Behaviour in schools receives a good deal of public attention, much of it negative. The Steer Report (DfES, 2005b) puts this into perspective:

> *Our experience as teachers, supported by evidence from Ofsted, is that the great majority of pupils work hard and behave well, and that most schools successfully manage behaviour to create an environment in which learners feel valued, cared for and safe. It is often the case that for pupils, school is a calm place in a disorderly world* (p. 6).

The report goes on to say that most of the behaviours that teachers struggle with are minor disruptions and that major incidents are rare and perpetrated by a small number of students. There is evidence that in general pupil behaviour is improving. This suggests that teachers arrive in classrooms with predominantly positive expectations.

Any unacceptable behaviour, however, whether low level or extreme, can be very challenging as it both damages teacher confidence and undermines learning. Poor behaviour can be a trigger for teachers to leave the profession and can often restrict the life chances of pupils (NUT, 2005). Sharing, developing and actually *doing* what works is therefore essential for the current and future wellbeing of all involved.

> *The knowledge and skills of staff are the single most important factor in promoting good behaviour* (Steer Report, p. 83).

WHAT THIS BOOK AIMS TO DO

- To go beyond behaviour management to develop more positive pupil behaviour
- To foster the relationships that will help keep vulnerable and challenging students connected with school and learning
- To promote the wellbeing of all, including teachers
- To share research evidence and effective practice.

Although much of what is included here will help in responding effectively to challenges, the aim is to go beyond behaviour management – to explore what schools and teachers can do to change pupil behaviour over the longer term.

Behaviour management often comprises the strategies employed when behaviour threatens to disrupt teaching. These primarily aim to meet the needs of teachers and the rest of the class. Management can also include how to pre-empt difficulties by paying attention to how the curriculum is delivered, the physical layout of the classroom, your teaching style and what Kounin (1977) calls 'with-it-ness'. Although these are essential skills for an educator and will be addressed throughout the book, when behaviour management becomes an end in itself, there is little consideration about what this behaviour means for the student and how we can support behavioural change.

Some teachers believe fear is an effective management strategy and that if students are intimidated this will take care of any discipline problems. Although this might work in the short term – for that teacher – the longer-term costs of this approach are considerable.

When distress is not heard, a focus on sanctions alone can make things worse. Although it is vital to maintain high expectations for behaviour, when we say: 'that will teach them!' we need to think carefully about the lessons we really do want students to learn. How can we help children and young people choose to be considerate and cooperative? How can we motivate them to stay engaged with learning? How can we help them see school as a refuge and resource that helps them maintain a positive sense of self and learn to deal with adversity elsewhere in their lives? This is not being soft on difficult students; it is using both intelligence and research evidence to break a negative cycle.

Our challenging pupils are those most quickly marginalised by the system and most likely to be suspended and excluded from school. If you go into any prison you will find many inmates who had a negative and disconnected school experience. The same is true for others who are socially excluded. The research evidence is that a sense of belonging promotes pro-social behaviour, resilience and improved learning outcomes (Benard, 2004; Blum & Libbey, 2004). The second aim is therefore to help schools do everything they possibly can to keep children and young people connected. Promoting positive relationships and positive school experiences can intervene in a negative cycle of disadvantage.

Teacher wellbeing is symbiotic with student wellbeing. Keyes and Haidt (2005) say that many adults in society are 'languishing' rather than 'flourishing' – and some of these adults are in the classroom. The third aim is therefore to promote wellbeing and relational quality throughout the school and clarify what that means. Small consistent differences in the way people interact can lead to great changes over time. When teachers use emotional literacy and develop their own resilience they have a more satisfactory and effective working life. When teachers work together to build social capital in schools they feel supported, even under stress. This not only promotes wellbeing for teachers new to the profession, it can also revitalise experienced practitioners who have become jaded and cynical. Everyone benefits from a focus on wellbeing.

There is a discourse on 'discipline' in education that does not always help schools move towards more effective practice in improving behaviour. The word discipline has connotations of doing as you are told and conforming to rules laid down by those in authority. This element of external control can lead to students doing what they can get away with out of the sight of authority figures. The internalisation of pro-social values means changing behaviour from the inside out.

〰️ **Questions for reflection and discussion**

What are your aims as a teacher?

What are your aims for your students?

LEARNING TO BE: LEARNING TO LIVE TOGETHER

The report to the United Nations on education in the 21st century (Delors, 1996) identified four pillars of education:

- Learning to know
- Learning to do
- Learning to be
- Learning to live together.

Much of the focus of education in the 20th century has been on the first two pillars – knowledge and skills. There is now increasing evidence that the last two are not only just as important, but also underpin effectiveness for the first two (Zins et al., 2004).

Learning to be and learning to live together are the foundations for changing behaviour. This incorporates how we think and feel about ourselves, and our perceptions of the world and those with whom we share it. This is a very different approach from providing rewards for conforming to the rules, and consequences for breaking them.

The social and emotional dimensions of learning (SEL) are beginning to be acknowledged across the world. The Collaborative for Academic, Social and Emotional Learning (CASEL) is an influential body of researchers and educators promoting the value of SEL in the United States. CASEL defines SEL as '*a process for helping children and even adults develop the fundamental skills for life effectiveness. SEL teaches the skills we all need to handle ourselves, our relationships, and our work, effectively and ethically*' (CASEL, 2007). Payton et al. (2008) analysed three large-scale reviews of research on the impact of social and emotional learning (SEL) programmes on elementary and middle school students from Kindergarten to Grade 8. These were divided into studies of SEL for all children (universal), those for targeted groups (early intervention) and after-school programmes. Collectively the three reviews included 317 studies and involved 324,303 children.

Their findings were:

- Universal, targeted and after school SEL programmes raised achievement test scores an average of 11, 17, and 16 percentile points, respectively.

- Universal and targeted programmes increased social-emotional skills in test situations.
- All three types of programmes improved social behaviour such as getting along and cooperating with others and decreased behavioural problems such as aggression and disruptiveness.
- All three types of programmes led to more positive feelings about self, others and school.
- Universal and targeted programmes reduced levels of emotional distress such as anxiety and depression.
- Positive outcomes were enhanced when classroom teachers delivered programmess rather than researchers and where attention was given to the quality of implementation.

In the UK the Social and Emotional Aspects of Learning (SEAL) programme was introduced to primary schools in 2005 and secondary schools in 2007 (DfES, 2005a). It is estimated that the majority of primary schools and a significant proportion of secondary schools are now using the programme. Evaluation of SEAL in 84 primary schools in Sheffield between 2005 and 2007 indicated high levels of success (Pullinger, 2008), including improvements in behaviour and the way children were able to express feelings. Some pupils had learnt to sort out low-level conflict on their own and incidents of bullying were reduced.

Taking account of the social and emotional aspects of learning acknowledges the importance of teaching the whole child and maximising their potential in all domains of development. Where education systems emphasise individual success in academic outcomes they are not fully congruent with this approach. Although personalised learning is receiving greater attention, educational testing and government directives on academic targets risk undermining the work of many teachers who are concerned their students also learn the skills that will facilitate their lives. Academic achievements alone do not guarantee a fulfilling life. If you have not learnt to manage yourself well, or developed the personal qualities to overcome adversity, nor learnt how to establish and maintain supportive relationships you are unlikely to flourish and sustain wellbeing.

📁 Case study

Mark was a straight 'A' student and is now doing very well in his career, earning a high salary and the status that comes with this. He is a good-looking young man and a keen tennis player, married to an intelligent and caring woman who has given him two young sons. You would have thought he had everything it takes to be happy and fulfilled, but Mark has not learnt to consider the needs of anyone but himself and in some ways has the maturity of a toddler. When things do not go exactly as he wants he explodes into uncontrollable rage and can be verbally abusive to anyone who gets in his way. His family life is now at risk as he has done this once too often at home and work colleagues are beginning to avoid him. Unless Mark can learn 'how to be' and 'how to live together' more effectively, he may lose much of what he has worked so hard to achieve.

〜〜 **Questions for reflection and discussion**

What did you learn at school that has helped you with your work and personal life?
What else would have been valuable?

VULNERABLE AND CHALLENGING

Vulnerable children and young people often struggle with these important social and emotional elements of learning and development. They may not have had positive role models, experiences or guidance to help them learn to cope with difficulties or connect with others. Often they are overwhelmed by chronic or acute challenges and put their energies into trying to protect themselves from further threat and harm – perceived as well as real.

The behaviour of these students can be very difficult to manage in the classroom. This may lead teachers to give up a career in education and go off to find something less stressful. Teaching, however, can be an immensely rewarding career, despite – and sometimes because of – the challenges it presents. Teachers need to build both their confidence and resilience so they are not overwhelmed when the going gets tough.

The way we think about children and young people impacts on how we feel about them and also about ourselves. These thoughts and emotions determine the actions we take in relation to behaviour. In can be hard to appreciate in the stress of the moment that there are choices, some of which give everyone a better time in the classroom. It would seem sensible to choose what is effective and seek support to stick with it. This is not always the easiest option and can be personally challenging at times.

FOCUSING ON WHAT WORKS

This book tells you what works, not what people think works. Each chapter shows what has been proved to be effective over the longer term – avoiding the lurch from one challenging experience to the next, from one crisis to another.

The views expressed here are evidence-based. Although studies are not cited at every turn, very little appears here which is not rooted in scientific enquiry. The reference list at the end of each chapter is there to follow up if you wish. Also included are resources to extend your knowledge and skills and suggestions for materials that may be directly useful in the classroom.

This book goes beyond management techniques to what you might do to change behaviour in the longer term. There is neither a simple nor quick fix but consistently good practice will make a significant difference to positive outcomes – for your students, their achievement and their futures. It will also make a positive difference to the quality of your life every day at work.

Much of what you will read here may seem obvious. Unfortunately, common sense is not so commonly practiced. It is harder to do what is sensible, ethical, thoughtful and effective when you are under stress and the ethos of the environment in which you are working is not supportive.

A teacher in training recently let me know he was having a miserable time on his school placement. The students, in his view, were just horrible, they didn't want to work and several did everything they could to disrupt his well-prepared lessons. The class teacher did nothing to support him. I sympathised with his predicament and asked him what he was doing about getting to know the students. His response was depressing but also not untypical: *'I teach science in a high school. I'm not there to have relationships'.*

Another young teacher, however, came up to me after a presentation on teacher–student relationships and said:

> *I'm in my second year of teaching. When I was in training my supervisor said it would be better if I kept my distance and let students know who's boss. I didn't feel comfortable with that and I have been doing what you have been suggesting in this workshop to make connections. I now know from my own experience that this works. Even the students that others struggle with, sometimes even experienced teachers, are mostly OK in my class. I love my students and I love my job.*

Relationships and emotions exist all day every day in school. What you do and say, and the expectations that students develop of you, will impact on the way they respond to you. It makes sense to promote the positive wherever you can. This does not mean condoning what is unacceptable and 'letting kids get away with it' – what matters is the way that you deliver consequences.

📁 Case study

Erin Pizzey, founder of the domestic violence charity, Refuge, grew up in a high status but dysfunctional household. Her mother was cold and distant and her father, who was a diplomat, could be a violent bully. Erin says that she had many behaviour difficulties at the convent school she attended, including violence and outright defiance. She particularly remembers one Sister who was always calm, warm and accepting but maintained high standards of behaviour. Whenever Erin misbehaved she had to help out in the kitchen. One day she was caught stealing. The Sister simply looked at her and quietly said: 'Well, that is going to be a lot of washing up'. Erin says that her respect for this Sister helped in coping with a very difficult time of her life.

THE THEORETICAL BASE

This book is based in and builds on the following theories – ways of thinking about the world.

Positive psychology

Instead of identifying problems and deficits and finding ways to treat pathology, positive psychology explores strengths, solutions and factors that maximise wellbeing to enable people to flourish.

Personal construct theory

This says that we all try to fit new experiences into our understanding of the way the world works. We therefore interpret new events on the basis of what we have already experienced. It is hard to change beliefs by giving information alone. This challenges us to consider the experiences we are providing for students and how these may be mediated.

Social constructionism

This approach sees behaviour as shaped by social context and social processes. We interpret student behaviour in the light of the dominant discourses around us. If a silent classroom is seen as a good thing in a school a student who asks many questions may be considered out of order. If noisy discussion is perceived as an indication of high engagement with learning then questions will be welcomed.

Systems and ecological approaches

This way of thinking also moves beyond the individual to their local context and the way the system in which they are embedded can promote or undermine change. Everything is interconnected and interactive. Changing or even tweaking one part of the system will have an impact on others. A focus on teacher wellbeing for instance may relieve stress, which in turn increases positive student–teacher relationships, and so on.

THE EVIDENCE BASE

Throughout the book you will find references to studies in the following areas:

- Mental health and resilience
- Effective education
- Social and emotional learning
- Multiple intelligences
- The determinants of student and school wellbeing
- Behavioural issues in school
- The promotion and learning of pro-social behaviour
- Values education
- Neuropsychology and the way the brain works
- Restorative approaches

- School culture and leadership
- Reducing cycles of violence
- Relationship research.

Three specific qualitative studies provide supportive evidence for the approaches suggested and also many of the quotes found in the text. These are described briefly here. More information can be found in the publications cited in the references.

The views and constructs of parents on the home–school interface for behaviour

Nineteen families whose children had been identified with challenging behaviours were interviewed about their experiences in schools. They were asked what had been supportive and helpful and what had not (Roffey, 2002).

The development of emotional literacy in Australian schools

This study took place in six schools focused on establishing emotional literacy and relational quality across the learning environment. Interviews took place with students, teaching staff, school counsellors and principals. Some schools were building from a strong values base, others starting where there was little respect, care or community spirit. It took these schools many years to 'turn around' but they did so with remarkable outcomes (Roffey, 2008).

Circle Solutions: creating caring school communities

Eighteen undergraduate students supported the implementation of Circle Solutions in eight schools. Circle Solutions is a framework for group interaction based in the principles of democracy, inclusion, respect and safety. This study is an analysis of student experiences, observations and reflections (McCarthy, 2009).

RE-VISITING THEMES

As you go through the book you will find that similar themes come up time and again. The same things are said in different ways and in varying contexts.

There are references to **relationships, relational values, belonging and connectedness** and ways of promoting this. Your own **emotional literacy** will be revisited both in terms of expressing emotions in confident and helpful ways, responding to difficult situations and staying resilient. Another major theme is maximising a **strengths and solution focus** to ensure your interactions are positive experiences for everyone. Paying attention to the **words** you use is important. **Discourse** is an important theme – the way we think and talk about behaviour, students and families influences the lens through which we interpret different realities. **Pedagogy** is included – what teaching approaches are most successful in getting and keeping pupils engaged. Student **agency and participation** means handing responsibility back to students and giving them both the skills and opportunities to make considered decisions about their behaviour and how they want to 'be' and 'live together'.

Reading this book may affect the way you see your job and the students you teach. It gives ideas and concrete strategies to build student confidence as successful learners and worthwhile people, promote the positive and respond effectively to challenges. What you do and say will impact on how pupils think of themselves and their school experiences, what they feel about being in your classroom and the behaviour they choose to engage in while they are there.

You will still come across students who are very difficult and damaged – particularly in high school. Whatever you do will not change their behaviour much. But, by keeping to the principles recommended here, you will be giving them an alternative experience – a way of understanding that there are different ways of being – which may impact on their future. You might never know the difference you make. Keeping to these principles will also give you a sense of professional accomplishment and boost your own resilience. It is a relief to know that you do not have to win every battle to be a good teacher.

CHAPTER CONTENT

There are four sections, each divided further into chapters. The first section addresses effective teaching. Chapter 2 includes what students perceive as a 'good teacher' and then details recent research on effective practice.

What does it mean to become and be an emotionally literate teacher and what difference does this make to the promotion of positive behaviour and effective responses in the face of challenges? These questions are addressed in Chapter 3.

Chapter 4 is about students themselves, making the important link between vulnerability and challenging behaviour. We look at the risk factors that may exist in a young person's life and the protective factors that help them be resilient in the face of adversity. Schools can make a significant difference.

The second section focuses on learning and choosing pro-social behaviour. Chapter 5 explores various ways you might conceptualise students and their behaviour. How you think about something makes a difference to how you feel and what you do. Chapter 6 details what is involved in establishing a pro-social classroom, ensuring that students feel valued and accepted and have a sense of their own strengths and achievements. Chapter 7 is closely aligned to this, and covers aspects of positive relationships, including what teachers might do to establish connection with their most challenging pupils. Chapter 8 highlights the importance of student agency and participation in decision-making.

Section Three addresses behaviour that is challenging. Chapter 9 aims to help teachers discriminate between different behaviours, the contexts in which they appear and developmentally appropriate responses. Chapter 10 explores the interactions between feeling, thinking and actions and what might be possible to change. This chapter covers behaviours you are likely to come across in your everyday work.

Responding professionally to a continuum of challenges is the focus of Chapter 11. Within this we demonstrate how restorative approaches enable students to stay connected with their school community whilst also taking responsibility for their behaviour. This chapter also addresses teacher wellbeing. Teachers who are burnt out are unlikely to respond calmly and professionally in challenging situations.

Section Four is on whole school issues. Chapter 12 explores ways in which a focus on student and school wellbeing might be addressed at every level in an ecological spiral of positive practice. The culture of a school is critical to how behaviour is conceptualised, what happens for vulnerable and challenging students and how teachers are supported in their efforts to establish and maintain positive relationships and maximise engagement with learning.

READING, REFLECTING AND TAKING ACTION

In each chapter you are invited to interact with what you have been reading in the following ways.

Questions for reflection and discussion are placed below sections of text to encourage you to think about the meaning for you. Sometimes you may just want to take a moment or two to remember your own experiences and how these apply to your current situation. You may then wish to discuss this with a colleague.

Throughout each chapter are suggestions for intervention to both promote positive behaviours and respond effectively to challenges. These strategies are summarised for you in bullet points at the end.

Each chapter provides professional development activities to enhance your knowledge and skills, together with Circle Solutions activities for students. Both include paired discussion, small group activities and discussions of hypothetical situations.

CIRCLE SOLUTIONS

Circle Solutions activities are included to engage your students on some of the issues discussed. Some of these are suitable for younger pupils, others for older students – many can be amended to suit all ages, including adults.

I first came across Circles in New Jersey in the early 1990s. The principal of an elementary school I was visiting told me that 'Magic Circles' happened every day in every class after recess and made all the difference to the running of his school. It was not long afterwards that others, notably Murray White, Barbara Maines, Theresa Bliss, George Robinson and, in particular, Jenny Mosley, developed Circle Time in the UK. Circle Solutions is built upon the work of these pioneers within positive psychology and social constructionist paradigms, emphasising strengths and solutions, student agency for defining solutions to classroom issues, developing a sense of belonging and changing whole class conversations.

Circle Solutions is a framework for group interaction based in the principles of democracy, inclusion, respect and safety. Everyone sits in a Circle with the teacher as participant facilitator. The aim is for students to find out about themselves and others, learn about what is involved in positive relationships and make decisions for their own class group:

- Circles begin with a statement of the principles and a check-in or greeting.
- Participants are then mixed up so they interact outside their usual social groups – this helps to break down barriers between people.
- Following activities can be paired, small group or involve the whole Circle – the content is chosen by the facilitator according to the age and needs of the class: students can lead these activities when they are familiar with the framework.
- All Circles end with a closing, calming activity such as relaxation, visualisation or reflection.

Circle sessions take about 20 minutes with young children, longer with older students. They need to happen regularly to have a sustainable impact, daily is optimal and once a week the minimum.

Many activities are presented as collaborative games. Playing games is engaging to young people, rarely threatening if not individually competitive and involves social and emotional learning as part of the process. The playfulness and laughter in games reduces stress and bonds people together in shared enjoyment. Games that do not depend on academic skills for participation promote the inclusion of many students who may otherwise struggle (Hromek & Roffey, 2009).

Issues in Circle Solutions are often addressed in an indirect way, using stories, the third person or hypothetical situations. These are primarily solution focused – what we want rather what we want to get rid of. For example, rather than deconstructing a problem such as spreading rumours, pupils explore what trust is about and the difference it makes to how people feel about themselves and each other. What it means to be trustworthy and why you need others to be reliable so we can all function as a supportive community.

Expectations in Circle Solutions are that everyone gets a turn to speak if they wish, but they do not have to say anything if they choose not to. They are already participating by watching and listening. Respect is shown to each other by listening to what each person has to say, only naming individuals in a positive way and not putting anyone down.

Circle Solutions focus on the positive:

- To ensure the Circle is a safe place for both students and teachers
- To emphasise direction and goals rather than eliminating problems
- To promote positive feelings and a sense of belonging
- To have fun together in a safe and respectful way
- To aim for the future rather than bemoaning the past
- To foster optimism, hopefulness and resilience.

The way Circles are facilitated makes all the difference to their usefulness in the classroom and beyond. Facilitators need to run Circles in line with the principles of respect, inclusion, safety and democracy (McCarthy, 2009) and make connections between the activities and the learning that is taking place.

Each chapter concludes with references, suggestions for further reading and useful resources.

REFERENCES

Benard, B. (2004). *Resiliency: What have we learned?* San Francisco: WestEd.

Blum, R.W. & Libbey, H.P. (2004). Executive summary, Issue on School Connectedness – Strengthening Health and Education Outcomes for Teenagers. *Journal of School Health*, 74(7), 231–2.

Collaborative for Academic, Social and Emotional Learning (CASEL) (2007). *Background on social and emotional learning*. www.casel.org/downloads/SEL&CASELbackground.pdf. Retrieved 15 Jan. 2010.

Delors, J. (1996). *Learning: The treasure within.* Paris: International Commission on Education for the Twenty First Century, UNESCO.

Department for Education and Skills(DfES) (2005a). *Social and emotional aspects of learning.* London: DfES.

Department for Education and Skills(DfES) (2005b). *The Steer Report: Learning behaviour: The report of the practitioners group on school behaviour and discipline.* London: DfES.

Hromek, R. & Roffey, S. (2009). Promoting social and emotional learning with games: 'It's fun and we learn things'. *Simulation & Gaming*, 40(5), October 2009, 626–44.

Keyes, C. & Haidt, J. (eds) (2005). *Flourishing: Positive psychology and the life well lived.* Washington: American Psychological Society.

Kounin, J.S. (1977). *Discipline and group management in classrooms.* Huntington, NY: Kreiger.

McCarthy, F. (2009). *Circle time solutions: Creating caring school communities.* Sydney: Report for the NSW Department of Education.

National Union of Teachers (NUT) (2005). *Learning to behave: A charter for schools.* London: NUT.

Payton, J., Weissberg, R.P., Durlak, J.A., Dymnicki, A.B., Taylor, R.D., Schellinger, K.B. & Pachan, M. (2008). *The positive impact of social and emotional learning for kindergarten to eighth-grade students. Findings from three scientific reviews.* www.casel.org/sel/meta.php

Pullinger, N. (2008). *Evaluation of the Sheffield SEAL programme.* Sheffield Education Services.

Roffey, S. (2002). *School behaviour and families: Frameworks for working together.* London: David Fulton Publishers.

Roffey, S. (2008). Emotional literacy and the ecology of school wellbeing. *Educational and Child Psychology*, 25(2), 29–39.

Zins, J.E., Weissberg, R.P., Wang, M.C. & Walberg, H.J. (2004). *Building academic success on social and emotional learning: What does the research say?* New York: Teachers College Press.

SECTION ONE

BEING AN EFFECTIVE TEACHER

Teaching is all about communication. It is not, however, just formal knowledge that is transmitted. When a teacher also communicates passion about her subject, interest in students' progress, delight in their attainments, sympathy with their difficulties and patience with their efforts she is more likely to have students who are engaged and behave well. When a teacher communicates self-respect and respect for others, concern about his students, a willingness to listen and also share a laugh he is likely to have students who are more cooperative and responsive to direction. Not only do students say this is what they want and need, it is also confirmed by research on effective education.

Socially and emotionally competent teachers support the development of positive behaviour and respond with professional integrity in times of crisis. Jennings and Greenberg (2009) have identified that such teachers:

- set the 'emotional tone' of the classroom
- model respectful communication
- model expected pro-social behaviours
- develop supportive and encouraging relationships with students
- establish and implement behaviour guidelines in ways that promote intrinsic motivation – rather than impose non-negotiable rules
- design lessons that build on student strengths and abilities.

These teacher behaviours are associated with an optimal classroom climate, characterized by low levels of conflict and disruptive behaviour, smooth transitions between activities, appropriate expressions of emotion, respectful communication and problem solving, engagement with tasks, and supportive responsiveness to individual differences and students' needs (La Paro & Pianta, 2003).

Effective teaching is also increasingly associated with personalised learning. Teachers need to know their students, not just their subject. Each individual has many stories that inform the person they have become. Our most challenging students are often vulnerable and at risk. Even if we know only a fragment of their personal stories, establishing the protective factors that promote resilience ensures everyone learns in an environment that responds to the 'whole child' and maximises wellbeing. This means high expectations, fostering a sense of belonging and believing in the best of each student, letting them know we think they are worth the effort.

REFERENCES

Jennings, P.A. & Greenberg, M.T. (2009). The pro-social classroom: Teacher social and emotional competence in relation to student and classroom outcomes. *Review of Educational Research,* 79 (1), 491–525.

La Paro, K.M., & Pianta, R.C. (2003). *CLASS: Classroom Assessment Scoring System.* Charlottesville: University of Virginia Press.

2 BEING A 'GOOD' TEACHER

Chapter objectives

- To understand what the qualities of a 'good' teacher are for students
- To summarise research findings on effective teaching
- To make links between 'good' teaching and behaviour in the classroom
- To think through what it means to teach the 'whole child'
- To consider how best to respond to the challenges and sometimes conflicting demands in schools and the education system
- To explore your own strengths as a teacher.

WHAT DO STUDENTS SAY ABOUT 'GOOD' TEACHERS?

There are many studies on effective education. But what do pupils themselves say about teachers and what do they consider makes a 'good' teacher?

Four hundred and thirty children and young people between the ages of 4 and 19 were asked about issues of concern to them (NSW Commission for Children & Young People, 2004). The most significant factor in schools was their relationship with teachers. All the respondents said they love having 'good teachers', and for many students they are what is best about school.

Liking your students

An important finding in the above study is that children want teachers who like them. It is sad if not worrying that some children seem to spend every day in school feeling their teachers simply don't like them.

If they like me, I like them – and I feel better (student).

They should like us; they chose the job so they should like us (student).

Treating pupils with respect

Feeling respected includes feeling acknowledged, valued and that your views are taken into account. Respect means not putting students down:

I think they make the mistake that they expect you to respect them before they give you respect (student).

We have found that when teachers respect students they usually respect them back (teacher on values project).

Keeping order

It may come as a relief to learn that most students want to be at school and are interested in learning. The younger they are the more likely this is to be true. Because they enjoy finding out new things and discovering more about themselves and the world they live in, they do not like environments in which this desire is thwarted. They do not like being in wild classrooms where there is a lot of disruption.

A teacher who can 'keep control' therefore, is seen as a 'good teacher'. The big issue is how they do that. Maintaining order and keeping a situation under control so that chaos does not take over is not the same as controlling pupils. Although it may be difficult at first to see the difference, it is essential to discriminate between the two. Trying to assert authoritarian control over students is rarely a good idea and frequently backfires. It also does nothing to teach children and young people about developing self-control.

Clear positive expectations

Establishing accepted standards for behaviour that are framed in the positive is more motivating for students than a list of 'don'ts' and sanctions for disobedience. 'Good' teachers make their expectations clear so students know what they should be doing. Classroom management is even more effective if classroom rules or guidelines are negotiated with students at the outset. Making choices together about how the class will be managed is more likely to lead to compliance with agreed standards than having regulations imposed: see Chapter 8 for how to do this.

Lively lessons

Pedagogy matters to pupils. Teachers who vary activities and incorporate collaborative, interactive strategies for learning are considered 'good' teachers who can engage the class.

When you have a teacher who does discussion and interaction as part of their lesson you enjoy it more (student).

Some of my teachers incorporate games ... make it more interesting, while staying on the subject of what we're meant to be learning (student).

Having a laugh

Students love being in classes where they anticipate humour and joviality. It is highly motivating when the teacher is someone you can have a laugh with but does not relinquish control. The first quote below is from a primary school student and the second from a pupil at high school.

Teachers are very funny – if you are having a hard day they come out with a joke and it makes you feel better, less stressed.

I reckon a good teacher is willing to actually try and make it fun to learn …

There is evidence in the positive psychology literature that supports the educational value of sharing laughter in the classroom (more on this in Chapter 6).

Showing you care

Sometimes teachers think they are being caring, but pupils do not always recognise this – there can be a mismatch in perceptions. It would seem useful for teachers to understand the several dimensions of what it means to care in the school environment. It includes being empathic and understanding, relating in a friendly way and being helpful.

She was genuinely concerned – she wanted to help kids – she was sort of very reassuring (student).

It is also about being accessible and sensitive to individual needs.

A lot of teachers make time. They walk around at lunchtime and recess. Others wait until everyone is out of the class so they can talk to people (student).

The teacher in the story below was initially embarrassed about her reactions in this situation but it was clearly a powerful demonstration of care for the student.

📁 Case study

Farad was a toughie – he sent out messages that it would be unwise to mess with him. An invisible shield kept up the hard man image, no-one ever got close to him. One afternoon he ran across the school field to try and leap onto the back of the moving lawn tractor. His teacher, Mrs H, fearing for his safety, shrieked his name at the top of her voice. He ran back, thrust his face into hers and screamed back 'what?!' Mrs H, a usually composed person, became tearful, 'I was so scared you would fall under the blades and get hurt'. Farad couldn't quite believe she was that upset on his behalf. He realised she really did care about him. From that moment on their relationship changed. Farad was much more considerate and friendly. When he left primary school at the end of that year he told his teacher how much he would miss her.

Believing in the best

This includes focusing on strengths rather than weaknesses and not jumping to negative conclusions and attributing blame. 'Believing in the best of someone' was vividly illustrated in the *Unteachables* documentary (Channel 4 UK, 2005) when the teacher, Phil Beadle, worked hard to identify strengths his challenging students could be proud of. He let them know he valued these things about them. One boy said that he should be cloned, 'every school should have a Phil'.

Being positive and consistent

Students associate their own and their teachers' positive emotional states with good teaching and good learning (Moore & Kuol, 2007). Pupils warm to teachers who are usually cheerful and optimistic. This impacts on classroom atmosphere and enhances learning. There will be understanding from students if on occasions such a teacher has a down day. Teachers who are moody, however, are unpredictable, and this makes students anxious, particularly those who rely on the stability of school to compensate for lack of security at home.

Enabling students to feel comfortable

A good teacher is one you can approach for help, who does not make you feel that you are being 'stupid' for asking questions or not understanding the first time around. These teachers accept mistakes as part of learning.

> If you are too scared you can't learn. If you are scared of what they are going to do if you do something wrong (student).

Speaking slowly and quietly

Students do not approve of teachers who shout. Not only can yelling make younger children anxious and older pupils angry, it also raises the noise level in the classroom. One piece of advice I received as a newly qualified teacher was: 'the quieter you are, the quieter the children will be'. I have found this to be true for all age groups, from 5-year-olds to undergraduate students. The few times I raised my voice it had an effect because it was unexpected. If I had used it frequently not only would I have been exhausted, but everyone would have gotten used to the volume and simply raised their voices to an even higher decibel level. Speaking quietly does not mean mumbling or being inaudible; communications need to be clear. It is helpful if they are also concise.

Students also appreciate teachers who give instructions at a slow enough pace for them to follow. Speaking too fast is confusing and pupils may end up feeling they don't understand and therefore can't do assigned tasks. If they then get into trouble asking someone else this sets up an unnecessary negative spiral.

Repetition is useful. Sometimes students feel incompetent if they do not follow the first time, but most of us benefit from having instructions repeated – and being shown what to do helps even more.

Being fair

Teachers who are seen to be even-handed and fair win pupil approval. Favouritism is toxic to an atmosphere of trust. Students can become resentful if they see the able and achieving students get the most positive teacher attention. Sometimes boys feel that girls get this too. It is not helpful for teachers to compare siblings either favourably or unfavourably – each family member should be treated as an individual. There is, however, a common understanding that those who are struggling need extra time and attention. This is not usually seen as unfair.

Teachers need to be positive, not too critical and negative. They need to value effort. Comparing to high achievers doesn't help. Effort needs acknowledgement (high school student).

Appropriate behaviours

You cannot expect pupils to behave in appropriate ways if their teachers are not modelling this. Students do not think it is 'cool' for teachers to dress provocatively, to use mobile phones in the classroom, to swear or try to 'be your friend'. They want to be able to look up to and respect their teachers.

A study in Turkey (Baloglu, 2009) asked over 1,000 students in three high schools about negative teacher behaviours that undermined positive student behaviour. Aggressive behaviour was cited as the most common problem: insults and threats were given as examples; this included threatening failure and low marks. Speaking too fast and favouring some students over others were also considered unhelpful.

Questions for reflection and discussion

In which ways does your idea of a 'good teacher' compare with what students say?

What is the difference between being friendly and being a friend? Why is one a hallmark of a good teacher and the other not?

WHAT DOES THE RESEARCH SAY ABOUT BEING AN EFFECTIVE TEACHER?

This section is based primarily on John Hattie's meta-analysis of 800 meta-analyses of effective education (Hattie, 2009), which incorporates studies of several million students. All of these studies are quantitative, based on measurement and statistics.

Hattie summarises what he calls six signposts towards excellence in education:

- Teachers are among the most powerful influences in learning.
- Teachers need to be directive, influential, caring and actively engaged in the passion of teaching and learning.
- Teachers need to be aware of what each and every student is thinking and knowing, to construct meaning and meaningful experiences in the light of this knowledge and to provide appropriate feedback.
- Teachers need to know the learning intentions and success criteria of their lessons and know how well they are attaining these criteria for all students so they know where to go next.
- It is not the knowledge or ideas, but the learner's construction of this knowledge and these ideas that is critical.
- School leaders and teachers need to create school, staffroom and classroom environments where error is welcomed as a learning opportunity, where discarding incorrect knowledge and understandings is welcomed and where participants can feel safe to learn, re-learn and explore knowledge and understanding.

Some teachers may find this advice overwhelming but doing things slightly differently rather than additionally will address much of what is suggested. The findings in Hattie's research discussed below impact directly on what you might do in the classroom to maximise positive behaviour.

Feedback

It is not only the feedback that teachers give to students that matters but also the feedback that students give to teachers about their learning. This ensures that the learning is at the appropriate level for the student so they continue to make progress. This maintains engagement and motivation.

Making mistakes

The learning environment needs to be one where students expect to make mistakes as part of learning. Getting things right all the time indicates low expectations.

High expectations

Hattie's findings show that too often students are written off. He maintains that high expectations for ALL students are essential for effective education. This is synonymous with one of the major protective factors for children at risk.

Clear direction

Teachers need to know what goals they aim to achieve and communicate that so that students know what they are doing and why.

Meaningful learning

Teachers need to see learning through the eyes of their students so they can make it as meaningful as possible. They also need to encourage pupils to personalise learning to make it meaningful for themselves.

> *Those students, regardless of prior ability, who used the classroom and its activities to further their own interests and purposes learned more than those who dutifully did what they were told but did not want or know how to create their own opportunities* (Nuthall, 2007).

This suggests that teachers structure their pedagogy to incorporate ways in which students can 'hook' learning into their own interests, needs or experiences.

Cooperative learning strategies

There is universal agreement that cooperative learning is effective. This also promotes more positive relationships amongst individuals from different ethnic backgrounds and between able and disabled students (Roseth et al., 2008).

Personal bests

Martin (2006) found that one way of assisting students to set goals was to introduce the idea of personal bests, where pupils compete with their previous best performance rather than with each other. Martin found that setting personal bests was related to educational aspirations, enjoyment of school, participation in class and persistence on task.

A school ethos that facilitates a learning environment for all

Student disruption in a class impacts on the learning for all. How well teachers plan, prevent, pre-empt and respond to that disruption, therefore matters for everyone.

〰 Question for reflection and discussion

How much congruence is there between what the research says about being a good teacher and what students say?

TEACHING THE 'WHOLE CHILD'

The five outcomes of the Every Child Matters Agenda (DfES, 2004) acknowledge that children's achievement is affected by other aspects of their wellbeing. A central feature of student and school wellbeing is a focus on teaching the 'whole child', maximising the potential in all domains of development, cognitive, social, psychological, physical and emotional. Teaching the 'whole child' is not about doing an array of different things – it is about doing a range of things differently.

An analogy can be made with medical practice. The doctor who only sees a patient as a 'back problem' or 'a shingles case' may lose vital information in treating them. When I go and see my GP she relates to me as a whole person – not just a bundle of symptoms. She smiles at me, uses my name and asks how things are going. She often remembers to ask a small personal question such as did I enjoy my holiday. She follows this up with more specific questions, which inform how she treats any presenting problem and what might help improve my health and wellbeing in general. She not only has a high level of medical knowledge, she also knows how to relate to people so their treatment is optimal. The trust I have in her means I follow any instructions she gives and do not feel reluctant to ask for further advice when I need it. She sometimes spends extra time with patients if the occasion warrants this so does not always keep tightly to appointment schedules. Her patients know that when it is their turn she will have time for them.

A student is not just an empty vessel waiting to be filled with information – he or she is a complex person who has needs, ideas, interests and experiences all of which they bring into the classroom. Each individual has their own way of interacting with their educational experience and we need to take account of the social, emotional, psychological, physical, spiritual and intellectual domains in our teaching to maximise positive learning and behaviour.

PHYSICAL NEEDS

It is more difficult to function well if you are tired, ill, or hungry. Some schools ensure that the first thing their students do when they arrive is have breakfast. One company is supporting this endeavour as their contribution to the community.

📁 Case study

The Greggs Breakfast Club programme was started in 2000 with the aim of providing a free, nutritious breakfast for primary school children in areas of particular social disadvantage. It is now taking place in more than 120 schools in the UK. The supply of cereals, fresh bread and milk has contributed to improved attendance and classroom performance and to strengthening the relationship between the schools and their local community. A vital element in the success of the clubs are the volunteer groups from the school community who serve the food and generally run them. They tend to be parents and grandparents of some of the children who attend the clubs. This enables the primary school pupils to enjoy a fun and healthy start to the day and allows local people to get involved in vital school activity.

Head teachers have been very positive about this initiative and say that not only does it provide nutrition for pupils but also valuable opportunities for informal conversation between staff and children. It improves social skills and of course punctuality.

∿ Question for reflection and discussion

What actions might you take if you knew that some of your students were arriving in school hungry?

Sleep

Sleep is another major issue in some schools. Parents may avoid the battles involved in getting their children to bed early enough for a good night's rest. Students then arrive in the morning tired, cranky and not ready to learn. There is no easy answer to this but the following is worth a try.

Provide repeated information to parents about different kinds of sleep, how much children need and how necessary it is for learning, mood regulation and health. This could be when children start school and throughout the year. Parents will also find it helpful to have some ideas about how to get their children to bed earlier. Ask your educational psychology service or a counsellor to help with this.

For children who really are exhausted is it possible to give them a place for a short sleep? It might be better to have them rest for half an hour than spend several hours not settling to anything and disrupting the group. If children sleep heavily on several occasions invite parents to discuss ways of changing this pattern.

I found out that one of my young students shared a bed with his older brother who often kicked him out. He ended up cold and sleepless on the floor. I kept a duvet and pillow in a cupboard and let him curl up in a corner when he was too tired to do anything else (primary school teacher).

📂 Case study

Monkseaton High School in Tyneside has instituted a 10am start to the day for its older pupils after Paul Kelley, the head teacher learnt about the 'two-hour shift' in teenagers which means that their biological sleep cues, from melatonin levels to body temperature, come a couple of hours after those of young children and adults. Although it is too early to predict results, Kelley says that the omens are good: 'The children say that they prefer it – and they do seem brighter when they arrive'. The school is monitoring student performance with researchers at Oxford University.

The social, emotional and psychological domains of the whole child will be addressed throughout other chapters.

CONFLICTS IN THE SYSTEM

A difficulty for many in education is that a 'good' teacher is not necessarily defined in the system as someone who enables each student to reach their potential but as someone whose students perform exceptionally well on test scores.

In some schools the process by which this occurs is not a concern – and any student who disrupts learning for anyone else is quickly shown the door. There is still a focus on exclusion for those who are seen to be persistent troublemakers. The Academies in the UK want to be seen as Schools of Excellence and getting rid of 'the bad apples' promotes this ideology. It is a strategy that not only fails children, but is ineffective in the longer term. The report by the American Psychological Association on 'zero tolerance policies' in schools in the US (Skiba et al., 2006) found that school exclusion was not only an inevitable 'school to prison pipeline' for some individuals but that an authoritarian ethos undermined relational trust in schools between all teachers and students. This impacted negatively on both behaviour and achievement for all students – not just those with the most challenging behaviour. The report recommends a more 'community' approach in schools, including a consideration of restorative practices.

An even more dramatic example for schools to ensure everyone feels they matter is a recent analysis of the eight schools in the United States where, since 1999, students have gone on a killing rampage. All these schools had high levels of stratification where bullying was rife (Wike & Fraser, 2009). The original headline in the *New Scientist* (Geddes, 2009) on this study claimed 'Teen Killers Don't Come from Schools which Foster a Sense of Belonging'.

A democratic and inclusive approach in the classroom is upheld by the research on effective education – both in terms of improved behaviour and academic outcomes. Authoritarian schools and autocratic teachers are the result of an erroneous belief in the efficacy of high control, not the evidence of what works.

SUMMARY OF STRATEGIES AND APPROACHES TO PROMOTE POSITIVE BEHAVIOUR

- Make expectations clear and positive.
- Have high expectations for all students.
- Negotiate ground rules with class groups.
- Be fair and even-handed.
- Speak slowly, quietly and clearly.
- Repeat instructions and demonstrate what is needed.
- Vary activities and incorporate collaborative and interactive strategies for learning.
- Be approachable – never make a student feel stupid for asking for help.

- Stay cheerful as much as you can – incorporate humour in your lessons.
- Accept and value mistakes as part of learning.
- Demonstrate self-respect.
- Teach the whole child – taking account of their needs in all domains of development.

SUMMARY OF STRATEGIES AND APPROACHES TO DEAL WITH DIFFICULTIES

- Consider whether basic needs are being met and if this is contributing to the behaviour.
- Let students know what you like about them.
- Be in charge of a situation, rather than in control of a pupil.
- Explore ways to increase school connectedness.

Professional development activities for teachers

Memorable teachers

Talk with friends or colleagues about the teachers you remember the most.

Draw a line down the middle of a piece of paper. In one column write about teachers who are just a bad memory and in the other column those who were a positive influence.
- What did these teachers do and say?
- What did these teachers make you and your friends feel about yourselves and your capabilities?
- How did they influence your attitude towards school and learning?
- How will this impact on your own practice?

Low and slow

Experiment with keeping your voice low and slow. When someone needs attention, go and speak to them directly rather than raising your voice across a room. If a student is behaving inappropriately use the proximity praise technique first by giving positive feedback to those close by and then asking generally if everyone understands what they are to do next. Use expressions and gestures, for example thumbs up gestures for those who are doing well. Ask individual students quietly and politely what they need to get going.

Check out what difference this made at the end of the lesson:

- Did you have more energy left over than usual?
- Did your voice quality make any difference, positive or negative, to how students got on with their work?
- Is it worth trying again? (Bear in mind that if students are used to a high volume level it will take a while to see the changes you want.)

(Continued)

(Continued)

Whole child

The five outcomes of the Every Child Matters agenda in the UK (DfES, 2004) are for children to:

- Be healthy
- Be safe
- Enjoy and achieve
- Make a positive contribution
- Achieve economic wellbeing.

Discuss with a partner ways in which this agenda might improve behaviour in school. Discuss the difference between teaching a subject and teaching the whole child.

Your own strengths as a teacher

Developing your effectiveness checklist. If you are brave enough you might like to give this to your students!

Table 2.1 Ten Teacher Strengths

Strength	How I have demonstrated this strength	What would help develop this further?
I like children and young people and enjoy teaching		
I believe in education and want to make a difference		
I value all students, regardless of their ability		
I treat all students fairly and with respect		
I have high expectations of all my pupils but accept mistakes as part of learning		
I am creative in planning so lessons are usually varied, interactive and often fun		
I give regular feedback and seek detailed feedback from students about how they are going		
I am positive, optimistic and usually cheerful		
I have self-respect and confidence		
I am a good communicator – I speak clearly and listen well		

Circle Solutions activities with students

These activities will:

- Help you understand what students think is important
- Show you are listening to what they have to say
- Help students understand the many skills required to be a 'good teacher'.

All Circles begin with a statement of the principles:

- When one person is speaking everyone else listens.
- You may pass if you do not want to say anything.
- There are no put-downs.

Sentence completions

- I feel respected at school when …
- I feel comfortable in school when …
- I learnt best when …

Mix up activity

Stand up and change places if you:

- had a good laugh in class this week
- learnt from a mistake
- achieved a personal best in something.

Pair share

Students talk about 'good' teachers they have known and decide what two things they both liked the most about these teachers. They feed back one each to the Circle: 'One thing about a good teacher is that they …'

Being a teacher: small group activity

(This will need to take place over more than one Circle session.)
Give each group of 4–5 students a different topic for which they must plan a 10–15 minute lesson. Each lesson must have at least one clear learning outcome, be interesting, fun and respectful to students. It must cater for students who find learning easy and need to be challenged and also those who find learning difficult and need encouragement.

Large group activity

Each group delivers their lesson to the whole Circle, taking it in turns to play the teacher role.

In the Circle the whole class reflects and feeds back on:

- Which groups did well and why?
- The learning from this activity.

RESOURCES

DCSF, *Personalised learning: A practical guide* (2008, DCSF). This can be downloaded from www.teachernet.gov.uk/publications

Gianna Knowles. *Ensuring every child matters* (2009, London: Sage). Chapter 6 on 'Enjoying and achieving' is particularly helpful for teachers.

Nel Noddings, What does it mean to educate the whole child? *Educational Leadership*, 2005, *63*(1), 8–13. Nel Noddings, an educational philosopher, makes the links between educating the whole child, democracy and a civil society. You can download this article by putting the relevant search words into Google.

Whole Child: A primary school programme that combines themed stories with Circle activities. There are three age levels and five themes: Getting Along; Emotions; Health and Wellbeing; Family and Community; and Citizenship and Human Rights. Two examples are *Jazzy's party* by Meredith Costain and *Changes* by Libby Gleeson. The first is for middle primary students on relational bullying and the second for upper primary students on parental re-marriage, both issues that many students face. The three teachers books are by Sue Roffey. This resource is available from Pearson Education.

REFERENCES

Baloglu, N. (2009). Negative behaviour of teachers with regard to high school students in classroom settings. *Journal of Instructional Psychology*, 36(1), 69–78.

Channel 4 / Talkback Thames (2005). *The unteachables*. (Four one-hour TV programmes). Details and further information: www.channel4.com/life/microsites/U/unteachables/index.html

Department for Education and Skills (DfES) (2004). *Every Child Matters: Change for children in schools*. London: DfES.

Geddes, L. (2009). Some schools may be breeding grounds for teen killers. *New Scientist*, 18 March.

Hattie, J. (2009). *Visible learning: A synthesis of over 800 meta-analyses relating to achievement*. London and New York: Routledge.

Martin, A.J. (2006). Personal Bests (PBs): A proposed multidimensional model and empirical analysis. *British Journal of Educational Psychology*, 76, 803–25.

Moore, S. & Kuol, N. (2007). Matters of the heart: Exploring the emotional dimensions of educational experience in recollected accounts of excellent teaching. *International Journal for Academic Development*, 12(2), 87–98.

Nuthall, G.A. (2007). *The hidden lives of learners*. Wellington NZ: New Zealand Council for Educational Research.

NSW Commission for Children & Young People (2004). *Ask the children: Children and young people speak about the issues important to them*. www.kids.nsw.gov.au/kids/resources/publications/ask-children

Roseth, C. J., Johnson, D.W. & Johnson, R.T. (2008). Promoting early adolescents' achievement and peer relationships: The effects of cooperative, competitive, and individualistic goal structures. *Psychological Bulletin*, 134 (2), 223–46.

Skiba, R., Reynolds, C.R., Graham, S., Sheras. P., Close Conely, J. & Garcia-Vasquez, E. (2006). *Are zero tolerance policies effective in the schools? An evidentiary review and recommendations*. Zero Tolerance Task Force Report for the American Psychological Association.

Wike, T.L & Fraser. M.W. (2009). School shootings: Making sense of the senseless. *Aggression and Violent Behaviour*, 14(3), 162–9.

3 BEING AND BECOMING EMOTIONALLY LITERATE

Chapter objectives

- To explore what it means to be emotionally literate
- To reflect on your own intra- and interpersonal skills and their development
- To examine how emotionally literate teachers promote pro-social classrooms
- To increase awareness of emotions in challenging situations
- To learn to deal with unacceptable behaviour whilst not undermining teacher–student relationships
- To emphasise the power of words – what we say and how we say it
- To learn how to avoid fruitless battles!

EMOTIONAL INTELLIGENCE AND EMOTIONAL LITERACY

Intra- and interpersonal intelligences have been on the educational agenda since Gardner wrote his first groundbreaking book on multiple intelligences (Gardner, 1983). The profile of emotional intelligence was raised further when Daniel Goleman (1996) argued that it reduces aggression and contributes to better learning, decision-making, and other foundations for successful living. He claimed that increasing emotional intelligence leads to *advantage in any domain in life* (p. 36).

There continues to be debate around the concept of emotional intelligence in academic circles but agreement across many disciplines that handling yourself and your relationships well improves wellbeing, performance and teamwork. Many prefer the term emotional literacy, as it does not have the connotation of an individual innate trait. It also suggests that social and emotional skills can be learnt and developed.

DEFINITION OF EMOTIONAL LITERACY

The following definition acknowledges the interaction between the personal, the interpersonal and the systemic.

Emotional literacy is a values-based concept concerned with all aspects of relationships. This includes not only the development of knowledge and skills within individuals but also the ethos of the systems and communities in which we live and work. The following summarises what this means at different levels.

Emotional literacy for individuals encompasses:

- *personal awareness, understanding, knowledge and skills related to what we feel and why*
- *knowing how to regulate emotion safely*
- *having awareness of what maintains emotional resources*
- *having a repertoire of ways to express emotion safely and being able to put this into practice in challenging situations*
- *awareness and knowledge of others and skills in relating to them*
- *the ability to tune into the affective to manage situations well*
- *a focus on the positive*
- *personal and professional integrity: identifying values and acting consistently across contexts on the basis of these*
- *a sense of personal effectiveness and an internal locus of control*
- *acting thoughtfully rather than on impulse.*

Emotional literacy between people promotes:

- *the demonstration of acknowledgment, acceptance and value*
- *positive and constructive communication*
- *effective interactions, including appropriate assertiveness*
- *honesty, transparency and trust*
- *support and the mutual maintenance of emotional resources*
- *willingness to resolve conflict by negotiation and compromise*
- *focusing on issues rather than personalities*
- *exploring competencies and possibilities rather than making judgements and attributing blame*
- *skills to de-escalate potential confrontation*
- *the ability to withdraw from situations appropriately and safely.*

Emotional literacy at a systems level (classroom, school, family, community):

- *enhances emotional safety*
- *gives agency and ownership to decision-making*
- *is ethical and fair*
- *encourages a constructive, positive and solution-focused approach*
- *promotes responsibility*
- *values diversity*
- *is flexible and creative*
- *has high expectations*
- *is modelled by leaders.*

Emotional literacy means working in the following ways to develop social and emotional capital:

- *collaborating to promote inclusive wellbeing rather than a blame culture*
- *proactively addressing underlying issues rather than reacting to and 'treating' symptoms of distress*
- *being reflective, listening to people and withholding hasty judgement*
- *focusing on the humanity we all share, respecting difference, valuing diversity and promoting a sense of belonging.*

Emotional literacy is neither sentimental nor self-indulgent. It has great potential to enhance both individual and community well-being. Re-evaluating the way we think about ourselves and how we interact with others can be challenging. (Roffey, 2006 pp. 2–3)

The promotion of pro-social behaviour requires teachers who are socially and emotionally competent themselves so they provide appropriate models as well as responding effectively in conflict situations.

When it comes to challenging students, negative emotions often run high. It takes sound levels of self-awareness and formidable skills to not let strong feelings overwhelm sensible action.

DEVELOPING EMOTIONAL LITERACY

The framework shown in Table 3.1 has 11 dimensions of social and emotional literacy (Roffey, 2010). Under each heading are questions designed to develop your knowledge and skills so you become a more socially and emotionally competent teacher. You are asked to identify ways in which you already demonstrate these skills and reflect on the next steps to take.

The framework begins with an exploration of your values and beliefs. Some people refute facts that do not fit in with their own belief system. For instance, there is strong agreement between scientists that human behaviour is contributing to climate change but those with a vested interest in thinking otherwise do everything they can to deny the overwhelming evidence. If you do not value relationships or believe educators should take these into account you are unlikely to be willing to develop your own emotional literacy. Since all the evidence says relationships are central to effective learning these beliefs might be the first thing to examine and re-consider.

THE EMOTIONALLY LITERATE TEACHER AND THE PRO–SOCIAL CLASSROOM

Authoritative teaching, which I have renamed facilitative teaching to distinguish it more clearly from authoritarian (Roffey, 2004), is a combination of high expectations with high levels of support. This mirrors the parenting style proved to have optimal outcomes for children. Parents who are warm, responsive and flexible but clear about their expectations for high standards of behaviour have children who are likely to become well adjusted, independent, motivated and empathic (Baumrind, 1966; Kaufman et al., 2000). Children from authoritarian households where there are high levels of control but low warmth, or permissive families where there is love but few boundaries, do less well on achievement, mental health and pro-social behaviour (Chan & Koo, 2008; Lexmond & Reeves, 2009). Facilitative teachers, unsurprisingly, promote both positive academic and behavioural outcomes (Baker et al., 2009).

Table 3.1

Dimensions of social and emotional learning	Questions for development
Self-awareness: • Being and becoming • Values, beliefs, strengths and goals.	Why did I become a teacher? What do I believe are the qualities of a 'good' teacher? What do I want for my students? What am I really good at? What skills do I most need to develop?
Emotional awareness: • Aetiology • Triggers • Embodiment • Social construction.	What do I understand about the biology of emotion? To what extent am I in control of my emotions or do they control me? What have I noticed about the way my thoughts and feelings interact with each other? What triggers strong reactions in me? In which ways am I aware of the personal, social and cultural influences on what I feel, the way I think about things and how I interpret events?
Emotional skills: • Regulation • Expression • Resilience.	How do I face and deal with my own difficult feelings? How do I calm myself down or cheer myself up? How do I express what I am feeling? What sustains my emotional wellbeing and helps me be resilient in adversity?
Conceptualising the 'other': • How we position others in our world.	How do I appreciate my unique characteristics and strengths? How do I value unique qualities in others? In which ways do I focus on the positive in people rather than their deficits? In which ways do I acknowledge and value 'the whole child'? To what extent do I think about people as individuals rather than assuming characteristics from a stereotype? How do I look for what I have in common with others?
Interpersonal skills: • Skills needed to establish and maintain positive relationships.	How do I demonstrate interest in others? In which ways do I show respect, reliability, kindness, care, warmth, trust and support? How do I know I am an active listener? What skills do I have that help me collaborate well with others? How do I celebrate the success of others?
Situational skills: • Tuning into the emotional context.	How do I find out about issues affecting students? How do I show empathy to others? What helps me to read and interpret emotional expression in students, parents and colleagues? How do I check the meaning of student behaviour? In which ways do I avoid making judgements on limited evidence? Am I aware that problem-solving is ineffective in times of high emotion?
Leadership: • Taking responsibility • Empowering others.	Do I set myself achievable goals? What enables me to take initiative? How do I empower others, especially students?

(Continued)

Table 3.1   (Continued)

Dimensions of social and emotional learning	Questions for development
	How do I involve them in decision-making?
	How do I both take responsibility for my own actions and disperse leadership?
	In which ways is my confidence growing?
Promoting the positive: • Feelings, thoughts and actions.	How well do I focus on the things that are good in my job and good about students?
	In which ways is my communication positive?
	How do I maintain an optimistic outlook?
	In which ways do I encourage students to have fun in my lessons?
	What do I do to keep things in perspective so I don't get pulled down unnecessarily?
	How do I show I don't take myself too seriously?
Conflict and confrontation: • Dealing well with relational difficulties.	How do I show that I am willing to negotiate a win–win outcome in a conflict situation?
	What do I know about being appropriately assertive?
	What skills do I have to de-escalate a confrontation?
	What problem-solving skills do I have?
Repair and restoration: • Mending what is broken.	How often do I admit mistakes or that other ways of doing things may have been better?
	How do I show that I am willing to rebuild a relationship?
	Do I respond positively to others who seek resolution of difficulties?
Ethics and integrity: • Moral / human rights dimensions of SEL.	To what extent am I honest with myself and with others about things that matter?
	In which ways am I an ethical person?
	To what extent have I developed a philosophy of life that guides my own behaviour across contexts?
	Would others say I walk the talk and live my values?

Questions for reflection

Which questions in the framework stand out as being most relevant for you?

Are there others you would add?

Case study: the popcorn dilemma

I stood behind a mother with her young daughter in the cinema queue. The little girl had a big box of popcorn and as she was stuffing this in her mouth much of it dropped onto the floor. The mother ignored the mess. This was permissive parenting. The little girl was learning that she was not responsible for her actions, that someone else would clean up after her and that she did not have to consider the impact of her behaviour on others. If her mother had scolded or shouted at her and made her clear up the mess all by herself this would have been authoritarian and controlling. The girl would have learnt that you got into trouble even when you didn't know why and that doing as you were told was not enjoyable. The third, facilitative, way would be to point out gently to the child what she was doing, tell her why we couldn't leave it like that (others would get popcorn all over their feet and they might slip) and then help her clear up, modelling expectations. The child would learn that her behaviour has consequences, that we are responsible for the wellbeing of others and that she could have fun with her mum doing things together so that even chores could make her feel good. If her mother had then praised her for being helpful and thoughtful she would begin to see herself this way and take pride in being so.

Questions for reflection and discussion

Identify authoritarian, permissive and facilitative teachers you have known.

What did they do and what was the impact on pupils.

What impacts might be less visible?

FEELINGS ELICITED BY CHALLENGING BEHAVIOUR: FEAR, FURY AND FRUSTRATION

The following are some of the feelings teachers have when faced with challenging situations, either the anticipation of them or the actual occurrence, with some suggestions for pre-empting these so you have more control over your responses.

Fear

Many teachers experience anxiety and even fear in relation to behaviour. Inexperienced teachers in particular may lack confidence in their abilities to manage the complexities of a class. Anxiety can make you hyper-alert: you sleep badly, are not relaxed, do everything you can to prepare for challenges and are therefore on the lookout for them. This can lead to being hypersensitive, perceiving minor behaviour infringements as unacceptable when a more laid-back approach will quickly smooth over a situation. It can become a self-fulfilling expectation.

Fear is toxic and can colour everything you are doing. If you wake up feeling nauseous at the thought of the day ahead, with your heart pounding and wanting to hide under the blankets, then you are not going to be able to think straight and teach well. Take action at the first signs of anxiety.

The biological reason for fear is to prepare the body to flee from a potential threat. Hormones such as adrenaline are pumped into the body in preparation. The part of the brain known as the amygdala initiates this response. Sometimes responses are instinctive but the amygdala will also go into action if it has learnt that the trigger is a potential threat.

As this organ is the seat of emotional memory some reactions are linked to our earliest memories – perhaps sudden noises or being left alone. The amygdala sends messages to our body to prepare it for action much faster than the neo-cortex (the thinking centre of the brain) kicks in. This is sometimes known as an emotional hijack. Unless there is immediate physical danger, it is better to wait a moment before acting on an emotional cue.

Fear in school is usually connected with a perceived threat to your sense of self. Some fears relate to students, some are about your own responses and others relate to colleagues and managers. If you are in an authoritarian school the chances are you will be more afraid of the head teacher than the students! Some fear is hyped by staffroom conversation, your managers or what the papers say. You need to sort out how much fear is being fuelled by others and your own history rather than by the situation itself.

Many anxieties are related to the unknown. We cope much better when we have some useful knowledge. Let's look more closely at what you might be afraid of:

- Fear of not knowing what to do
- Fear of losing control of the class
- Fear of losing control yourself – with tears or anger
- Fear of losing face
- Fear of being seen as a poor or weak teacher
- Fear of looking foolish or losing the respect of others
- Fear of being in trouble yourself
- Fear of not having sufficient resources to keep going
- Fear of having made a bad career choice
- Fear for other students
- Fear on occasions for your own safety: being physically attacked by students is comparatively rare but receives much publicity when it does happen.

> There are many fatally poisonous snakes in Australia and a lot of people are scared of them. Very few people, however, are actually killed by being attacked by snakes. Nearly all deaths occur where someone either deliberately or inadvertently threatens the snake, such as poking a stick at it or treading on it. As long as you make enough noise or keep a respectful distance so the snake keeps theirs, the fear is unfounded. Sometimes teachers poke metaphorical sticks at students and then wonder why they get bitten!

Facing down fear

Check realities

Fear often lives in our imagination and can be assuaged by knowledge. Check what is really going on. How much of your day are you under threat – by how many students and in which ways? It is likely that you will find it is much less than you thought.

Put things in perspective

Are you allowing the few things that go wrong to dominate how you feel? We all have a tendency to do this. It takes conscious effort to keep negative feelings from overwhelming the positive. Be firm with your negative inner voice!

Check intentions

Do not go for the worst possible interpretation of events. Does the student mean to be insulting or has she just not thought through the impact of her words/facial expression/body stance? Does he intend to question your authority and make you look incompetent or is he just having a bad day? Are people laughing at you or at a situation?

Refocus

One answer to fear is to refocus away from the potential threat. Think about what the behaviour means for the student rather than what it means for you. All action has a meaning for the person doing it.

Davies and Laws (2000) give the following example of how we position students and jump to conclusions about the meaning of their behaviour. It also addresses how fear might be manufactured and how the application of 'consequences' puts all the onus for change on the young person.

Case study

Shane was suspended from his regular school. In assembly he was wearing his baseball cap. When he was asked to take it off, he refused; got up, turned his back on the principal, said nothing and walked out in front of a couple of hundred students. Shane was suspended for this action … 'Consequences' were brought to bear and Shane was sent away from the school: 'He must learn about consequences and so shape his actions accordingly'.

Shane later told Cath that he had had his hair cut short and did not want it seen. But of course he could not say that at the time. To provide such an explanation in front of the assembly would be embarrassing. Further, to do such a thing was neither a recognisable pattern of behaviour that he could imagine anyone taking up and it was certainly not one of the repertoires of action that he could take up and in doing so be recognised as behaving acceptably. So he walked out. An obvious choice really, but it could not be read by the school this way. His action was read as powerful and disruptive. Staff at the school were extremely upset by his refusal to comply, and perhaps even a little afraid of what they saw as his challenge.

Build confidence

The antidote to anxiety and fear is confidence – confidence in yourself and your abilities, confidence that you do not have to control everything, confidence that even your most difficult students are not all bad and confidence that there are colleagues who will help and support you.

Confidence can be built by the following thoughts:

- Most students want to be in school and learn.
- Some students have issues that are highly stressful for them.
- You have choices in the way you perceive behaviour.
- You do not have to be in control all the time – there are ways in which you can stay in charge of a situation: this means learning useful things to say and do.
- Colleagues have also been through tough times, you are not the only one.
- There are people to support you – check who these are.

Confidence can be developed by taking the following actions in challenging situations:

- Not taking student behaviour personally
- Not going on the defensive
- Focusing on the positive
- Looking for student strengths
- Learning to breathe regularly to reduce the physical symptoms of fear
- Looking confident; standing tall and making good eye contact not only makes you feel better about yourself but students are also more likely to respond to your authority – a bent posture and looking away does the opposite
- Giving the student space to calm down – this also gives you some time to think
- Giving yourself affirmations
- Finding something light-hearted to say where possible and appropriate: it can take the heat out of the situation; self-deprecation works, sarcasm does not.

Confidence is shown by using questions and phrases that show respect and self-respect:

- I can see you are having a hard time here.
- What can I do to help?
- Do you need a quiet moment?
- I cannot control you, only you have the power to do that.
- All I can tell you is what will happen if you make certain choices – it is up to you to choose.
- I believe in your ability to … (calm down, take control of yourself).
- It matters to me that you are making progress in your learning.

Fury

Anger, like other emotions, is on a continuum. It can begin with an unease that something is not right which grows into a rage if this is not addressed. Or it can be explosive in response to an event or perception – usually of perceived injustice. Explosive anger may result from the culmination of events – only one of which may be immediately visible. This is another reason why interrogating a student on 'why they are behaving like this' is not useful.

Anger can be valuable in motivating people to make the world a fairer and more humane place. It is not anger that is the problem but the way it is expressed. Although anger can lead to aggression it is not itself aggression and it is useful to discriminate between the two.

Anger is also strongly associated with loss and change and is recognised as part of the grief process. You can often 'scratch a mad child and find a sad child'.

There are often good reasons to be angry with students whose behaviour is unacceptable. Some of this is personal, the way they treat you, and some is about social justice, how they treat others. Such behaviours can include:

- Unkindness, callousness and cruelty
- Their lack of acknowledgement or appreciation of your efforts
- Lack of responsiveness
- Refusal to take responsibility
- Unreasonable demands
- Being self-centred
- Expressing values that are counter to yours – perhaps racist or sexist.

What happens when students behave in ways that affect you personally? They do not listen, are insolent, do not follow instructions, talk over you and/or make fun of you. The way you engage students in the first place will stop some of this happening.

📁 Case study

Miss Banbury was our English teacher. She always looked as if everything was a worry. Her lessons were dull and uninspiring even for those who had chosen to study English Literature. She spoke in a monotone, interacted at a minimum level with her students and did not seem at all enthusiastic about her subject. Our class thought she was fair game. In the middle of a lesson one morning someone began to tap under the desk with a pencil – and others joined in. Miss Banbury had no idea where the noise was coming from at any one time and had no way to stop it. Whenever she approached someone they put their hands on the desk and the tapping continued elsewhere. She got more and more angry. We thought it was a great laugh – until she burst out of the room in tears. We'd gone too far.

〰 Questions for reflection and discussion

What did this behaviour mean?

What would have made a difference to the outcome?

Emotions are highly contagious. We have mirroring neurons in our brains that may spur us to copy the emotions being expressed by others around us. This means that when a student is angry we may immediately feel angry ourselves. It is essential to be aware of this and wherever possible model calmness. This will help students calm down faster.

The physical manifestation of anger prepares you to defend and fight rather than run. It is natural to go on the defensive to protect yourself. This is rarely helpful and can often escalate a situation.

> 📁 **Case study**
>
> Jess comes into school after lunch having had a row with his girlfriend. He is still upset. He arrives late to class, throws his school bag into the corner of the room and kicks a chair over. Mr Hardy, his teacher, shouts across the room to him: 'Pick that up, how dare you come into my class like that'. Jess sneers back: 'Don't want to be here anyway, your lessons are rubbish'. Mr Hardy retorts back that it isn't his lessons that are the problem but Jess's attitude to work. He intimates that Jess has low ability. Jess, with no holds barred, begins to tell Mr Hardy what he thinks of him as a teacher while others in the class listen in. Mr Hardy shouts at Jess to 'get out'. Jess complies but kicks over two more chairs in the process. The next time he comes to Mr Hardy's class he is already spoiling for a fight.

This situation is not uncommon in schools. Jess's behaviour was certainly unacceptable and he needed to know that – but the teacher taking his behaviour personally and being defensive made the outcome much worse for them both.

> 〰️ **Questions for reflection and discussion**
>
> Have you come across teachers expressing anger in this way?
>
> What happens?
>
> Going on the defensive is a common response in human behaviour: do teachers have a responsibility to react differently?

When your anger is about injustice to someone else it can be even more difficult to deal with. Students may seem callous, selfish and arrogant. One thing to do here is to appeal to their ambivalence about what they are doing in terms of their 'best selves', for example:

- I expect better from you – this behaviour does not show your … (e.g. strength of character, innate sense of fairness, ability to make good judgements).
- I am not sure this fits with how you want to be.
- I wonder if you are feeling great about yourself just now? I bet you felt better about yourself when (identify a positive here if you can).

Harnessing anger

You can regulate anger in the following ways:

- Remind yourself that students bring many issues to school – not everything is about you.
- Dissociate and externalise: see your anger as giving you information but not taking over.
- If you possibly can delay a little before dealing with an incident: this will enable you to calm down and use your energy more wisely – it will also help the student. Following up incidents afterwards is often a better strategy than jumping in.

How do you express anger well in the school situation?

- Ensure the student knows it is the behaviour that is unacceptable, not them.
- Use 'I' statements rather than accusatory 'You' statements.
- Own and give voice to your emotions: this is not only helpful to you but models the behaviour you want in students.
  I am feeling furious with you just now – I need to calm down before we speak about it otherwise I may say things I regret. Please wait outside so I can finish what I am doing here and have a moment to get myself together.

Frustration

This is a common emotion and particularly strong in teachers who care about education and their students. When frustration builds up it can give rise to despair and so can be toxic to healthy learning environments. Frustration is not just about student behaviour but the myriad of issues that impede teachers from working at an optimal level.

Frustration comes about because:

- things do not go to plan
- there is never enough time
- you might not get through the demands of the curriculum
- the resources you need are not there
- the support you need is not available
- you cannot use your initiative or creativity
- you do not feel consulted
- others undermine your work.

This list suggests that it is not just students that lead to teacher frustration but the accumulation of issues within and beyond the school. This requires whole school approaches – see Chapter 12.

Although they may not realise they are doing this, teachers may express their frustration with students rather than with colleagues or the school leadership because the classroom is a safer place. A teacher may already be primed for a showdown and the first student who presents a challenge gets the full force of their pent up feelings. This just exacerbates a negative cycle.

⌇ Question for reflection and discussion

What similarities can you find between a teacher who takes their frustration out on students and pupils who are better behaved at home than at school?

Dealing with frustration

Frustration, like anger, can give you energy. In a professional development activity teachers talked about how they dealt with frustration and several said they took a long walk, another said she thumped a cushion, others said that they talked things over with trusted friends and colleagues. It is not possible, however, to use these strategies in the classroom!

One way to become less frustrated is to become more flexible. This enables you to be more laid-back in your response to situations. Go to Plan B when Plan A falls apart.

🗁 Case study

I was the fourth and last person to speak at a seminar. All the others had gone over time and I could feel the audience getting restless before lunch. I sat there getting increasingly frustrated and irritable. When it was my turn I should have cut down my talk to two minutes and finished promptly. Instead, I ploughed through what I had prepared, lost the attention of the audience and probably their respect. It was a lesson I have tried not to forget: respond to the situation rather than stick to the plan!

Creativity helps. Look for alternatives. If you don't have the material you need, how can you improvise? Ask students for ideas.

Another way is to express your frustration in ways that bring humour into the situation. This will do you many favours – it shows you are not taking yourself too seriously, you can take the heat out of a situation and you are able to make others laugh. It helps you feel in control.

Avoid attributing blame or accusing students – this simply makes things worse. Good time management may also help – see Chapter 11.

GETTING NOWHERE BUT KEEPING ON TRACK

There are times when you will come across students whose experiences have so damaged them that your efforts to connect with them lead nowhere. If you imagine what it must be like to ask someone to trust you when you have been let down over and over again you can understand how hard it might be for these individuals. You present a threat to them, because to establish something positive with you just risks another rejection when you move on. In these circumstances all you can do is to keep to your own codes of behaviour, give these students as many positive experiences as you can and look to your own support networks and coping strategies. If you do not take their rejection personally you will be able to protect yourself emotionally. Fortunately there are comparatively few students like this – most have redeeming features, something to like and an ability to respond positively at times. Keep things in perspective and hold on to your sense of humour!

SUMMARY OF STRATEGIES AND APPROACHES TO PROMOTE POSITIVE BEHAVIOUR

- Set a positive 'emotional tone' in the classroom.
- Be actively and positively engaged with both your students and your subject.
- Model the behaviour and communication you want to see in students.
- Be encouraging and supportive in your relationships.
- Think about what it means to look and be confident.

SUMMARY OF STRATEGIES AND APPROACHES TO DEAL WITH DIFFICULTIES

- Be aware of emotional hijacking and where possible wait for your thinking to get back on track before responding.
- Be flexible – respond to the demands of the situation.
- Acknowledge and validate feelings in students.
- Check realities to stop imagining the worst.
- Do not take things personally and go on the defensive.
- Beware mirroring negative emotions.
- Use self-deprecation, never sarcasm.
- Show belief in students' ability to take positive control themselves.

Professional development activities for teachers

Emotional tone of the classroom

In pairs, think of three different classrooms you have each experienced and rate them out of five for 'emotional tone' with five being the most positive. What was actually going on? How did you feel about being in these classrooms? What action by the teacher would have moved the emotional tone of the least positive one step in the right direction?

Setting SEL targets

In which three dimensions might you develop your emotional literacy? Talk with others about how will this help you in responding to behavioural issues in school?

Mirroring emotions

Think of a time when someone in the vicinity was expressing a high level of emotion such as anger, laughter, excitement, sadness or fear. What happened to you? Did you experience a similar feeling? Discuss your experiences with a partner. What does this tell you about emotions in school?

Hypothetical discussions

Consider the scenarios featuring Kas, Justine and Billy set out below. There are no right or wrong answers to these dilemmas. The aim is to generate ideas that may be helpful to all concerned. The questions below are to guide your discussion.

- What are your priorities in this situation?
- What does it appear the student is feeling?
- What might be contributing to these feelings – both in the short and longer term?
- What information here is relevant to this situation and why?
- What other information would help?
- What might help the student calm down?
- What might be your immediate feelings?
- What might be contributing to these feelings?
- What might be your immediate response based on these feelings?
- In which ways might your response be different after thinking about it?
- What would help you be in charge of this situation?
- What are the issues for other students and how they might be feeling?
- List your options – some may be conditional on other factors.
- What are the likely outcomes for you of different responses?
- What are the likely outcomes for the student?
- Could anything have prevented this scenario arising in the first place?
- What might you do in the longer term to support the student and promote their emotional wellbeing and learning?
- Do other students have a role here? In which ways?
- What is the role of the whole school?

  How can you apply the learning here to other similar scenarios?

Kas

Kas is 14. He is not doing well in school – all his standardised test scores hover below the average. He has a particular skill in cooking and is usually cooperative and attentive in home economics lessons. He has begun to drop out of school, missing one in every few days. In most lessons he constantly talks to others, turns in his seat and aims to raise a laugh. He is not unpopular, and peers seem to enjoy his sense of humour.

You have already discovered that his father left before Kas was 3 and he never sees him. He has had two stepfathers, both of whom have also disappeared. He is very protective of his mother and three half-sisters. He loves his bike and spends a lot of time keeping it in good condition. He worked Saturdays for a local garage for several weeks but last week had a row with the manager and walked out.

One Monday morning Kas arrives in school very late. He glowers as he walks into your lesson and slams the door behind him. You ask him to take his seat and speak with you later. As he stomps to his seat you hear him swear at you under his breath.

Justine

Justine is 9 and has been a concern since the day she arrived in school. She seems isolated, is rejecting of others, has no stable friendships but hangs about on the edge of groups. With the encouragement of staff some girls invite her to play sometimes but this usually ends in tears as Justine does not follow the rules, runs off with other people's things and can be verbally and physically aggressive if she doesn't get her own way.

At the end of one Friday lunchtime a group of girls approach you to say that Justine has taken several school bags and thrown these over a high fence next to the school field. The owners are furious and one told her bluntly what she thinks of her and her behaviour. Justine is now sitting by the fence crying and refusing to come into class. The bags have been retrieved.

Billy

A pupil runs into your room and says that you have to come immediately. Billy, who is 16 and has already been suspended from school, is attacking someone in the schoolyard. Apparently he has got a broken bottle and is ablaze with anger. His target is another boy who is a member of another 'gang' in the school.

Affirmations

Affirmations are statements that promote a positive mind-set. You say them to yourself to foster a sense of wellbeing, purpose and confidence. These can be statements such as:

- I can be calm.
- I am able to see the best in others.
- Today I will not take myself too seriously.

(Continued)

(Continued)

In a group of three write down 20 affirmations on cards which will help in dealing with challenging behaviour in school. Now agree your favourite five to share with the group. Why did you choose these five? How will they help?

Circle Solutions activities with students

These activities will:

- help students understand more about their emotions
- support ways of regulating feelings.

All Circles begin with a statement of the principles:

- When one person is speaking everyone else listens.
- You may pass if you do not want to say anything.
- There are no put-downs.

Mix up activity: what do feelings look like?

Go round the circle giving each student one of these words in turn:

- Excited, surprised, scared, relaxed
- Ask them to change places when their emotion is called. They move according to the emotion they have been given. Add the words 'a little bit' or 'a lot'.

Pair share

Ask students to talk to each other about what makes them cross and irritable. Then ask them to discuss what helps. Can they find two things in common?

The face of feelings

Ask students to face each other in pairs. One student is asked to look happy. Their partner studies their eyes, mouth, neck and shoulders carefully and then tries to mirror this in their own expression and body language.

They reverse roles. The second student is asked to look unhappy. Their partner studies carefully at how this is expressed and mirrors what they see.

Did students begin to experience the emotions themselves? What else did they notice? They report to the Circle anything they discovered.

Calming breathing

When we are anxious our breathing and heart rate become erratic. Emotions and their embodiment is a two-way process. We can reduce anxiety by controlling our breathing.

Ask everyone to imagine their breathing is being monitored by a thermometer. When they breathe in the mercury rises to the top, when they breathe out it falls. The aim is to get the mercury moving up and down smoothly. Ask them to breathe in to a count of three and then out again to a count of three. Continue for a full minute. Students now have a strategy for regulating difficult emotion.

RESOURCES

Type *Children See, Children Do* into Google or YouTube. This very short video shows how important adult models are for children in learning how to be and live together.

Check out Elizabeth Morris and Julie Casey's book *Developing emotionally literate staff* (2006, London: Sage). There is an excellent section on the analysis of an emotional hijack.

REFERENCES

Baker, J.A., Clark, T.P., Crowl, A. & Carlson. J.S. (2009). The influence of authoritative teaching on children's school adjustment: Are children with behavioural problems differentially affected? *School Psychology International*, 30, 374–82.

Baumrind, D. (1966). Effects of authoritative parental control on child behavior, *Child Development*, 37(4), 887–907.

Chan, T.W. and Koo, A. (2008). *Parenting style and youth outcome in the UK*. Oxford: University of Oxford.

Davies, B., & Laws, C. (2000). Poststructuralist theory in practice: Working with 'behaviourally disturbed' children. *Qualitative Studies in Education*, 13(3), 205–21.

Gardner, H. (1983). *Frames of mind: The theory of multiple intelligences*. New York: Basic Books.

Goleman, D. (1996). *Emotional intelligence: Why it can matter more than IQ*. New York: Basic Books.

Kaufmann, D., Gesten, E., Santa Lucia, R.C., Salcedo, O., Rendina-Gobioff, G. & Gadd, R. (2000). The relationship between parenting style and children's adjustment: The parents' perspective. *Journal of Child and Family Studies*, 9(2), 231–45.

Lexmond, J. & Reeves, R. (2009). *Building character*. London: Demos.

Roffey, S. (2004). *The new teacher's survival guide to behaviour*. London: Sage Publications.

Roffey, S. (2006). *Circle time for emotional literacy*. London: Sage Publications.

Roffey, S. (2010). Content and context for learning about relationships: A cohesive framework for individual and whole school development. *Educational and Child Psychology*, 27(1), 156–67.

4 KNOWING THE STUDENTS YOU TEACH

Chapter objectives

- To summarise risk factors for students
- To summarise what we know about resilience
- To focus on the protective factors schools can provide
- To identify what you cannot change in a student's life and what you can
- To avoid making assumptions on limited knowledge
- To focus on solutions rather than dissecting problems
- To emphasise that universal wellbeing is in everyone's interests.

Counsellors in training have said they wished they had known more of their students' stories when they were teachers. Knowing what students are dealing with has given them greater insight into behaviour and needs in the classroom. There is no way, however, that a teacher can know all the stories any one student brings. The best we can do is not jump to conclusions about what is going on. All action is meaningful to the person doing it, even if we do not understand why. The following is an example of what can happen if we do not, at least to a minimal extent, explore the meanings of behaviour and the stories that are underneath.

📁 Case study

Haran was walking up the steps on his way to the front of the school to report in late. He was preoccupied and didn't see the deputy head teacher until he was almost upon him: 'Not only are you late, young man, you are not in proper uniform. Where's your tie?' Haran shrugged. He'd forgotten it. The deputy put his hand on the boy's arm: 'And look at me when I'm speaking to you.' Haran looked up, brushed the teacher's hand away with some force, sneered and swore vehemently. He then turned round and walked out of the school gates ignoring demands to return. All hell broke loose. Meetings were held in which

Haran's 'poor attitude' to school, 'aggression towards teachers', 'unacceptable language' and 'major attendance problems' were all cited as reasons for his eventual exclusion. He ended up as a student in a pupil referral unit where he was invariably polite and well behaved – though still frequently late or absent.

Haran was a very mature looking 13-year-old: a big lad with a shadow of a moustache on his upper lip. He was the eldest male in his household as his father had gone missing before the family fled to the UK as asylum seekers three years earlier. His mother spoke very little English and Haran spent much of his time translating for her with various agencies. That morning he had gone with her to the doctor's where it had become clear that not only was she physically unwell, she was also very depressed. Haran's school tie had been the last thing on his mind.

〜〜 Questions for reflection and discussion

Identify some of the stories that Haran was bringing to that situation.

The deputy head had alternative ways of addressing the situation that would not have taken any more time. What could he have done or said differently that may have had a more positive outcome?

What strengths and positive qualities can you identify for Haran?

WHAT WE KNOW ABOUT RISK AND RESILIENCE

There have now been a number of studies that have helped to identify risk factors and protective factors for children and young people (e.g. Benard, 2004). One of the most well known of these is a longitudinal study which explored the life trajectory of nearly 700 babies born in Kauai in Hawaii in 1955 (Werner & Smith, 1992, 2001). All of these infants were born to families where there were four or more risk factors.

Risk factors

Risk factors in families include the following: neonatal stress, very young parents, poverty, long-term unemployment, alcoholism and other addictions, mental health issues such as depression or schizophrenia, disability or chronic illness, violence, criminality and social isolation. To these can be added growing up in a war zone, displacement, bereavement and loss, and major trauma including abuse and family conflict. Adversities are interactive. Several of the difficulties above could lead to poor attachment, which in turn contributes to psychosocial problems, poor attention and difficulty with learning (Gerhardt, 2004).

One or two adversities might cause you some problems but having four or more increases your chance of negative outcomes by a factor of 10. A mirror image then follows in which young people growing up with such experiences are at risk of repeating them in their own lives in an inter-generational cycle of risk and disadvantage. They not only often struggle with learning but may also develop anti-social behaviour, depression and other mental health difficulties. They may find it hard to establish and maintain healthy relationships, seek solace in drugs and alcohol, not be able to hold down a job and are more likely to be involved in criminal activity. They also tend to be sexually active at an early age and become young parents themselves.

Everyone experiences adversity at some time or other – it is part of the human condition. One or two risk factors are unlikely to impact on our life trajectory. Children born to young parents may do very well, people recover from major trauma or eventually adapt to a loss in their lives. Some adversities are, however, powerful predictors of negative outcomes. For instance, individuals who are sexually abused in childhood are much more likely than others to suffer from serious mental illness (Kendler et al., 2000).

RESILIENCE

The valuable finding in the Kauai study, replicated in several studies since, is that although two-thirds of those individuals born with major risk factors had the predicted negative outcomes listed above, the other third had risen above the adversities in their early life to do well. The study identified the factors that contributed to the development of this resilience. These protective factors can be divided into personal factors and environmental factors, though clearly there are interactions within and between categories.

Personal factors:

- A positive outlook
- A sense of humour
- Pro-social orientation – wanting to connect with others
- Persistence – not giving up at the first hurdle
- Willingness and ability to talk about issues
- Intelligence and problem-solving abilities
- Confidence and self-esteem
- Androgyny – not being too gender stereotyped.

Environmental factors:

- Someone who believes in you as a worthwhile person
- A sense of belonging – opportunities to participate in your community
- High expectations – being encouraged to do your best in all situations.

Personal protective factors

A positive and optimistic outlook on life is powerful and interacts with other factors such as having a sense of humour and getting things into perspective. When life has handed you a raw deal you may begin to see everything as conspiring against you. The ability to overcome this tendency, be aware of and thankful for anything positive, make the most of opportunities and stay hopeful about the future makes a difference to what actually happens to you. Blaming others for your situation has short-term benefits in making you feel better but in the longer term makes you feel helpless. Blaming yourself just leads to a negative self-concept and hopelessness. Being able to accept that some of what happens is down to other people, some to you and some just a matter of chance is helpful. A positive approach also fosters an interest in setting achievable goals. Achievements can build confidence and self-esteem.

Intelligence is protective – with the proviso that this does not lead to 'over-thinking' and rumination on the negative. The ability to problem-solve however, adds a personal repertoire of strategies to cope with adversity. It stops a situation from being overwhelming.

Being willing and able to talk about issues is protective. Highly macho males who believe their self-image will be damaged by talking things through are therefore more at risk than those who are able to discuss personal issues. Girls and women are also less at risk when they are able to be assertive rather than submissive.

Wanting to connect with others and having the ability to do so is another powerful factor in resilience and links to one of the three environmental factors, a sense of belonging.

Helen McGrath and Toni Noble (2011) have written the Bounce Back resiliency program to help primary aged children learn some of these important skills. Using a wide range of activities and incorporating many well-loved children's stories, teachers encourage students to understand that adversity is part of life and bad things happen to everyone from time to time. It is important to get this into perspective and not let the bad overshadow the good. When you are having a difficult time it can be helpful to talk to other people. Pupils are taught that some things are open to change but others are not. Most importantly, they come to appreciate that how you think about what happens to you can make a big difference.

Questions for reflection and discussion

What personal protective factors do you practice?

How do they help in times of stress?

How many of these strategies do our students have access to?

Environmental protective factors

Having someone in your life who communicates to you that you are a worthwhile person is a major protective factor against adversity.

In order to develop normally, a child needs the enduring, irrational involvement of one or more adults in care of and in joint activity with that child. In short, somebody has to be crazy about that kid (Bronfenbrenner, 2004 p. 262).

For most children their parents fulfil this role – but for some, other family members are equally and sometimes more significant. Grandparents, siblings, aunts and uncles can be powerful influences for wellbeing, especially when parents are emotionally, if not physically absent.

> 📁 **Case study**
>
> Jennifer's mother, Xenia, was able to look after her daughter's physical needs but was emotionally very volatile and therefore unpredictable. Sometimes Xenia was loving, but more often demanding of love. Jennifer was never quite sure why she made her mother so angry. Sometimes Xenia screamed abuse, blaming her daughter for all the ills in her life – especially the breakdown of her marriage. Although she never hit her, occasionally she shut her daughter in a cupboard. When at her most unstable Xenia was admitted to the psychiatric ward of the local hospital and Jennifer went to live with her paternal grandmother. It was this woman who Jennifer says 'rescued' her. She was always there, always loving, always predictable, and in many ways let the little girl know that she was a person worthy of love and affection.

Teachers often underestimate how important they can be in the lives of their students. In a thousand small interactions that convey warmth, welcoming and consistency they can provide the psychological input that lifts someone out of a major risk zone. Ways in which you might build this relationship with your vulnerable and challenging students are addressed in Chapter 7.

Feeling you belong somewhere, that you matter – not only to the individuals in your world but to the community in which you are situated – is increasingly recognised as important to sustained wellbeing (e.g. Libbey, 2004). Communities are many and varied. They include the family, the local neighbourhood, cultural and/or religious communities, sports clubs and other similar organisations. It can be reasoned that sporting events have significance in propping up a sense of belonging where more traditional forms of community connectedness are frayed.

Schools are significant communities in the lives of children. School connectedness goes beyond the wearing of a uniform or cheering on your team. Students benefit from a sense of belonging in which they feel included and valued – more on this in Chapter 6.

Developing a sense of belonging will foster inclusion. Exclusive belonging is where the members of a particular community may foster antipathy towards those 'outside' in order to maintain a sense of supremacy. Although this boosts resilience for those inside it can undermine wellbeing for others. In an extreme form it is at the root of racism, social injustice and violence.

The third important factor identified in the research is high expectations. This means not writing anyone off by dismissing them as unable to learn or having negative qualities that will not change, thereby giving the message they are not worth the bother. High expectations do not mean setting the bar so high that pupils will fail but high enough so that they are challenged. High expectations need to be combined with a focus on strengths and a belief in the best of someone.

〰 Questions for reflection and discussion

Can you name one teacher who believed in you and made you feel that you could achieve? What difference has this person made to your life?

BUBBLE-WRAPPED CHILDREN

There is another group of students that teachers are coming across more frequently. These children are growing up in what is becoming known as 'risk averse families' (Gill, 2007). These parents, wanting the best for their children but not fully appreciating what that is, do not allow them to experience and learn to deal with any adversity. They promote the message that their children deserve the best of everything and need to be protected and defended at all costs. Self-esteem is based in feeling good about yourself because you are a treasured child, rather than reaching for goals and attaining these. At the extreme end of the spectrum these parents give children everything they ask for, do their projects for them and go into battle for them at every opportunity. Less obviously they make few demands on their children to be responsible members of their communities.

As a result these children and young people are also at risk. They are not resilient, do not become independent or develop the personal and social resources that enable them to deal well with the inevitable challenges that life presents. They have not been encouraged to take account of others so do not develop positive relationships that require elements of empathy and conflict management. Their behaviour at school may also be hard to manage.

USE ENERGY WISELY

It is possible to use up energy wringing your hands about the problems, blaming parents and trying to change people, when resources would be better spent on what does make a difference. You can do little, if anything, about the risk factors in a child's life – there is a great deal you can do to promote resilience and wellbeing.

WELLBEING AND WELFARE

It is useful to know something of a student's background but in the busyness of everyday classrooms it can be hard to respond to each individual. We do not always know which of our students are vulnerable. A focus on universal wellbeing is therefore a good use of time and effort.

Welfare or pastoral care is where you respond to difficulties after they have arisen. It is the strategies that are put into place for individuals when the need becomes apparent. Many schools have strong welfare or pastoral teams, special needs co-ordinators, educational psychologists or counsellors who often do a wonderful job in picking up the pieces for students when they are in crisis, monitoring their progress, developing individual education plans and keeping these under review. There will always be such students with this level of need – but fewer of them need intensive help if difficulties are prevented from arising in the first place or are dealt with as very early intervention.

Wellbeing is a strategy for everyone. It comprises the way the school environment promotes mental health for all students. This includes school vision, the centrality of the whole child, ethos and organisation, relationships, social and emotional learning, behaviour policies, curriculum and pedagogy. Rather than student welfare being the province of senior staff and specialists, schools can promote the message that 'every teacher is a teacher for wellbeing'.

A focus on wellbeing includes a strengths and solution-focused approach, looking for what is positive and what might be built upon. This is at the whole school level (see Chapter 12) but also for individual students.

SOLUTION-FOCUSED ASSESSMENT

Often we rely on standardised tests to tell us about students. There is a danger we focus on what children and young people can't do – a deficit model. This leaves us with a blank. An alternative to this is solution-focused assessment. This seeks to discover what is happening when students are cooperative, attentive and behaving in pro-social ways. It looks for exceptions to poor behaviour.

Assessment can apply to people and also to situations. We assess a situation and judge what to do on the basis of the knowledge we ascertain. How can assessment help us to know our students so that we can more effectively meet their needs and respond well in times of difficulty?

Use the solution-focused assessment in schedule Table 4.1 adaptively and creatively. After each question reflect on what this tells you about the student and what it suggests you might do next to either find out more or to inform an intervention.

Table 4.1   Solution-focused checklist for behavioural issues

Name of student:	Date of assessment:
QUESTION	RESPONSE
When is this student most engaged with learning?	
In which subjects and with which teachers?	
What other factors support engagement for this student in school?	
When is the student most engaged outside of school and with what activities?	
What positive qualities does this student think they have?	
What positive qualities can teachers identify in this student?	
Who is the most supportive person in this student's life?	
Who is the most supportive person in the school for this student?	
Who else is important?	
When during the week is this student most calm and cooperative?	
In which classes is this student most calm and cooperative?	
What helps this student stay calm?	
What helps this student be cooperative?	
On a scale of 1–5 (1 = very little, 5 = a great deal) how much self-control does this student feel they currently have? What do they think would help them move one step in the right direction?	
On a scale of 1–5 how happy is the student with the way things are going in school? What is happening so they are not at the lowest point (if applicable)? What would be happening if they were at a 5? What would move them one step in the right direction?	
Who does the student look up to? Who is a role model?	
What is it about this person that the student admires?	
Who are positive peer influences for this student?	
What does the student enjoy most about school?	
What would they like more of?	
What is the best day they can remember at school? Why was it so good?	
In which ways are they already a 'good' student?	
What do they think would help them become more of a 'good' student?	

SUMMARY OF STRATEGIES AND APPROACHES TO PROMOTE POSITIVE BEHAVIOUR

- Help students learn the personal protective factors that help them with adversity.
- Provide resiliency seminars for parents to show what will foster authentic wellbeing for their children.

- Focus on how to provide environmental protective factors:
  - ○ High expectations and support to meet them
  - ○ A facilitative relationship
  - ○ A positive sense of belonging.

- Develop personal bests for students in both behaviour and academic subjects.

SUMMARY OF STRATEGIES AND APPROACHES TO DEAL WITH DIFFICULTIES

- Do some research – find out about students
- Check what the behaviour might mean for the student – what are they trying to communicate?
- Do not jump to conclusions on limited knowledge
- Use solution-focused thinking to assess strengths in individuals and situations.

Professional development activity for teachers

Knowing your students

Identify three challenging students: What do you know about them? First complete the checklist below to summarise your current knowledge and then go and find the answers from files, previous teachers, other professionals and students themselves. Some information will be highly confidential. Be sensitive in your enquiries.

Table 4.2

Educational history

How long has the student been at school?
How many schools have they attended?
What interventions have been put in place
  to support the student in the past?
Were interventions monitored and reviewed?
  How successful were they?

Background

Any known risk factors

Protective factors

Is there anyone in this student's life who thinks
  they are a valuable person? This might be a
  grandparent, uncle, sister, cousin, youth worker or teacher.
What communities does this student feel that they
  belong to – family, school, church, sports club, youth club?

Table 4.2   (Continued)

Where has the student been successful? What has helped them?
What do they believe they have achieved in life so far?
Student's interests outside school?

Conversations with the student

Three wishes
Three personal goals
The most significant event in their lives
What is most important to them – what to they value the most?
What would they most like to have achieved in 10 years' time?

Small group discussion

What has this activity told you about the students you find challenging and how you might respond to them in the classroom?

Circle Solutions activities with students

These activities will help you discover some issues of risk and resilience for your class group. Circles need to be a safe place for everyone. Questions are posed in an indirect way or with a focus on the positive.

All Circles begin with a statement of the principles:

- When one person is speaking everyone else listens.
- You may pass if you do not want to say anything.
- There are no put-downs.

Thumb signals

Each person in the Circle takes a turn to show how they are feeling today by:

- a thumbs up if they are feeling really positive
- thumb to the side if they are feeling neither good or bad or perhaps a bit wobbly
- thumbs down if they are not feeling so good.

This provides a quick check on which students might need a bit more help getting through the day.

Mix up activity

Change places if you:

- have a sister
- are the youngest person in your family
- belong to a club.

(Continued)

(Continued)

Pair share

Talk with each other to find out two things you have in common about your family or the people you live with.

Silent statement mix up activity

The aim here is to show that many people have similar experiences.
  Stand up and change places if:

- you know someone who has moved home more than five times
- you know someone who is looking after a parent who is not well
- you know someone who has lost a parent through death or divorce.

Sentence completions

  I feel I belong when …
  The best day of my life was when …
  I am looking forward to…

Pair share

Talk about your dreams for the future. Find something the same for both of you.

RESOURCES

Kate Thomsen, (2002). *Building resilient students* (2002, Thousand Oaks, CA: Corwin Press). This has a particularly good chapter on violence prevention and a checklist for assessing students' multiple intelligences.

www.wellbeingaustralia.com.au/wba has a section 'All about Resilience' listing articles, books and further websites.

REFERENCES

Benard, B. (2004). *Resiliency: What have we learned?* San Francisco: WestEd.

Bronfenbrenner, U. (2004). *Making human beings human: Bioecological perspectives on human development*. Thousand Oaks: Sage Publications.

Gerhardt, S. (2004) *Why love matters*. London and New York: Routledge.

Gill, T. (2007). *No fear: Growing up in a risk averse society*. London: Gulbenkian Foundation.

Kendler, K.S., Bulik, C.M., Silberg, J., Hettema, J.M., Myers, J. & Prescott, C.A. (2000). Childhood sexual abuse and adult psychiatric and substance use disorders in women: An epidemiological and cotwin control analysis. *Archives of General Psychiatry,* 57, 953–9.

Libbey, H. (2004). Measuring student relationships to school: Attachment, bonding, connectedness, and engagement. *Journal of School Health,* 74(7), 274–83.

McGrath, H. & Noble, T. (2011). *Bounce back. A wellbeing and resilience program.* Melbourne: Pearson Education.

Werner, E.E. & Smith, R.E. (1992). *Overcoming the odds: High risk children from birth to adulthood.* Ithaca, NY: Cornell University Press.

Werner, E. & Smith, R.E. (2001). *Journeys from childhood to midlife: Risk, resilience and recovery.* Ithaca. NY: Cornell University Press.

SECTION TWO

ENCOURAGING POSITIVE BEHAVIOUR

What does it mean to behave well in school, and how can we encourage students to choose behaviour that is both conducive to their learning and contributes to a positive classroom environment? This section brings together research and practice that details what schools and teachers are finding effective.

Being 'good' is not as obvious as it might first appear. A Jewish proverb says 'we do not see things the way they are, we see things the way we are'. Who we are determines the lens through which we filter our experiences and interpret them. Perceptions are coloured by our values, beliefs about how things 'should' be, how others talk about issues and what you read in the press. How someone thinks about a student and their behaviour directs both what they feel about it and what they do.

A wise teacher puts effort into what is within their influence to change. We cannot 'make' another person change – we can only change what we do. Do not underestimate the power of this approach. The evidence shows that consistent small positive differences in what we say and do, the expectations we have and the support we provide to meet these, have the potential over time to impact on improved motivation, engagement and behaviour in even our most challenging students.

As difficult behaviour is often the expression of negative emotions it makes sense to explore how to construct positive feelings in school in an authentic and meaningful way. How can we encourage students to feel good about being there and engaging with learning? Schools can, and many do, provide experiences that give children and young people consistency, security and a positive sense of themselves. This fosters both connection with school and engagement with learning. The key to promoting pro-social behaviour lies in how teachers develop positive classrooms, the mindful promotion of healthy relationships across the school and maximising student participation and responsibility. This section shows how you might go about doing this.

5

THINKING ABOUT BEHAVIOUR

Chapter objectives

- To reflect on what it means to be a 'good' student
- To explore alternative ways to think about behaviour
- To examine conceptualisations of students whose behaviour is challenging
- To think about how pro-social behaviour develops
- To appreciate that some students need help to learn behaviours expected in school.

WHAT DOES IT MEAN TO BE 'GOOD'?

When new parents describe their baby as a 'good baby' they usually mean she sleeps most of the time and doesn't make too many demands. This has little to do with being 'good' in the moral sense but is about being easy on caregivers. When infants reach the 2-year-old stage marked by independence, defiance and tantrums, this may be conceptualised as 'bad behaviour' rather than a necessary part of development. Children need to take account of others as they grow, but learning to stand up for themselves is also important.

Similar issues apply to school behaviour. It is difficult to be 'good' when:

- You might not know what that means
- The learning you have outside school does not fit with what you are supposed to do in school (e.g. 'hit 'em back')
- You have to be compliant and do as you are told by those in authority but also take responsibility for your own behaviour
- You have to fit in but also take risks with learning.

MacLure and Jones (2009) found that teachers usually want to develop cohesive classes where everyone knows and responds to the formal and informal rules. This is an understandable aim but can lead to low tolerance of diversity if those on the margins of the group are not actively included. Children who do not know how to perform 'the good student', or lack the skills to do so, may be publicly disciplined and become labelled as naughty. Others then marginalise them as 'outside' the norm, which has implications for their future.

> *Once a child's reputation has begun to circulate in the staffroom, dining hall and amongst other parents, it may be very difficult for her behaviour not to be interpreted as a 'sign' of such imputed character traits. Children who have acquired a strong reputation may therefore find it harder to be recognised as good* (MacLure & Jones, 2009, p. 5).

WHAT BEHAVIOUR DO WE WANT IN SCHOOL?

Here is a list of possibilities:

- Understand and obey the rules.
- Listen carefully.
- Respond positively and quickly to adult direction.
- Be considerate to others.
- Follow school routines.
- Move about the building 'appropriately'.
- Deal with conflict in 'mature' ways – i.e. without resorting to verbal abuse or punch-ups.
- Be polite and courteous.
- Do your best at all times.
- Keep things tidy.
- Be careful.
- Work with others when required.
- Work independently when required.
- Keep hands and feet to yourself.
- Sit on chairs 'properly'.
- Speak at 'appropriate' times.
- Do not argue.
- Share teacher attention.
- Try before asking.
- Ask when not sure.
- Do not interrupt or clamour for attention.
- Have what you need in school.
- Give things in on time.
- Respect authority.
- Be 'sensible'.
- Be on time.

And do we also want students to … ?

- Think about what they are being taught
- Ask challenging questions
- Take risks and learn from mistakes

- Be creative
- Take initiative
- Be confident
- Be sensitive to others
- Be positive
- Have energy and enthusiasm
- Be friendly and inclusive
- Be honest and trustworthy
- Be fair
- Have pro-social values.

〰 **Questions for reflection and discussion**

What do you notice about these expectations?

Do they fit with your experience in schools?

How many behaviours are personal, how many social and how many related to the routine and regulation of schools?

The following case study demonstrates that being a traditionally 'good' student is not necessarily the best training for success in life.

📁 **Case study**

Kiara had achieved high grades in school and was now working as an intern in an overseas aid agency. All her school reports had commended Kiara for her cooperative behaviour and diligent work. She was a traditionally 'good student' in all respects, especially in her desire to please others. What Kiara had not learnt however was genuine self-confidence, to risk making a mistake, deal with ambiguity or manage conflict when things were not going well. The busy agency needed her to work independently and quickly. Kiara only felt comfortable working on specific tasks for which she was given clear direction. When offered more open-ended suggestions in which she needed to use her initiative, Kiara would check every hour or so for the next step. Within a few weeks the agency began to look for someone who could be given an idea and run with it.

〰 **Questions for reflection and discussion**

In which ways did your education encourage or discourage your self-confidence?

What three school practices might have helped Kiara increase her competencies in this work situation?

BEHAVIOUR IS CONTEXT DEPENDENT

Behaviour can be construed as good or bad according to the context in which it appears. Children not only have to learn what adults want from them, they also have to learn what is acceptable when, where and with whom. Shouting in a library is frowned upon: shouting at a football match is what you do! If you have ever been out of your comfort zone in a social situation you will realise that it is not always easy to pick up what is expected. You also realise how complex social behaviour is when faced with a young person on the autistic spectrum who says and does things regardless of place and audience. We therefore need to provide children with many clues and every chance to learn what is 'appropriate' school behaviour. Students need clear direction, good models, lots of practice and reminders before reprimands. Although this is particularly true for younger pupils, teenage students also get confused about appropriate behaviour. They may, for instance, become over-familiar with a teacher and not be aware they have overstepped the mark.

Expected behaviour at school may be at variance from what students do outside. This can be around behaviours such as finishing a task, tidying up, social interaction and what is considered 'good manners'. This requires direct teaching.

 Questions for reflection and discussion

Do you have to behave in certain ways to be thought of as a 'good teacher' in the eyes of authority?

Are there any conflicts for you here?

What parallels can you see with students?

THINKING ABOUT STUDENTS WHOSE BEHAVIOUR IS CHALLENGING

As there are many ways of thinking about behaviour itself there are also different conceptualisations of students who present with challenges. Each way of positioning a student impacts not only on what we feel about that student but also on how we position ourselves in relation to that young person. This then influences what we do.

The 'bad' child in need of discipline

Conversations in staffrooms and in the media can focus on 'discipline' where young people are positioned as 'bad', 'out of control', 'refusing to learn', and 'needing a firm hand'. Their behaviour may be seen as deliberate, wilful and stemming from an innate lack of positive qualities. This model says that problems exist within the student and it is the student who must see the error of their ways and change their behaviour. When you position a pupil in this way you position yourself as the person who must ensure that control is maintained. You see yourself as the keeper of the peace – a police officer in the classroom.

> *Once I knew a bit more about this boy from the things he said in our Circle, I stopped imagining that he was just spending time thinking up ways to make my life a misery. I had believed his behaviour was a deliberate attack on me and it wasn't. It was everything that was happening in his life. Once I began to see him differently I could relate to him differently and things between us got much better* (teacher).

The 'mad' or 'abnormal' child with something wrong with them

This way of thinking is known as the 'medical' or 'within-child' model. It has been discouraged in the past in the UK, where an interactive model for special educational needs has been encapsulated in legislation and guidance since 1981. Language changed to reflect this. Schools for 'maladjusted children' for instance, were renamed schools for 'children with emotional and behavioural difficulties'. The difference may seem trivial but is highly significant, as the words we use determine how we see things.

The Diagnostic and Statistical Manual of Mental Disorders (DSM-IV-TR: APA, 2000) has been highly influential around the world in promoting a 'mental illness' model of difficulty. In many educational jurisdictions, schools cannot get funding for additional help for students whose behaviour is hard to manage unless they have been diagnosed with a disorder. There is increasing disquiet about this for many reasons. Crucially, it implies something wrong with the person rather than with their circumstances: 'oppositional defiant disorder' (ODD) for instance, is diagnosed for young people who are not complying with authority and being uncooperative and disobedient generally. They may have their own good reasons for behaving in this way – it does not mean they are 'abnormal'.

Some labels are grounded in genetic, pervasive conditions such as autistic spectrum disorder. Autism requires long-term specific intervention and diagnosis is often helpful. Other 'disorders', however, are not so clear-cut. Once a cluster of behaviours has been named a 'disorder' a drug can be developed to 'treat' it, and the involvement of pharmaceutical companies with the DSM has been brought into question. There is also a concern about the potential for misdiagnosis and over-diagnosis. The number of children being prescribed drugs for attention deficit hyperactivity disorder (ADHD) has increased dramatically in the last 15 years. A recent longitudinal study, however, shows little evidence for the efficacy of medication on behaviour and indications of some long-term educational and health risks (Smith et al., 2010).

When you position a young person as having a 'disorder' they are then seen as outside your sphere of influence. You can position yourself as not responsible – they can't help it and neither can you. Many in education then say they do not have the skills or resources needed and the child should therefore be somewhere else.

∿ **Questions for reflection and discussion**

Why do you think that 'within-child' models of behaviour have developed?

What are the disadvantages of this way of thinking in a classroom?

The 'sad' child in need of a different history

The family is usually seen as 'the problem' but sometimes it is traumatic experiences, such as exposure to violence or displacement, which have been damaging. The student is positioned as 'sad' rather than bad: perhaps disadvantaged, neglected or indulged. As a teacher all you can do is sympathise. In this model, you position yourself as caring but helpless. The person who is seen as responsible for intervention is the counsellor/therapist who helps the young person learn to cope with their experiences and the fall-out from these.

It is increasingly common for teachers to blame parents for permissive and overprotective parenting. They see problems in school as emanating from a lack of boundaries and low expectations. Children learn to consider no one but themselves, so become demanding and uncooperative. Blaming parents is understandable but does not move the world forward. It can undermine any chance of working well together. Miller (1994) found that of 24 primary school teachers all but three cited home factors as being implicated in student behaviour difficulties. When the same teachers were asked why they felt student behaviour had improved all mentioned factors within their control, especially positive attention to the child followed by selecting work at an appropriate level of interest.

FROM HELPLESSNESS TO ACTION

Whatever a child or young person brings with them to school is either exacerbated by what happens there or modified. Schools can and do make a difference.

The following approaches are more hopeful. They explore behaviour as the outcome of the interaction between the student and the school environment.

Ecological systems approaches

Systems theory looks at what it is possible to change, rather than what is outside your sphere of influence. You cannot do anything about a student's family, background, history, past experiences or personality – so putting time and energy trying to change what you cannot just makes you feel worse. As with all ecologies everything is interconnected so although you only pay attention to what *you* can do to make a difference, the outcomes can be more far-reaching than you might imagine. An individual teacher has influence on the following:

- Relationships at all levels
- The emotional climate of the classroom
- Expectations
- The learning opportunities presented
- Pedagogical approaches
- Provision for individual needs
- The ways students are spoken to and about
- Support networks
- The physical environment – how rooms are set out and what is on the walls.

In matters of human behaviour there is rarely a straight line between cause and effect. Outcomes are the result of what builds up interactively over time. This spiral can either be in a positive or negative direction. Here are examples of both for the same student.

📁 Case study

Poppy, aged 6, was in trouble in school. She had enjoyed playing when she first came to school but the teacher had mentioned to the year 1 class teacher, Ms A, that Poppy did not settle well to directed tasks and would need 'a firm hand'. Ms A was on the lookout for off-task behaviour and when Poppy did not meet expectations told her in front of her classmates that her work was not good enough. Within a couple of months Poppy started to tear up her books and throw pencils. Annie, her mother was asked into school but only ever heard negative things about what her daughter was doing wrong, including from other children. After a while she began to dread going near the school. Annie and Poppy's relationship deteriorated at home and the little girl began to say she felt ill on school days so she would not have to go.

Ms A went on maternity leave at Easter and a temporary teacher, Mrs M, began to take the class. She was a retired lady with a great deal of experience. She soon noticed that Poppy seemed able to grasp the concepts being taught but avoided formal pencil and paper work. She decided to ask advice from the educational psychologist who thought that Poppy had dyspraxia – a difficulty with motor co-ordination, organisation and sequencing. Annie was asked into school to talk about her daughter and confirmed that she did struggle with doing up buttons, jigsaws, drawing and getting things in the right order.

Mrs M focused on getting Poppy to feel successful as a learner and to raise a positive sense of self in the class before she introduced some activities aimed at supporting her writing skills. She also talked to the class about how well Poppy was doing, despite her difficulties. Poppy's behaviour improved, the relationship between mother and daughter became more supportive and Poppy began to look forward to going to school again.

Behaviour perceived as meeting needs

In the following theories behaviour is seen as an attempt to attain basic psychological needs. If these needs are actively addressed for all students the incidence of behavioural difficulties may diminish.

Self-determination theory

This theory (Ryan & Deci, 2000) says people are motivated to meet their needs for competence, autonomy and relatedness. The first refers to the need to experience yourself as competent in controlling your own environment so you can predict what will happen. The need for autonomy is defined as determining your own behaviour. What you do is your choice; you are not coerced into action. The need for relatedness includes feeling a sense of wellbeing from participating in a social world. There is a strong correspondence in this theory with the protective factors in resilience.

Choice theory

Glasser's theory (1998) says that all human behaviour aims to satisfy one of five needs: survival, love and belonging, power, freedom and fun. The only behaviour we can control is our own. Once this is recognised we take appropriate responsibility for ourselves. More on Glasser in Chapters 6 and 7.

Behaviour as a special educational need

Students who have physical or sensory difficulties have provision made for them so they can access the curriculum. Students with emotional/behavioural difficulties also have needs but there is often less willingness to make adjustments in such cases. The following analogy puts this into a different perspective.

> If a child needed a wheelchair you would give her a wheelchair. You would not insist that every student in the class have a wheelchair so it was 'fair'. You would also not say that she 'should' be walking at the same pace as others. Children who have social and emotional difficulties may also need adjustments to ensure their needs are met. Other students often understand this better than adults.

Behavioural difficulties are often part of a child's repertoire of special educational needs – more on this in Chapter 9.

DEVELOPING PRO-SOCIAL BEHAVIOUR

Over time we learn how to be and how to live together by the interaction of the following:

- Our experiences
- The mediation of these experiences that help us understand them in certain ways; e.g. the conversations children have about family break-up can prevent them feeling rejected or to blame

- Our personality, abilities and the development of our self-concept – who we believe we are and what we can do
- Expectations of others in the formation of our sense of self
- Our relationships; who is significant in our world, who we copy and who we want to please
- What we discover meets our needs, especially social, emotional and psychological
- Direct teaching and reinforcement of expectations and relational values, knowledge and skills
- Structured opportunities to reflect and talk about personal and relational issues
- How our worlds are socially constructed – what we come to believe is the 'right' way to be.

Behaviourist model

This says we learn how to behave by repeating what we find rewarding and avoiding what is painful. Despite being a dominant model in schools it has limitations, especially for those who have had multiple negative experiences. Such individuals are less likely to receive rewards and more likely to have sanctions applied. This can entrench rather than remediate their behaviour.

Punishment is more to do with retribution and 'justice' than learning. If punishment worked well as a deterrent our prisons would be empty. For many individuals it is shameful to get into trouble and for these students a serious conversation may be all that is needed for them to reflect and change. For others punishment can be meaningless or even a badge of pride. For some students anything a school can hand out doesn't come close to what they have already had to deal with. Meaningful consequences handed out by people who matter may have an impact on how a young person thinks about themselves and their community, but a blunt delivery of detention, suspension or anti-social behaviour orders (ASBOs) is unlikely to change behaviour and can reinforce negative self-concepts and relationships. Simply punishing students can increase aggression, vandalism and truancy (Mayer, 1995; Skiba & Peterson, 1999).

Meaningful rewards can, however, reinforce positive behaviours. Those especially worth having include:

- Acknowledgement of specific achievement and effort – although tangible rewards may be given it is the acknowledgement that really matters

Some schools have developed a system where teachers give out 'Gotcha' cards to students to reinforce positive behaviours. Staff are noticing an inverse correlation between the number of Gotcha cards an individual teacher gives out and the number of behaviour referrals they make. The more acknowledgement for positive behaviours, the less problems there are.

- Positive messages home – letters, certificates, merit awards
- Second-hand praise: say something positive about a pupil in the knowledge this will get back to them – this is particularly helpful for students who resist direct praise

- Privileges such as free time or choice of activity can be an incentive to reach a specific target. Primarily extrinsic motivators, however, do not internalise pro-social values. When students understand that certain behaviours increase their sense of wellbeing or connection to the group they begin to choose actions for different reasons.

Restorative justice approaches

Our judicial system is set up to identify evidence of wrongdoing, make judgements which attribute blame to the guilty and hand out appropriate sentences. Restorative justice questions the wisdom of a model that disconnects individuals from their communities and offers even less motivation to behave responsibly. Restorative justice requires a shift in belief about the appropriate way to respond to wrongdoers. It builds on the importance of relationships and connection – themes constantly revisited here.

In restorative practices an incident of wrongdoing is seen as affecting the whole community. The basic philosophy is that:

- Many unwanted behaviours are violations of people and/or their relationships.
- Violations create obligations and responsibilities.
- Restorative justice seeks to heal the harm caused and put right the wrongs.

Rather than upholding values of vengeance, retaliation and reprisal, restorative justice promotes values of compassion, reparation, thoughtfulness and generosity of spirit. These are qualities we are aiming to instil in our students, especially those who are struggling to learn them. More on putting restorative approaches into practice in Chapter 11.

Teaching wanted school behaviour

Some students need to replace behaviours they have already developed with those that are more helpful to them in the social context of school. This requires all staff to clearly communicate and reinforce expectations. The following example demonstrates how not to do this!

> Along with other parents I went to see my son in his primary school assembly. As we took our seats along the sides of the hall the head teacher walked through the rows of children seated on the floor. She had her hands behind her back and every so often she would shoot out a finger to point at a child who was talking, fidgeting or not sitting up straight. They would be loudly reprimanded. She was probably aiming to show the parents what great control she had in her school. I wondered how the children felt.

The following principles focus on the positive and apply to all students:

- Make expectations explicit: give both visual and verbal clues as to what is wanted (do not emphasise what is not wanted – the 'don't think of an elephant' principle); for some students pictorial 'cue cards' to remind them of expectations such as waiting their turn or saying thank you can be helpful.

- Give a rationale so that students know these expectations are for their benefit, not just yours.
- Expect students to comply.
- Be surprised rather than angry if they don't: it shows you think well of them.
- Model and demonstrate the behaviour required.
- Make requests succinct – too many words can be confusing.
- Keep things simple. We do not expect students to learn curriculum targets all at once – divide behavioural targets in a stepped sequence where necessary.
- Give prompts and positive feedback.
- Give reminders before reprimands.
- Discuss with the students how they are doing.
- Pay particular attention to the beginnings and endings of activities, as this is when most behavioural difficulties occur.

A life-sized paper shape of a child on the window, or puppet, teddy, rag doll or similar, can be helpful in establishing expected behaviour with young children. The image has a name, is a member of the class and provides a 'third person' to whom the teacher addresses remarks such as:

- Well, Teddy, what do you think of this class for waiting for me so nicely? Aren't they just wonderful?
- I am a bit sad today, Teddy, some children were fighting. You don't feel safe when there is fighting do you? You think children need to sort out their arguments without fighting? Perhaps we can all talk about that in our Circle.

Bill Rogers (2009) suggests that sometimes when students are not complying with expectations mirroring their errant behaviour can be a strong motivator for change and brings humour to the situation. Students usually see the funny side of this so long as individuals are not embarrassed in front of others.

When students are having difficulties complying with expectations they may also need opportunities to understand why their behaviour is not helping them be part of the class group and support to learn specific behaviours that will help their inclusion. They need opportunities to practice. Once they have mastered a skill, such as not interrupting, they can become models for others. This will reinforce and sustain their new learning.

🗁 Case study

Max was not an easy child. He was energetic, curious and single-minded. This meant that he was demanding of teacher attention, did not always listen to instructions and was not always cooperative. In his second year in school his parents separated and Max began to be moody and aggressive as well as highly active. His mother was brought into the school several times to talk over concerns about his behaviour but things continued

(Continued)

(Continued)

to deteriorate. Max began to lock himself in the bathroom in the mornings. His mother was at her wits' end.

The following year a new approach was taken in which it was decided to give Max a red star in a special book every time he waited his turn, had a playtime in which played well with other children and when he completed a task set for him by the teacher. The teacher made sure that Max was successful by reminding him of his targets, giving him tasks where he was going to be successful and asking staff on playground duty to reinforce positive behaviour. When Max had a page of stars he was given a certificate to take home to show how well he had done. Within a few weeks Max's behaviour began to improve and although still very lively he eventually settled into the routine of the class and made progress with his learning. His relationships at home also improved.

Focusing on strengths to develop a positive self-concept

Children develop a view of themselves that they have been given by adults since their early years. These may include 'naughty', 'lazy' or a 'nuisance'. If you tell a 4-year-old how helpful she is she will try and be helpful, if you tell a 7-year-old often enough that he is clumsy and careless this is how he will see himself and have nothing to aim for. This is not ignoring problems but focusing on what is going well and looking towards goals. Working from a strengths perspective is more motivating than addressing entrenched deficits and problems. It can be powerful for students to have their strengths identified and acknowledged. More on strengths in Chapter 10.

SUMMARY OF STRATEGIES AND APPROACHES TO PROMOTE POSITIVE BEHAVIOUR

- Catch students being 'good'.
- Be clear and concise – say briefly what you want students to do.
- Provide a model to copy – show students what to do.
- Enhance confidence – it is OK to not get it right the first time.
- Construct a positive self-concept.

SUMMARY OF STRATEGIES AND APPROACHES TO DEAL WITH DIFFICULTIES

- Focus on encouraging and teaching wanted behaviours rather than trying to get rid of unwanted behaviours – in small steps if necessary.
- Acknowledge that changing behaviour takes time and that there are no quick fixes.

- Give reminders before reprimands.
- Aim to be 'significant' to challenging students so their relationship with you matters.
- Respond to unacceptable behaviour in ways that maintain connection to community.

Professional development activities for teachers

The good student

Identify three students whose behaviour you find challenging.

Observe these students over a period of a week and identify all the times they perform 'the good student', that is doing what is expected in school. What happens when they do?

Discuss your findings with a small group. Are there any common threads?

Changing behaviour

Paired discussion

Think of a time someone wanted you to change in some way.

Which factors influenced what you did (or didn't) do?

Being 'in trouble'

In a small group discuss times you or close friends were 'in trouble' in school. What happened and what did you think/feel about the outcomes?

Teaching and learning behaviour

With a partner go through the list of behaviours wanted in school and choose three for students you are teaching. Write five to ten things you might do to help a student learn these.

Circle Solutions activities with students

These activities will help students learn about change and help you learn about them.

All Circles begin with a statement of the principles:

- When one person is speaking everyone else listens.
- You may pass if you do not want to say anything.
- There are no put-downs.

You may like to add 'What is said in the Circle, stays in the Circle', and also remind students they should only talk about what they are comfortable to share.

Silent statements

Stand up and change places if...

- You know someone who has had some tough things to deal with.

(Continued)

(Continued)

Pair share

Students talk to each other about what has helped them get through some tough times. They find two things they have in common and feed this back to the Circle:

- We have found it helps when …

Changes

Put the following words on cards:

- Past history
- Eye colour
- Hair colour
- Personal qualities
- Family
- Health and wellbeing
- Physical development
- Likes and dislikes
- Learning
- Outlook on life
- The future
- The weather
- Confidence
- Friendships.

In the Circle give one of these words to pairs of students. Ask pairs in turns to place their card in one of two piles – what can change and what cannot. Give them time to think and talk about this. The pair say why they have placed the card in their chosen pile. Invite other students to comment.

Now ask students to place cards into three piles. In one are things that are up to them to change, in another are things that are a mix of themselves and others (and sometimes chance) and in the third are things that they cannot influence.

Ask students to think of one thing they value about themselves and one thing they would like to change. They write these on a piece of paper, screw this up and then everyone throws their paper across the room. After three throws the teacher asks students to pick up a paper near them and each gets read out anonymously to the Circle. Comment on similarities between students.

RESOURCES

Bill Rogers' *Behaviour recovery* (2004, London: Sage) is an excellent resource for teaching expected behaviours to students who are really struggling and looking at what is involved in developing an individual plan with them.

Find out more about the Glasser Quality School model at www.wglasser.com/

Read the first four chapters of Tom Billington's book *Separating, losing and excluding children: Narratives of difference* (2000, London: Routledge) for a clear exposition of the power of discourse.

John Burningham (2007, London: Red Fox) has written a children's book called *Edwardo: the horriblest boy in the whole wide world*: it illustrates very simply that the more we tell children they are lazy, untidy, cruel, noisy and rude the more they will be these things. The more we tell them they are kind, helpful, strong, polite and gentle and give them opportunities to be so, the more they are likely to develop these qualities instead.

REFERENCES

American Psychiatric Association (2000). *Diagnostic and statistical manual of mental disorders: DSM-IV-TR, fourth edition (text revision)*. Arlington, VA: American Psychiatric Publishing.

Glasser, W. (1998). *Choice theory*. New York: HarperCollins.

MacLure, M. & Jones, L. (2009). *Becoming a problem: How children develop a reputation as naughty in the first years of school*. ESRC: Manchester Metropolitan University.

Mayer, G.R. (1995). Preventing antisocial behavior in the schools. *Journal of Applied Behavior Analysis*, 28, 467–92.

Miller, A. (1994). Parents and difficult behaviour. In P. Gray, A. Miller, & J. Noakes. (1994). *Challenging behaviour in schools: Teacher support, practical techniques and policy development*. London and New York: Routledge.

Rogers. B. (2009). *How to manage children's challenging behaviour, second edition*. London: Sage Publications.

Ryan, R.M. & Deci, E.L. (2000). Self-determination theory and the facilitation of intrinsic motivation, social development, and wellbeing. *American Psychologist*, 55, 68–78.

Skiba, R. & Peterson, R. (1999). The dark side of zero tolerance. *Phi Delta Kappan*, 80(5), 372–6.

Smith, G., Jongeling, B., Hartmann, P., Russell, C. & Landou, L. (2010). *The Raine Study: Long-term outcomes associated with stimulant medication in the treatment of ADHD in children*. Perth: Government of Western Australia, Department of Health.

6 POSITIVE FEELINGS IN THE PRO-SOCIAL CLASSROOM

Chapter objectives

- To explore the social and emotional aspects of the classroom
- To outline multiple ways of being intelligent
- To appreciate how cultural diversity impacts on behaviour
- To identify strategies to promote a sense of belonging in the classroom
- To show how humour can reduce stress and enhance positive peer relationships.

CLASSROOM CULTURE

Many school mission statements refer to maximising the potential of each student and developing a culture of respect and inclusion. In schools where this is genuinely promoted the emotional tone in the school is conducive to an effective learning environment and any behavioural challenges are dealt with well. Teachers feel more supported and everyone is happier (Jennings & Greenberg, 2009).

Building a pro-social classroom involves the understanding and promotion of relational values, the active teaching of social and emotional skills, the modelling of pro-social behaviours, opportunities for students to reflect on how they want their classroom to be and the agency that hands them responsibility for the ethos. This is a far cry from simply telling students how to behave.

PRO-SOCIAL BEHAVIOUR

Pro-social behaviour fosters healthy relationships, it shows you are able to take someone else's perspective, be empathic with their situation and considerate of their needs. Sometimes pro-social behaviour is context specific – people only demonstrate this with those in their immediate world – sometimes it is broader based and shows responsiveness to an unknown community. You see evidence of this when great disasters happen and people do what they can to help – they feel for the situation that others have found themselves in. If you believe people deserve what happens to them you are less likely to feel sympathetic. This 'belief in a just world' (Lerner, 1980) can both demonise the unfortunate, such as refugees, and also lead you to believe you are a bad person when something bad happens – you must have done something to deserve it. This can result in depression. Many things happen by chance. Sometimes you are just in the wrong place at the wrong time. Students need to hear both messages – they are not helpless and can effect what happens to them, but neither are they responsible for everything that goes wrong.

It is harder to develop pro-social behaviour when this has not been part of your experience nor the expectations placed on you. If you suspect the worst of others you may put your energy into protecting yourself the best way you know how.

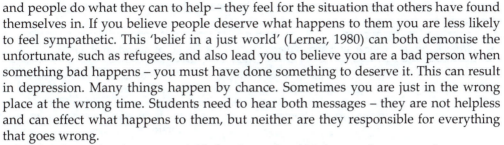

Question for reflection and discussion

To what extent do you believe in a 'just world'?

How does that impact on your thoughts and feelings about students who struggle?

POSITIVE FEELINGS

Positivity is not to be taken lightly! Students who experience many negative emotions have difficulty with concentration, cognitive tasks and relationships. You will know that if you are feeling sad, angry or anxious it is hard to think straight. On the other hand, there is increasing evidence that positive feelings promote creativity, attention, problem-solving skills, cooperation and pro-social behaviour. They reinforce our personal resources and reduce the impact of negative events (Fredrickson, 2005). All teachers might consider how they are promoting the positive to reduce challenging behaviour.

When we raise our awareness of the quality of both relationships and feelings in the classroom we begin to understand the extent to which are they negative or positive and what is contributing to this. What is it possible to do to make everyone feel better about themselves, each other and their learning? How much can we affect what is happening so there is both pro-social behaviour and maximum engagement with learning?

Tew and Park (2008) identified the affective features of an effective learning environment in the UK with the acronym CLASI. This is where students and teachers feel Competent, Listened to, Accepted, Safe and Included. This mirrors research in Australian schools (Roffey, 2008) where both teachers and students spoke about similar relational values of feeling respected, acknowledged, valued, consulted, trusted, supported and included. Table 6.1 summarises the qualities of a pro-social classroom and gives a rationale for why we should be paying attention to them in matters of behaviour.

Table 6.1   The rationale for promoting relational values and qualities in the classroom

Feeling/quality/value	Behaviour when in place	Behaviour when absent
Security	Being able to predict what will happen, having trust in others to do what they say. Knowing support is there enables you to take risks with learning.	If you do not feel secure you may be constantly anxious or feel chaotic. You might jump to negative conclusions, test boundaries or need to be in control of everything.
Acknowledgement	You are spurred to do better and are more committed to those who acknowledge your specific efforts.	When efforts are ignored people may lose motivation and the willingness to persist.
Respect	If you experience respect you are more likely to respect others and be prepared to listen to what they say.	When you feel marginalised you are likely to be disengaged or angry and dismiss what is said to you.
Acceptance	If you feel accepted you are more likely to have a positive sense of self and appreciate that others are also unique.	If you are rejected this may undermine your confidence. You may actively reject the values of the community.
Valuing diversity	You are more likely to want to please those who show they value you, your culture and your contribution.	If you do not feel valued you are less likely to value yourself or others. You may feel like an outsider.
Inclusion and belonging	When you feel you belong somewhere you develop a sense of loyalty and learn how to be part of a group.	When you are excluded you may feel resentful and need to maintain your self-esteem by any means. You may attach to whatever group will have you.
Trust and responsibility	Where trust is valued and promoted relationships thrive.	If you feel no one trusts you, there is no incentive to be responsible.
Competence	Nothing succeeds like success. You are more motivated to demonstrate what you are good at and aim for the next challenge.	If you doubt your ability, see minimal progress and yourself as incompetent you are likely to avoid making an effort. You may then be labelled 'lazy'.
Confidence	If you feel confident you know you can get over difficulties. A mistake or bad event doesn't knock you down for good and you have the motivation to persist.	If your coping strategies are undermined you may feel helpless and a victim of circumstances. You may become anxious, depressed, passive and/or blame others.
Feeling cared for	If you feel cared for you are more likely to have positive interactions with the person demonstrating this and over time to develop empathy and care for others.	If you feel someone does not care about you, you have little to lose if you don't take notice of them, their requests or their feelings.

Table 6.1   (Continued)

Feeling/quality/value	Behaviour when in place	Behaviour when absent
Safety	If you feel safe you are more willing to take initiatives and to reach out to others.	If you are afraid you may be hyper-vigilant and have less emotional energy to attend to learning.
Being listened to	When someone asks what you think and listens to the answer you are more likely to take them seriously and also feel valued.	When someone dismisses what you say and feel you may shout them down or express feelings in unacceptable ways.
Fun and enjoyment	Stress relief and emotional resilience is built by humour in the classroom.	When things are not stimulating or enjoyable you may switch off. You may also look for amusement elsewhere.

Security

Predicting what will happen in class includes having guidelines for behaviour, a teacher with a stable temperament, and students knowing what they are supposed to be learning. It is helpful for teachers to let students know the content of a lesson at the outset. Prior warning of transitions or changes of routine reduces feelings of panic in some children. Even where there is the opportunity for spontaneity a moment of getting used to the idea will help.

Where there are low expectations for behaviour at home, children will push boundaries until someone stops them. Children and young people rely on adults to ensure that their environment is predictable rather than chaotic. They like to know where they stand and that someone is in charge.

When children have suffered a loss or trauma their behaviour often deteriorates. Although empathy, understanding and gentleness is appropriate, keeping behavioural expectations high enhances feelings of security. When families are in transition students may feel everything is temporary and confusing. They may not know what will be happening next. The reliability and routine of schools can be a welcome relief to what is happening at home. When teachers jump on unwanted behaviour too hard or too fast they can undermine that security.

Peer relationships and security

Some students have an overwhelming need for security. This can translate into fear of losing friends, which in turn may lead to jealousy, clinging behaviour, manipulation or succumbing quickly to peer pressure. It is useful to encourage students to work with and get to know a range of peers in the classroom and address friendship issues, including peer pressure in SEL. Resisting peer pressure is difficult for adults who fear social ostracism – how much more so for young people with fewer resources at their disposal.

〜〜 **Questions for reflection and discussion**

What might a friend or colleague ask you to do that you would rather not?

How many different ways can you think up to say 'no', standing your ground but trying not to give offence? Ask students the same question.

Acknowledgement

How do students know that it matters if they are there? Are they greeted warmly? Are they addressed by the name they wish to be known by? Does someone notice when they are absent and welcome them back? Do they feel people at school are interested in them as a whole person? Are they asked questions about what is important to them?

You do not have time for long or regular personal conversations with every student. Twenty seconds once a week with more vulnerable students will however pay dividends in many ways.

> Mr B was a geography teacher in a high school. As he walked along corridors past students he would greet some of them with a personal comment:
> *'How did your sister do in the swimming gala?'*
> *'Like the haircut, suits you.'*
>   Perhaps he would wink at a teenage boy and say; *'saw you in town Saturday – pretty girl you were with'*. He was the most popular teacher in the school, students were desperate to get into his classes and never played up when they were there.

Regular Circle activities provide opportunities to build up a rapport with students on a regular basis.

Acknowledging efforts makes a difference. When students try to improve their behaviour and no one notices or says anything, they become angry, disappointed and de-motivated. Teachers who don't believe they should say anything positive 'because it's only what students should be doing anyway' are missing the point and laying up problems for themselves.

Acknowledgment is different from praise. It is letting someone know you have noticed. Any praise needs to be specific, genuine and deserved – it can be empty, meaningless and shallow otherwise. Students need to know what they have achieved that is praiseworthy and why. Some students are unable or unwilling to accept public accolades but appreciate a discreet nod or private word.

Peer relationships and acknowledgement

There are many ways students can be encouraged to acknowledge each other. Talking in pairs about the origin of each person's name and feeding back this information to the wider Circle provides information on each individual's history, culture and personal narrative. A 'Random Act of Kindness' board in the classroom or 'Tree of Friendship' can provide a place where students acknowledge positive behaviours. Comments must be for observable actions. Teachers may need to structure situations where more challenging students are given opportunities to show what they can do. This acknowledgement can change the way students see each other as well as themselves.

Feeling respected

There is still a belief in some quarters that adults should be respected because they are adults and that this respect is about deference – submission to their wishes. There are also groups of young people who behave in similar ways – if you don't submit to the gang leader you are not respecting them. Respect needs definition and clarification in school. It can be not jumping to conclusions about someone, not putting yourself above them, taking what they have to say seriously. We cannot love – or even like – some people, but we can show everyone respect by treating them with the dignity that acknowledges they are part of our shared humanity.

We are creating a community that looks after all the people in the community ... When I first came here no one cared about anybody – it was all about 'me'. We had to introduce policy, practices and guidelines which would bring about self-respect and mutual responsibilities ... there was discussion about bullying, respect and how we need to treat others as we want to be treated (school principal).

Question for reflection and discussion

Who do you respect and why?

Peer relationships and respect

It is useful for students themselves to define the meaning of respect. The following questions might be addressed over several Circle sessions to build an understanding of respect in the classroom. Ask students to work in small groups to come up with their thoughts on the following questions and share their findings with everyone:

- What does it means to be treated with respect?
- Is this the same for everyone?
- What does it feel like to be respected?
- What does it feel like when you are not respected?
- Is respect for an adult different from respect for a friend? In what ways?
- Do people have to earn respect or should we treat everyone with respect?
- What would someone have to do to earn respect?
- How do people learn to respect each other?
- List 10 different ways you can demonstrate respect.

Acceptance

Some students find it hard to understand that it is their *behaviour* we don't like and assume that we are rejecting *them*. Adults need to make it clear that they are referring to behaviour that is unwanted, not the student. If we do not accept our students, flawed and difficult as they may be, they will not accept themselves or others. Acceptance of yourself is the first step towards change.

No one is perfect. Acknowledging your own errors provides a model to students for taking responsibility whilst also demonstrating authentic self-respect.

Acceptance of difference refers to the promotion of an inclusive classroom where students of all abilities, race, religion, physical prowess, social status, family background and sexual orientation feel accepted for who they are. When this happens bullying diminishes.

Peer relationships and acceptance

Students who have been rejected by those who are supposed to care for them often see rejection at every turn, and may pre-empt this by rejecting others first. This then develops into a negative spiral. Some children are rejected because of their perceived difference from others. Rejected children are especially vulnerable to later mental health difficulties (Cowen et al., 1973) so we have a responsibility to intervene. Frederickson (1991), in writing about the rejected child, emphasises the need to address the perceptions and behaviours of others as well as helping the individual concerned to learn new skills and develop more useful perspectives. Short-term, add-on social skills training outside the social context in which the students spend most of their time, has short-term effects. Sustainable changes in relationships require an embedded, universal, multi-year programme that addresses beliefs as well as skills.

Circle of Friends is one way of helping isolated or rejected children find a place (Newton & Wilson, 2003). It was originally used to support children with disabilities but has now been adapted for students with other needs. This intervention involves a group of volunteer peers who support the 'target' child over several weeks.

Valuing cultural diversity

For the positive feelings described above to flourish in a classroom, cultural diversity must be honoured in both principle and practice. If the pictures on the walls and stories in books are predominantly one culture, students from other backgrounds can begin to feel they are invisible or there is something unworthy in their way of life. Institutional racism can be subtle but is highly damaging. It is not just bigots who are racist – otherwise kind and gentle people may be unaware of the many ways in which they convey the message that their race is naturally superior – and by extension, others inferior. The impact on students can be far-reaching in their connection to school, their behaviour, their learning and their future wellbeing. Slavin (2009) indicates the first steps required to address issues of equity in a school:

> The first step in multicultural education is for teachers, administrators, and other school staff to learn about the cultures from which their children come and to carefully examine all the

policies, practices, and curricula used in the school to identify any areas of possible bias (Slavin, 2009, p.112).

Weinstein and colleagues (2004) propose a conception of culturally responsive class-room management that includes the following five essential components:

- recognition of one's own ethnocentrism – being aware of how your own values and bias might impact on expectations for behaviour and your interactions with students who are from a different cultural background
- knowledge of students' cultural backgrounds
- understanding of the broader social, economic, and political context
- ability and willingness to use culturally appropriate management strategies
- commitment to building caring classrooms.

Students from cultural backgrounds other than the dominant one in the school often experience more difficulties than their peers. For instance: lively and loud African-Caribbean teenage behaviour can be negatively interpreted; Southeast Asian students may be regarded as insolent if they smile when being reprimanded rather than this being seen as a culturally acceptable communication of guilt and desire to appease.

When responses in the classroom do not take account of these cultural differences teachers can inadvertently exacerbate difficulties. Applying cultural knowledge can be an effective strategy all round. Ballenger (1999) writes about learning to work with Haitian children. Rather than pointing out immediate outcomes of behaviour to chil-dren: *'If you don't listen you won't know what to do'*; she learned to appeal to their sense of community: *'Would your mother and auntie be proud of you for doing that?'*

Some communities have a more collective approach that makes competitive pedago-gies uncomfortable for students. The notion of time is also a much more flexible concept in some cultures than that found in schools. Strict timetables may result in certain stu-dents getting into more trouble than those from the dominant culture.

Valuing diversity requires an active approach that gives students and teachers oppor-tunities to learn from each other and celebrate what they both share and uniquely bring to the community.

The Curriculum Corporation (2008) cites an Australian example in which art practice was used to explore community values, relationships and cultures by bringing students together from several schools to share dance styles, artworks and music.

⌇⌇ Questions for reflection and discussion

Think of a student who comes from a different cultural background to you.

What do you know about their culture?

How could you find out?

How will this knowledge support your teaching and your relationship with this student?

Peer relationships and valuing diversity

The biggest barrier to valuing diversity is ignorance. The more students know about each other and their stories the less they will stereotype. There are many ways to do this, especially in Circle activities. Have a postcard collection attached to a map on the wall which shows where families originated – nearly everyone has ancestors who have migrated or moved from one place to another. Why did they do this? Was it their choice or were they forced by others or circumstances? What can we learn from these experiences for the health, wellbeing and future of this society?

Feeling you belong

Belonging is a fundamental psychological need and determines values, beliefs and behaviour. It is the opposite of alienation. We want to be where we feel we belong. We take more notice of people in 'our' communities, have more commitment and loyalty and feel pride in 'our' successes. All of this can be seen in supporters clubs: the attendance at matches, the wearing of scarves and singing of songs, the despair when a team loses and ecstasy when they win.

A feeling of connection cannot be forced. You will feel pride if you feel a genuine alliance, you will feel you belong if you know others value your presence.

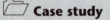 **Case study**

I was in hospital for several weeks when I was 7 years old. The class teacher arranged for the other children to make cards to wish me well. They all arrived in a big envelope. I have never forgotten how surprised and special I felt when I received this – and how I couldn't wait to get back to school and my class!

Where class groups actively foster a sense of connection they are more cooperative and more willing to work with each other to solve problems. Restorative approaches to wrongdoing will work because a hurt to the community is a hurt to all members of that community. There are many ways to build a sense of belonging in a class – here are some of them:

- Students have regular opportunities to get to know each other better – this breaks down exclusive cliques which can increase bullying.
- Cooperative learning is encouraged.
- Teachers use inclusive language so no individual is marginalised.
- Students are given responsibility for developing a positive and inclusive class ethos.
- Social and emotional learning is embedded in everyday classroom practice as well as in specific programmes.

- All students have opportunities to take lead responsibilities – not just those who are considered the 'natural leaders'.
- All students receive accolades for their strengths in diverse domains.
- All students know they will have their turn.
- No student is left out of class treats or outings.
- Everyone has a place of their own – somewhere to put their things.
- Students are welcomed – and welcomed back if they have been away.
- Everyone has a chance for their work to be publicly displayed.
- The classroom is a 'no put down' zone.

A sense of belonging can be undermined by public criticism or humiliation. Showing someone up in front of the class can start a wildfire of jeering by peers. Where a student does not feel they have 'a place' they may seek to belong by seeking attention in negative ways or by attaching themselves to a more marginalised group. Sometimes being the class clown is a way of having a place. Teachers may be more tolerant of this behaviour if they can understand the purpose beneath it.

Bettelheim (1994) has argued that a 'rightful place' can only be earned by contributing in a real way to the welfare of the community. To have a rightful place in the classroom students need to contribute in some important way to the operation and wellbeing of that classroom. Many teachers have stories about how they have 'turned around' a difficult student by inventing a special way in which the student could support the work and activities of the classroom (Ellis et al., 1998).

📁 **Case study**

My students all lacked a sense of community, and consequently they also lacked a sense of accountability. During my first few years as a teacher in this setting, I struggled to connect with students and to keep them engaged in the school environment. Some students did very well, but I was unable to reach others … The first change I made to begin building community was to rearrange my classroom management system to reflect the new focus of our classroom. I created 'Community, Inc.', a classroom management system that was 'publicly owned; created communities; invested in relationships and made a profit from the positive growth and relationships it created.' In this new system every student had a job, along with responsibilities to the overall 'company.' My classroom had 'corporate meetings' at least twice a day, and sometimes more frequently if we needed to address an issue in the classroom. 'Community, Inc.' pushed the typical boundaries of classroom rules to a system where the students decided the norms of behaviour in the classroom, along with how each student would be held accountable, not just to the teacher and administration, but also to the community as a whole (Webb, 2007).

From Webb, 'My Classroom's Journey with Restorative Practices,' reprinted with permission from the Restorative Practices eForum, January 7, 2010 © Deanna Webb, 2010.

〰️ **Questions for reflection and discussion**

What makes you feel you belong somewhere?

What do others say and do to make you feel wanted and included?

What do you feel when you are left out?

Feeling trusted and responsible

Students may have been let down badly by others in their lives. They have not learnt to trust others as reliable or consistent and are therefore likely to be irresponsible and untrustworthy themselves. Teachers therefore must only offer what they know they can deliver, keep to promises and never threaten. Trust is a fragile commodity and once broken is difficult to re-establish.

Students with negative experiences may have learnt to be manipulative, see lying as a means to an end, have little conscience about taking things that belong to others and cheat with a sense of impunity. As with other self-constructs, if we tell young people they can't be trusted that is how they will see themselves and consequently meet our low expectations. It is important to hold a middle path here. We need to provide opportunities for students to show they can meet higher expectations whilst not endangering the wellbeing and safety of others.

One way to develop trustworthy behaviour is to help students learn that their responsibility to others is part of belonging to a community and therefore in their interest. This can be hard to do in a society where individual greed and unethical behaviours are condoned. So long as it is within the bounds of the law people often do what they can get away with.

Peer relationships and trust

Trust is another word like respect that needs to be discussed and defined. What does it mean to trust someone, what does it mean to be trustworthy? How does this impact on how we feel about ourselves and others? What responsibility do we have towards others? Trust means being able to rely on your friends, that they will stick up for you and not be unkind about you behind your back. Trust is the antithesis of fear in a relationship.

🗂 **Case study**

Sunni arrived mid-term in a year 5 class, escaping family violence. It soon became apparent that she was taking all manner of things from the classroom, making up excuses when asked how certain items appeared in her bag. It was decided to use Circles to address issues of honesty and trust: What did these values mean and what feelings did they bring with them? What could everyone do to develop trust in the class? After a couple of weeks the stealing stopped and Sunni became more integrated into the class group.

This illustrates that providing structured opportunities to reflect in a safe place may be a powerful tool for changing behaviour. Discussing issues, not individuals, promotes the safety of the Circle. Students all took responsibility to create the ethos they wanted – and being part of a group endeavour is likely to have enhanced individual commitment.

Feeling capable

How do we help students feel capable? How can we develop their confidence? Any school system that only gives accolades to those who get high marks in exams or to sports stars risks making many more students feel they can't be successful.

> 📂 **Case study**
>
> Jonny is a 16-year-old who has struggled with learning most of his life. He can read fluently and has a good memory for facts, but understanding what he has read and being able to use information is very difficult for him. He has recently taken his 'mocks' before the real exams. 'How did you do Jonny?' I asked. 'Failed everything' he said, glumly. He now sees himself as incapable and makes even less effort to try.

The pass/fail dilemma is one that needs to be addressed for students like Jonny who have little way of perceiving themselves as successful. Norm referenced tests only measure performance against that of peers. With criterion referenced assessment students get credited for what they have achieved within a programme of study. Success is gained by meeting set criteria. It is aligned to the 'personal bests' model of learning in which students are in competition with themselves, not others. Many students not only give up when denied the opportunity to feel successful, they also begin to devise other ways to reduce the threat to their sense of self. The interaction between learning and behaviour is also addressed in Chapter 9.

Multiple intelligences: more than one way of being clever

Howard Gardner (1983) introduced the concept of multiple intelligences to refute the traditional idea of intelligence that was based in IQ tests of verbal and logical abilities. The argument was that a broader range of human potential was not receiving sufficient acknowledgement or attention. Gardner's updated framework (1999) included the dimensions of intelligence outlined in Table 6.2. The table defines these dimensions and links them to student interests, strengths and abilities.

Moving the concept of intelligence away from a narrow focus on verbal reasoning and logical/numerical abilities has both increased our understanding of how children learn and placed value on a wider range of abilities. When students struggle with the more traditional aspects of education it may be useful to help them identify other intelligences they may have. When the traditional pedagogies are not engaging students, they may learn more effectively using other learning strengths.

Table 6.2

Intelligence	Definition and area of strength	Likes and interests
Linguistic	Word smart – good with words and verbal reasoning. Often has a good vocabulary and is articulate and/or able to express meaning well in writing.	Likes books, stories, debating, discussing, reading and writing. Enjoys word games.
Logical-mathematical	Number smart – good at maths and working things out in logical steps.	Likes puzzles, problem-solving, measuring, comparing, sorting and statistics. Enjoys number games.
Spatial and visual	Picture smart – can visualise things in practice, good with anything that needs spatial orientation. Able to present things visually and/or diagrammatically.	Enjoys art, graphics, diagrams, graphs and maps, including mind-maps to structure project work. May be artistically creative.
Bodily-kinaesthetic	Body smart – tuned into the physical, fine and gross motor skills. Maximises potential ability in one or more of the following: movement, accuracy, speed, flexibility and/or strength. Is often energetic.	Often enjoys sports and physical activity. This includes those requiring strength, flexibility, stamina, good eye–hand coordination or coordinated physical movement. May be practical and/or skilled in craft subjects.
Musical	Music smart – being able to recognise sounds and define differences such as the quality of timbre and tone.	Likes listening to and/or playing music. May like to sing or play an instrument – alone or with others.
Intrapersonal	Self smart – having a high level of self-awareness. Good self-management in diverse situations; knows how to be resilient.	Enjoys reflecting on experience and personal development. May like to keep a diary, discuss coping strategies and problem-solving.
Interpersonal	People smart – being good with others; having empathy and high level of social skills to engage well.	Enjoys connecting with others. Will like group work and being in a team.
Naturalistic	Being attuned to the natural world, being good with animals and protective of the environment.	Will like being in natural surroundings and finding out about the natural world. Enjoys caring for animals.

〰 Questions for reflection and discussion

In which ways are you intelligent?

How do you know?

What activities might you introduce into the classroom to engage students who have specific intelligences?

Feeling confident

Confidence means not being scared of making a mistake or looking foolish. The willingness to have a go at something or persist in the face of difficulties is more likely to occur where mistakes are welcomed as part of learning and serious effort is valued, not just attainment. Oppurtunities to rehearse and practice new skills can also build confidence. An over-crowded curriculum can leave students with impaired understanding and a reluctance to put this to the test. It may be better for some students to learn some things thoroughly than attempt to skim the surface of everything in a programme of study.

Fragile confidence in anxious or sensitive pupils may be quickly undermined by sarcasm, public humiliation, being the underdog in competitive environments or rarely receiving accolades for skills learnt. Do not assume that students whose behaviour is challenging have thick skins.

Peer relationships and confidence

Peer support and buddying systems often boost confidence at school and foster adaption to change (Ellis, 2004). When individual students get to know each other and develop some joint strategies for managing aspects of school life they not only construct a more positive school experience together but also a safely net which encourages initiative – someone will be there to pick them up.

Feeling cared for

It is usual for teachers to explain their reasons for rules and expected behaviour in terms of consequences: *'If you don't settle down to work, you won't pass the test'*; *'The rule about not running is so you won't knock anyone over'*. With a slight adjustment you can express this directly in terms of your care for the student:

- I don't want to see you get hurt, so no running please.
- I would like to see you succeed at this; you have the potential to do it – so give it a go and show me how far you can get.
- I would rather you didn't get into trouble again, you don't need any more grief. How about sorting this out now?

📁 Case study

When Justine first arrived in school her behaviour was 'like a caged animal, completely wild'. She was unable to settle to anything and aggressive towards other children in both overt and covert ways. According to the deputy head it took 18 months of consistent care to establish a relationship in which Justine felt safe. Her background was 'about as dysfunctional as you could get' with a drug-addicted mother and brother who was eventually jailed for murder. Justine is now 11 years old, still struggles with learning but her behaviour is no worse than the average student. She is much loved in school by both teachers and her classmates.

Although this student was at the extreme end of risk and her behaviour reflected this, the school took it upon themselves to show her the everyday care and consistency that was missing from home. With regular circle work and trust-building she eventually became much more cooperative and less oppositional. It wasn't one thing that made a difference, it was everyone in the school pulling together. Justine was a regular focus of staffroom discussion about how best to support her and also the staff most involved with her.

Peer relationships, caring and kindness

There is a 'cool to be cruel' element in some schools. You can see this in dominant individuals who demand compliance from their 'gang' to reject others. It also underpins cyber bullying. Students may be uncomfortable about their involvement with this and it is worth working with this ambivalence. What sort of people do our students want to grow into? Do they treat people as they want to be treated? Making the school, or your classroom, a no put-down zone requires some prior discussion of what this means but can make a difference to the way students interact.

> When there was a put-down ... everyone in the class was sort of shocked and said 'we don't talk bad – I can't believe you said that' and they all stood up for this other girl. I didn't have to intervene and I found that the whole positive rephrasing, not using 'put-downs' has rolled over into every day (teacher).

Feeling safe

Although there is no longer physical punishment in schools, psychological threat can be just as hard to deal with and has the same emotional responses of fight or flight. Students who feel threatened will behave in unwanted ways.

Students feel safer in a classroom where they are not going to be embarrassed in front of their classmates, not asked direct questions they can't answer or required to do things publicly that they struggle with. They are confident the teacher will not make fun of their personal attributes or use sarcasm.

Peer relationships and safety

Bullying is a serious issue in our schools and can destroy young lives. There has been a wealth of research in the last two decades and wide discrepancy on the effectiveness of anti-bullying programmes – what works in one school may not in another (Rigby, 2006). Bullying is often a social issue – it can only flourish in cultures that condone it – even passively by ignoring its existence. Developing supportive relationships, respect, responsibility and resilience along with a whole school commitment to wellbeing would appear to be the best chance we have of addressing bullying behaviour and increasing safety in school.

> ### 🗁 Case study
>
> After having several students from the same tutor group referred for bullying behaviours the educational psychologist and behaviour support teacher worked with the whole class. After being shown a short film about bullying the pupils were asked to list associated feelings – what it was like to be bullied, be the perpetrator or be an onlooker. They agreed that helplessness, fear, anxiety, being out of control, feeling isolated or uncomfortable were not good feelings to have in a class. They realised that bullying may be accompanied by feelings of power but that this didn't last and perhaps people didn't like themselves afterwards or were worried they were out of control. It also became clear that bullying is a social issue – it requires others to let it happen. Students talked about the feelings they would like to have and then worked together to discuss actions they might take to support positive feelings and reduce bullying. Some of their strategies were simple – just tell someone to give it a rest and leave her alone. A term later the bullying had much reduced and students felt happier in their class.

Feeling listened to

Teachers talk for a living – they are usually good at it! The other side of communication may not come so easily. It takes time to listen properly in a crowded school day but it is worth thinking about structuring this so it works well for everyone. Listening is respectful. Active listening means looking at the person speaking and not being distracted by what else is going on, not interrupting, asking for clarification, responding and asking relevant questions. It also means listening for the feelings being expressed and not jumping in with the answers to a problem.

〰 Question for reflection and discussion

What is involved in listening to students and how can we do this in a busy school day?

When might it be inappropriate to engage in active listening?

Peer relationships and being listened to

Students are expected to listen to their teachers but also need to learn the art of listening within a conversation. Professor Robyn Alexander, a Cambridge academic, has developed Dialogic Talk, a teaching method advocated by advisers at the Secondary National Strategy for School Improvement. It is based on five key concepts:

- Collectivity: teachers and pupils address learning tasks together
- Reciprocity: teachers and pupils listen to each other

- Support: children speak freely without feeling embarrassed
- Cumulation: teachers and children build on their own and each other's ideas
- Purposefulness: teachers plan the lessons with specific educational goals.

This approach works well (Alexander, 2008). As students become more confident talking in a group forum they also become better listeners. They begin to consider other people's opinions and can disagree without shouting anyone down. These skills not only help in school subjects they apply to all areas of life.

Having fun

Some schools operate on the belief that learning is hard work and fun doesn't come into it. Students, however, identify a 'good teacher' as one who makes lessons enjoyable as well as having high expectations. Fun is identified in Glasser's choice theory (1998) as one of the five needs that human beings strive towards.

Lightness, fun and humour can lift the spirits of everyone for a more effective learning environment. It can motivate and energise. A good laugh releases oxytocin into the body. This both lowers the stress hormone cortisol and increases pro-social interactions (Kuchinskas, 2009).

According to Cornett (1986) and Kelly (1983), humour can facilitate learning in the classroom in the following ways:

- helping with the development of friendship and promoting a sense of belonging
- providing tension release in awkward moments
- developing cognitive skills such as the skills of prediction, decision making, recall, problem-solving, and visual imagery
- fostering creativity by helping students discover incongruous relationships and solve problems
- improving communication and developing vocabulary and reading skills through playing with language
- enhancing the study of other cultures
- promoting good health and stress relief
- developing a positive attitude and self-image which promotes positive behaviours, and assists with conflict resolution.

Humorous stories or examples also help students remember important information. Games can move learning forward while also having fun (Hromek & Roffey, 2009).

Teachers need to provide positive, not negative models for using humour in the classroom. There can be a temptation to raise a laugh by using sarcasm or ridicule of individuals. This is not only psychologically damaging to that pupil, it also impairs safety and connectedness between students. Laughing 'with' and not 'at' is an important distinction.

Peer relationships and having fun

I am so happy when we do Circle Time; it is so fun. I can't wait until next Tuesday when we will do Circle Time (student).

Laughing together strengthens bonds between students and reduces stress. Feeling happy also promotes creativity and cognitive skills (Fredrickson, 2005). Students need to learn the difference between having fun with and laughing at. Something is only a joke when everyone genuinely finds it funny.

SUMMARY OF STRATEGIES AND APPROACHES TO PROMOTE POSITIVE BEHAVIOUR

- Be welcoming.
- Take into account cultural differences and how these might impact on behaviour.
- Think about what it means to be treated with respect and model this consistently.
- Develop active listening skills – using these at appropriate times.
- Ensure students regularly have fun at school.
- Acknowledge diverse intelligences and incorporate these into curriculum delivery.

SUMMARY OF STRATEGIES AND APPROACHES TO DEAL WITH DIFFICULTIES

- When you need to criticise students ensure they know it is the behaviour that is unwanted, not them
- Reinforce rules or guidelines with a comment on your care and concern for the student
- Respond with a light touch whenever you can – save the heavy stuff for serious incidents.

Professional development activities for teachers

Taking action to promote the positive

List 10 feelings that might exist in a classroom. In groups of three go through the list and write an action for each to promote the positive in the classroom. Share effective practice you have already come across.

What does it mean to be intelligent?

In small groups discuss what makes a person intelligent.

Do you see this as a stable trait or does it fluctuate with the context?

What factors enable you to demonstrate your intelligence and what gets in the way? Share stories with others in your group that illustrate this.

Culturally responsive classrooms

Discuss in small groups: What types of cultural conflicts can arise in classrooms that might make it more difficult to have a safe, caring, orderly environment? What might be done to help address these?

(Continued)

(Continued)

Active listening

In pairs take it in turns to relate a recent experience. For the first minute the listener uses active listening skills such as looking at the person and giving them full attention, reinforcing what they are saying by nodding and asking good questions. For the second minute they switch these skills off. This means interrupting, looking and turning away, coming in with your own stories and not following up what is being said.

When you have both had a turn discuss what it felt like when someone was really listening and what it felt like when they were not. What does this tell you about students?

Circle Solutions activities with students

This is an extended section to build the positive classroom climate described above. These activities will:

- support students in learning about each other
- value cultural diversity
- foster a sense of belonging, connection and responsibility.

All Circles begin with a statement of the principles:

- When one person is speaking everyone else listens.
- You may pass if you do not want to say anything.
- There are no put-downs.

Pass a smile

The facilitator smiles to the person on their left who passes the smile to the person on their left until the smile has travelled around the Circle.

Mix up

Stand up and change places if …

- You can speak more than one language
- Your parents come from different countries
- You have friends who have different coloured eyes to you.

Pair share

Find two things that you have in common – say one each to the Circle beginning your sentence with: 'We both …'. You could start out with the following examples:

- Things you like to eat
- Places you have been
- Films you have watched.

Our class, our responsibility

Invite students to brainstorm all the feelings in the class – both good and bad. Write each onto a piece of card and distribute to pairs of students. Each pair places their feeling onto one of three piles, positive, negative or neutral. Do you have more in one pile than another?

Divide students into small groups and give each a positive feeling. Ask them to explore what is already happening in this class to promote this feeling, then decide on three actions to increase it. Each group reports the outcome of their discussions.

Sentence completions

The best thing about this class is …

I know someone respects me when …

Family life

Invite grandparents from local communities to tell you about games they played as a child. Ask them to come to Circle sessions to help you teach students how to play these.

Who am I? Small group activity

Give each group an item of clothing such as a hat or shoe. Students talk about the owner of the item and what they might be like. As they talk the facilitator goes round and hands out more pieces of information such as:

- This person plays the piano.
- This person is blind.
- This person has four children.
- This person has escaped from a war zone.
- This person reads the Koran.
- This person is in a wheelchair.

As each piece of information is given the students alter the picture they are building up of the person. After 10 minutes they introduce their person to the Circle and talk about the process, where they started and how their view of this person changed.

Sentence completions

I feel valued when …

I can make someone else feel valued by …

RESOURCES

An excellent website on promoting positive behaviour and relationships is www.it scotland.org.uk/supportinglearners/positivelearningenvironments/positivebehaviour/index.asp

A pack to support Circles of Friends interventions can be ordered from www.inclusive-solutions.com.

H. McGrath and T. Noble, *Eight ways at once* (2005, Melbourne: Pearson Education). Two teacher resource books giving many ways to apply multiple intelligences in the classroom.

You can also sign up for an emailed Multiple Intelligences newsletter from the MI network on www.ascd.org.

C.S. Weinstein, S. Tomlinson-Clarke and M. Curran, Toward a conception of culturally responsive classroom management. *Journal of Teacher Education*, 2004, 55, 25–38. This article is full of examples of how teachers have addressed behavioural difficulties – both individually and as a group – with students from different ethnic backgrounds. It is worth reading as a stimulus to further discussion.

Read more about Dialogic Talk at www.teachernet.gov.uk/teachers/issue52/secondary/features/Listenandlearn

Read Bonnie Benard and Sean Slade's chapter in the *Handbook of positive psychology in schools* (2009, edited by R. Gilman, S. Huebner and M.J Furlong, 2009, London: Routledge) on Listening to students: Moving from resilience research to youth development practice and school connectedness.

Download guidance from the Department for Children, Schools and Families on preventing and dealing with bullying and how to establish and maintain a safe school at www.teachernet.gov.uk/wholeschool/behaviour/tacklingbullying/

www.safeschoolscoalition.org/ is a website aiming to support and reduce bullying and harassment of gay or transsexual students.

REFERENCES

Alexander, R.J. (2008). T*owards Dialogic Teaching: rethinking classroom talk*, fourth edition. Cambridge: Dialogos.

Ballenger, C. (1999). *Teaching other people's children: Literacy and learning in a bilingual classroom*. New York: Teachers College Press.

Bettelheim, B. (1994). Seeking a rightful place. *The NAMTA Journal*, 19(2), 101–18.

Cornett, C.E. (1986). *Learning through laughter: Humor in the classroom*. Bloomington, IN: Phi Delta Kappa Educational Foundation.

Cowen, E.L., Pederson, A., Babigian, H., Izzo, L.D. & Trost, M.A. (1973). Long-term follow up of early detected vulnerable children. *Journal of Consulting and Clinical Psychology*, 41, 438–46.

Curriculum Corporation (2008). *At the heart of what we do: values education at the centre of schooling. The final report of the Values Education Good Practice Schools Project – Stage 2*. Melbourne: Commonwealth of Australia, Curriculum Corporation.

Ellis, J., Hart, S. & Small-McGrinley, J. (1998). The perspectives of 'difficult' students on belonging and inclusion in the classroom. *Reclaiming Children and Youth*, 7(3), 142–6.

Ellis, L.A. (2004) Peers helping peers: The effectiveness of a peer support program in enhancing self-concept and other desirable outcomes. Unpublished thesis, University of Western Sydney.

Frederickson, N. (1991). *Children can be so cruel: Helping the rejected child*. In G. Lindsay & A. Miller (Eds), *Psychological services for primary schools*. Harlow: Longman.

Fredrickson, B.L. (2005). Positive emotions. In C.R. Synder & S.J. Lopez (Eds), *Handbook of positive psychology*. Oxford: Oxford University Press.

Gardner, H. (1983). *Frames of mind: The theory of multiple intelligences*. New York: Basic Books.

Gardner, H. (1999). *Intelligence reformed: Multiple intelligences for the 21st century*. New York: Basic Books.

Glasser, W. (1998). *Choice theory*. New York: HarperCollins.

Hromek, R. & Roffey, S. (2009). Promoting social and emotional learning with games: 'It's fun and we learn things'. *Simulation & Gaming*, 40(5), October, 626–44.

Jennings, P.A. & Greenberg, M.T. (2009). The pro-social classroom: Teacher social and emotional competence in relation to student and classroom outcomes. *Review of Educational Research*, 79(1), 491–525.

Kelly, W. E. (1983). *Everything you always wanted to know about using humor in education but were afraid to laugh*. Paper presented at the Annual International Convention of the Council for Exceptional Children, Detroit, MI, April (ERIC Document ED 232 381).

Kuchinskas, S. (2009). *The chemistry of connection*. Oakland, CA: New Harbinger Publications.

Lerner, M. (1980). *The belief in a just world*. New York: Plenum Press.

Newton, C. & Wilson, D. (2003). *Creating Circles of Friends: A peer support and inclusion workbook*. Nottingham: Inclusive Solutions.

Rigby, K. (2006). What international research tells us about bullying. In H. McGrath & T. Noble (eds). *Bullying solutions*. Melbourne: Pearson Education.

Roffey, S. (2008). Emotional literacy and the ecology of school wellbeing. *Educational and Child Psychology*, 25 (2), 29–39.

Slavin, R.E. (2009). *Educational psychology: Theory and practice*, ninth edition. New York: Merrill Hill.

Tew, M., & Park, J. (2008). In the right mind: Feeling ready for learning. *Curriculum Briefing*, 7(1), 23–7.

Webb, D. (2007). *My classroom's journey with restorative practices*. Posted 2010-01-07 on www.safer sanerschools.org/articles.html?articleId=658

Weinstein, C.S., Tomlinson-Clarke, S. & Curran, M. (2004). Toward a conception of culturally responsive classroom management. *Journal of Teacher Education*, 55, 25–38.

7 THE POWER OF POSITIVE RELATIONSHIPS

Chapter objectives

- To explore what constitutes a healthy relationship
- To examine issues of power and control
- To identify ways to establish positive relationships with challenging students
- To explore repairing and rebuilding teacher–student relationships
- To reflect on engaging with families when behaviour is a concern
- To emphasise the centrality of peer relationships
- To explore collegiality and teamwork.

WHAT IS A HEALTHY RELATIONSHIP?

If you ask people what they want in their relationships they come up with the following:

- Mutual respect
- Trust and honesty
- Reciprocity – give and take
- Acceptance of you as a whole person
- Good, open communication
- Equality
- Warmth
- Reliable alliance – being there for you in good times and bad
- Feeling comfortable and enjoyment in each other's company.

Questions for reflection and discussion

How do you want to be treated by others?

What do others do and say that makes you feel comfortable and what do they do and say that makes you feel unsafe?

BEING IN CHARGE OR BEING IN CONTROL

A healthy relationship is where there is equality, shared decision-making and no individual controls what happens. A controlling relationship does not model healthy relationship skills, undermines protective factors in resilience, does not internalise pro-social values, can lead to resentment, is exhausting and reduces the chance of pro-social behaviour. It is at the far end of controlling relationships we find bullying and abuse.

Relationships between teachers and students are already unequal because a teacher has more power than a student. Using this authority to empower others is a more intelligent way to promote positive behaviour than asserting power over others.

A common discourse on teacher–student relationships is that a 'good' teacher has to be in control of their students. The evidence shows otherwise. A good teacher certainly does not let students run riot but does give them a say in what happens. A teacher who is able to be in charge of proceedings in the classroom, orchestrate events, lead, support, guide, encourage participation, provide timely feedback and be responsive to individuals as well as the group does not need to control students. An effective educator encourages self-control and believes in the ability of students to learn this.

Do we want pupils who do as they are told because they will get into trouble otherwise, or students who think for themselves and choose to behave in considerate ways? It is in everyone's interests to foster the latter. This is much easier when the whole school is behind this approach (see Chapter 12).

Glasser (1998) says external control is destructive to relationships and that being disconnected is the source of almost all human problems. He advocates seven caring habits to counter what he calls 'deadly habits' which undermine healthy relationships – see Table 7.1.

Table 7.1

Caring habit	Deadly habit	Example of a practical application in school
Supporting	Criticising	'How can I help you?'
Encouraging	Blaming	'Tomorrow is another day, let's try again then.'
Listening	Complaining	'What happened? What did you want to happen?'
Accepting	Nagging	'That didn't go well. How can we move on and make this better?'
Trusting	Threatening	'I will come back later and see how you have got on.'
Respecting	Punishing	'The decision is yours – but you need to know the consequences.'
Negotiating difference	Bribing, rewarding to control	'Let's see if we can both get what we want here?'

📁 **Case studies: alternative views**

School 1: A group of university students were aiming to introduce Circle Time with a year 5 class, keeping to the principles of respect, inclusion, safety and democracy. The pupils were not used to being given choice and freedom. One pupil offered the following advice: *'You have to control us you know, because we can't control ourselves'.* This is what they had heard and was now what they believed. When their teacher was not there to 'keep control', they behaved in the way they had been led to expect of themselves.

School 2: *'At first, when the children would not listen the teacher would intervene and shout at them, defeating the whole purpose of Circle Time. When she fully understood the principles she changed her approach and then we saw some real changes in the students'* (university student working in a school).

〰️ **Question for reflection and discussion**

Can you think of an example which clarifies the difference between being in charge of a situation and being in control of other people?

WHAT WORKS IN ESTABLISHING GOOD STUDENT–TEACHER RELATIONSHIPS?

Relationships between pupils and staff are widely recognised to be critical in creating healthy school environments and fostering pupils' mental wellbeing (Hornby & Atkinson, 2003). The literature points to the teacher–pupil relationship as being particularly significant for excluded pupils (Pomeroy, 1999, 2000) and 'hard to teach' pupils (Ennis & McCaulay, 2002; Spratt et al., 2006). Positive relationships are a significant factor in classroom behaviour. They inhibit difficult situations arising in the first place and provide a cushion when challenges do arise.

Relationships are enacted by what is said and not said and messages that are given about value and expectations. Words are powerful. We need to be aware not only of how we can use them to positive effect but also of the potential for damage. Imagine the following scenario – this is fictional but the example is all too real in some classrooms.

Ms Robinson sees herself as a friendly and tolerant teacher who maintains good standards of behaviour with her 7-year-old students. She smiles at children as they arrive and never raises her voice. Unfortunately some individuals, mostly boys, do not meet her high expectations. One such boy, Toby, often arrives late. As he creeps into the room, all the other children are sitting on the carpet. 'Well, look who's here' says Ms Robinson. She raises her eyebrows, which makes everyone else giggle and addresses the class.

'What are we going to do with him, children?' Someone calls out 'Make him miss playtime'. Others begin to join in with other suggestions. Toby stands alone, looking embarrassed. 'Just sit down Toby, you can see how upset everyone is with you'. Lateness is not the only thing that displeases Ms Robinson. Toby is untidy, does not always wait his turn and frequently asks others what he is supposed to do. Every day he is ridiculed for his slowness and other inadequacies and told how hopeless he is. The other children either shun or taunt him, following their teacher's example.

〰 Questions for reflection and discussion

Have you come across educators who attempt to control students in this way?

What do you envisage will happen (a) to Toby and (b) to the other students in his class if this continues?

What might change the teacher's belief that this is an appropriate response?

There are, however, countless stories of the positive difference that teachers have made to the lives of pupils experiencing adversity, either temporary or long-term.

I had a hard time at home and at school and this one teacher made a real difference for me. He showed that he cared whether I was there or not, whether I learnt anything. He didn't give up on me. It's because of him that I stayed in school. I don't think teachers should say 'it's up to you whether or not you learn' – it makes it seem they don't care about you. (trainee teacher).

Developing good relationships, especially with potentially more challenging students, means showing the student he or she matters as a person. Specific actions can be summarised as follows:

- Greet by name and smile so you look pleased to see them.
- Show an interest; find out something about their life and ask the occasional question; avoid interrogation!
- Find something you have in common – for example a team you both support, a TV programme you both watch: this provides safe ground for conversation and develops a relationship that is not about what is going on at school.
- Find something you can genuinely admire and comment positively on these qualities. Attributing to the student resourcefulness, humour, protectiveness, spirit in the face of adversity, etc. provides them with an alternative self-concept.
- Give regular positive feedback which is specific, genuine and brief.
- Let them know you believe they are worth your continued effort.

- Consistently show that their success, safety and wellbeing is of concern to you – just the phrase '*Are you OK?*' will help.
- Model courtesy – take a second to open a door for them, say please and thank you.
- Tell the student what you enjoy about teaching them – exaggerate a small positive if necessary!

Show acceptance of the person but not their behaviour by:

- Remembering that information is much easier to hear than accusation – state what students are expected to do
- Using 'I' statements: *'I need you to ...'* – rather than 'you' statements: *'You are ...'*
- Giving limited choices that offer the student some control and promote self-efficacy, for example: *'What would you like to do first, this or that?'*

Develop a sense of inclusion and belonging by:

- Providing experiences which guarantee success – however small
- Framing behaviour in terms of equity rights, for example: *'You are not allowed to hurt another student because other students are not allowed to hurt you'*
- Giving students a specific responsibility and positive feedback for this – this has to be something they are able and willing to do
- Using the words 'we' and 'our' to include, not to exclude
- Avoiding unfavourable comparisons or put-downs
- Doing everything possible to avoid or limit sanctions that exclude students
- Speaking about the student positively to others
- Repeating back to the student anything positive you hear from others – particularly valuable for students who arrive in school with a negative reputation, it helps reduce self-fulfilling expectations
- When they are in trouble show some sympathy: *'you're not having the best day'*.

WHY DO RELATIONSHIPS BREAK DOWN?

On the surface it may appear that teacher–student relationships break down because of specific interactions between individuals. Sometimes this culminates in explosive incidents where both parties blame the other. It is, however, the interaction of complex perceptions and feelings over time and within systems that determine how people relate at any given moment. What goes on in a classroom is influenced by school culture and differing values between stakeholders. It is also the result of emotions and expectations that have evolved over time. A young person who anticipates rejection or failure is more likely to respond negatively to innocuous comments and feel hurt and angry. The example below illustrates this.

📁 **Case study**

Thirteen-year-old Matt came into the counsellor's office with his cap on back-to-front and his head down. He had just returned from a three-day suspension. This had been handed out to him after his verbal abuse to his music teacher. Matt was not contrite. *'She just hates my guts – the moment I walk in the door she's at me. She never asks me, she just tells me and then if I don't jump to it she starts having a go. I hate her. Other teachers are OK – they let me be.'* Matt was not a student with long-term difficulties – there were problems at home that were making him edgy and reactive. Most teachers understood his current sensitivities and were careful not to throw fuel onto a burning ember. The music teacher was not prepared to make any allowances and their relationship had broken down. She was not having such a good time either.

〰️ **Questions for reflection and discussion**

What might this teacher have done differently here when Matt entered her lesson, when she wanted him to do something and when he was not immediately compliant?

What beliefs were influencing her actions and what might help her respond differently?

Emotions differ depending on what has been triggered recently. If the student has had a terrible weekend or a confronting incident in an earlier class then the teacher is likely to have a bruised ego to contend with. Feelings are also linked to expectations: if a student's past experience with history has been fraught then a history teacher might be in for a more testing time than a sports teacher where experiences have been happier. If, however, a positive relationship has been established then the impact of earlier events will be moderated by the student's expectations of safety and support.

Teachers also bring their own constructs and emotions into any situation. The school system impacts on these. A teacher may feel supported as a member of an emotionally literate culture or fearful of criticism within an authoritarian one.

A RANGE OF TEACHER RESPONSES TO STUDENT CHALLENGE

The following constructs determine how a teacher might respond in challenging situations. These are just a few of the possibilities:

- I will not be seen as a good teacher if this student gets away with not doing as I say.
- This young person seems to be having a hard time.
- I am going to pretend this isn't happening – it is safer to ignore this student.
- I'm in control here – how dare this person defy me.

- This student is making my life a misery.
- This student has a personality disorder.
- I need to reduce the tension in my classroom.
- I don't think it's right that I should have to deal with such behaviour in my class.
- I'm scared I might get hurt.
- People who don't want to learn shouldn't be here.
- Conflict can be resolved once things have calmed down.
- I just feel incompetent and stupid when this happens – it must be my fault.
- I need to find out more about what is going on.

 **Questions for reflection and discussion**

Which of the constructs above might be helpful in a challenging situation and which are not? Why?

REASONS FOR REBUILDING

An entrenched relationship breakdown often occurs because each individual feels the other does not like or respect them or wants to 'win' control over the outcome. Neither takes responsibility for their contribution to the breakdown and neither will back down. A situation may be relieved if someone in the relationship leaves but this does not address the root cause. Those who have not developed ways to rebuild relationships will continue to be faced with unresolved relational difficulties elsewhere. Making the effort to repair a relationship may have far-reaching outcomes for that young person's future, and is also beneficial to teachers over the longer term. It shows a young person they are worth the effort, keeps them connected to school, and provides a powerful model for skilled social interaction and personal effectiveness. Another reason for teachers taking the initiative to rebuild relationships is self-interest. Not only will life in the classroom be more peaceful with this particular student but relationship building brings credibility with others in the class. Once a teacher has developed positive relationship management with one student these skills generalise to other difficult situations.

OVERCOMING BARRIERS TO REPAIR

In students, the biggest barrier to repairing relationships is the extent to which they have lost trust in others or belief in themselves. For older students who have had few positive experiences and little reason to affiliate to school, the barriers may be harder, though not impossible, to shift. For younger pupils and those with more recent or temporary difficulties there is a good chance of rebuilding.

The barrier to repair in teachers may be because they blame the student, sometimes exclusively. Teachers may say students know what behaviour is acceptable and should therefore conform to what is 'right'. If the breakdown is squarely placed on the student it follows that they will be required to make the first step towards any repair. This may be a demand to apologise, make amends, or promise better behaviour in the future. Students who feel they have been treated unfairly are unlikely to respond positively to this 'opportunity' to acknowledge they are at fault, especially at the height of the conflict. They may later grudgingly do what is required to prevent suspension or other punishment but this does not do a great deal for future interactions – it simply serves to confirm the construct that those in authority are out to get you. Teachers have power and authority in the school system. They can use this to insist on student conformity to the rules or they can re-frame their role as a responsibility to initiate mediation. This does not mean condoning unacceptable behaviour but getting a fuller picture of the student's interpretations, acknowledging that misunderstanding or over-hastiness may have contributed to the breakdown and that there are times when emotions on both sides can get out of hand.

〰️ Question for reflection and discussion

How prepared are you to take some responsibility for a relationship not going well and make the first step towards reconciliation?

RELATIONSHIPS WITH PARENTS AND CARERS

The great majority of pupils enjoy school, work hard and behave well. A strong sense of community and positive engagement with parents are features of schools where behaviour is good (Ofsted, 2005, p. 5).

The statement above summarises both research findings and my own experiences. In schools where thought is given to working effectively with parents, especially where there are behavioural issues, situations often improve. The opposite is also true. Presenting parents with a list of misdemeanours their child is said to have perpetrated is unlikely to be helpful in establishing a collaborative relationship. Parents will either be overcome with shame and embarrassment or become defensive and/or angry. Teachers' frustration with 'not getting the message across' rarely acknowledges that parents have a different but equally important role to fulfil. This is to defend their child and get their needs met. Sometimes, however, parents reduce the threat to themselves by joining in with the negative, blaming discourse. This leaves the student with no advocate.

Research (Pianta & Walsh, 1996; Roffey, 2002) indicates that there are ways to engage parents of pupils with behavioural difficulties that are more effective than others. These guidelines can be summarised as follows.

Send positive messages home on a regular basis: Some parents have not had a good experience of school themselves. They may feel inadequate in their parenting skills or be fearful of judgement on these. Sending positive messages home promotes positive home–school interactions to break down potential negativity and intimidation and can serve to give ideas about good parenting skills. It also provides an opportunity for a positive interaction between parent and child. The following examples suggest ways in which this might be achieved with minimal effort.

We introduced reward postcards. Each day every teacher was expected to send one reward post-card home to a set of parents/carers. The focus for the reward would change on a weekly basis to ensure that the widest possible number of students became eligible. One week the focus might be on best homework produced, on another biggest improvement in effort, or highest quality of work achieved today. This had the effect of improving relationships with parents who were tired of receiving letters and phone calls when things went wrong (Steer Report, DfES, 2005, p. 18).

Phone hugs – once a week, choose two students and make a phone call home. Just let the parent know that the student is going along nicely and you wanted them to know that. This will make the next conversation much easier when you have not so good news (Hansberry, 2008, p. 2).

Have informal conversations where possible, the earlier the better: Many parents find formal meetings intimidating so a chat in the playground is the place to start if you can. Make sure no one can overhear anything confidential or negative. This informality is harder for working parents and in high schools but a one-to-one after school in the first instance may be all that is needed. This can also establish a good relationship with the parent, which will help later if things don't improve. Invite parents to see you with a letter or phone call saying that you would value their help in finding the best way to support their child. Begin the meeting with an initial positive statement followed by an open-ended question such as: *'How is [student name] finding school at the moment – what does she say to you at home?'* Then state your concern for the child: *'She seems to be unhappy much of the time/ having some problems settling to work/ getting along with other pupils. I'm not sure what's going on and want to help, do you have any thoughts about this?'*

Position parents as experts on their child: Parents may not be experts on education or child development but they usually know their child better than anyone. Ask questions about their history and development, interests, what comforts the child, what gains their cooperation and so on. Some parents will only want you to tell you about problems. It takes skill to empathise with but not condone a negative view. Ask them what support they have, what they have tried that works. They may say they use physically punitive methods to instil discipline. Unless this is a child protection issue that needs to be reported, this is not the time to confront parents. Point out that these strategies are not allowed in schools, so we have to look elsewhere. If you work to engage parents and increase their trust in you, there will be future opportunities to discuss more positive behavioural approaches. Such a conversation not only promotes a positive home–school relationship it also raises parents' sense of confidence, importance and responsibility in their role.

Be positive: In all verbal and written communications begin by saying something positive about the student. You may have to dig deep but this engages the parent and lets them know that you will be balanced in your approach and have the student's best interests at heart. It also reassures them about their parenting and promotes a more positive view of the child. Try such phrases as: *'Brandon is such an independent little boy'*; *'Martha has great spirit'*; *'I have seen a really caring side of Akbar this week'*.

Stay focused on the needs of the child: However tempted you may be, do not talk about your needs as a teacher or those of the class, it does not get parents on-side – it is their child they are interested in.

Seek commonalities: Parents may see things differently from you. Do not try to fight for your view to be dominant. Seek what you have in common and look at how you might work together in meeting the student's needs.

Make decisions together: Some parents will agree to anything at a meeting but find that their lives make it impossible to carry out such actions. Ask for their ideas and check what is realistic. One parent of a child with special needs (and other family commitments) once said that all the professionals she ever met announced that: *'This will only take five to 10 minutes a day'*. She felt constantly guilty about not fitting in all those 10 minutes of different interventions and feared the professionals would see her as someone who didn't care about her child.

Maintain good communication: Parents usually want to know what is going on at school and prefer contact that is regular, respectful, positive, private and two-way.

I can phone the school and leave a message (about things that have happened at home) and they understand. That's been helpful to act as a brake so the difficulties don't just escalate.

Listening to parents' concerns is crucial:

Teachers actually talked to me, explained things and listened to me. I think that was the most important thing – they listened to me.

Take account of family contexts: This could include work commitments and other demands such as caring responsibilities. Other concerns (health, finance, relational) may also be overwhelming. Although you may not be able to do much about these, it is helpful for parents to know you are taking them into consideration. For instance, ask when would be the best time for them to come to a meeting. The following quote is from a parent who is herself a teacher in tertiary education:

It wasn't just irritating, it was infuriating. Can you imagine what it is like to be in the middle of a lesson, you are called to the phone, you are completely distracted from your job – and it was nothing horrendous, boys' pranks, couldn't it have waited?

Structure more formal meetings with care:

- Give enough notice and ask what time suits parents best.
- Ask parents if they would like to bring a friend or supporter. This is particularly helpful for lone mothers. It provides emotional support, a person to talk to afterwards and someone who can help the parent remember what was said. They can also help with young children if necessary.

- Provide toys for young children who may be present.
- Do not have a pre-meeting between education professionals with parents waiting outside; it does not communicate respect.
- Limit the number of professionals attending if this is likely to be intimidating.
- Start meetings on time, check expectations about finishing and stick to what is agreed.
- Put everyone on the same level – sit in a circle on the same height chairs and use either first names or surnames for everyone: ask parents their preference.
- Beware of using educational jargon: words that are commonplace to teachers, such as 'curriculum' are not familiar to all parents. In particular do not use acronyms without explaining them first. Educators use short-hand all the time when speaking to each other without realising this can exclude others.
- Do not assume knowledge.
- Avoid giving parents material to read in a meeting: they cannot concentrate on this and they may have literacy difficulties.
- Be aware of cultural issues and provide an interpreter if necessary.
- Share air-space: actively encourage parental contributions to the discussion.
- Avoid interruptions: put a sign on the door and hold calls.
- Ask open-ended questions but do not interrogate.
- Smile, show warmth and empathy: avoid attributing blame, it leads nowhere.
- Keep the child's needs central to the discussion.
- Do not go on the defensive or become bureaucratic by frequently referring to rules and policies.
- Bring the meeting to a close by allowing five minutes to summarise what has been agreed about the way forward.
- Give parents opportunities to ask questions and make it clear they can do this at other times.
- Arrange a review meeting.

Allow parents to express feelings: It can be an emotional experience talking about your child's challenging behaviour. It may be difficult to separate this from feeling judged as inadequate as a parent. If a parent becomes tearful have a tissue on hand and tell them it isn't surprising they are upset. If they are angry they may accuse you and the school of all manner of things. Acknowledge their feelings and allow them to have their say until they run out of steam. Interrupting to deny the accusations will make it go on longer and may make the situation worse. No one in a highly emotional state listens to reason. When they pause for breath perhaps offer them a cup of tea and the opportunity to discuss what to do for the best. Stay calm yourself by thinking how you are going to reward yourself for being such a paragon of emotional literacy. As with students, the calmer you are the sooner they will be.

In cases where parents may be abusive

This goes beyond the expression of feelings to threatening language and gestures, constant shouting and swearing, intimidation and/or personal abuse. Ensure you are not alone in this situation.

Encourage everyone to be seated – this inhibits the escalation of aggression. If the parents have not calmed down within a short time tell them calmly but firmly that there are standards of behaviour in school which apply to both students and adults and that they are overstepping the line. You cannot deal with their concerns until this can be done in a mutually respectful manner. Ask when they can come and see you again. If parents are drunk or drugged on the premises ask them to leave and return when you can have a useful conversation about their concerns. If they refuse to go, leave yourself and inform senior staff members.

〰️ **Questions for reflection and discussion**

In which ways could you position a parent of a child with challenging behaviour?
What difference would this make to your interactions with them?

Parents whose children are affected by the behaviour of others

When parents send their child to school they expect teachers to act 'in loco parentis' and provide the same level of care and protection they would. When their child is hurt on the school premises they may be understandably upset and demand retribution. Listen and take their concerns seriously:

- Let them have their say in full without interruption.
- Agree what is not acceptable so you find common ground.
- Show concern for their child.
- Do not make excuses for the behaviour but point out how you are teaching students what is acceptable and not.
- Look for any strengths/positives in the situation – support from peers, etc.
- If applicable, talk about how pupils are expected to take collective responsibility for each other's safety.
- Adults cannot always protect children in every situation – our job is to help them develop skills to deal with adversity. Discuss ways in which their child is learning to deal with difficulties themselves and the support they need to do this.

It is wise to communicate behaviour policies with parents when their children first attend the school, with reminders as appropriate. Parents need to know how the school encourages pro-social behaviour and responds to behaviour that is unacceptable. They also need information on policies and practices designed to keep children safe. There are many adults who cannot see beyond punishment for problematic behaviour. Working to develop a different understanding takes ongoing communication about effective practice. This may also help parents learn facilitative parenting skills.

RELATIONSHIPS BETWEEN STUDENTS

(There is more on this throughout Chapter 6 and in all Circle Solutions activities.) Children and young people operate in two worlds. Their relationship with adults is one of dependence and inequality whereas relationships with peers are at the same level. To have friends children must reduce egocentricity and learn the 'rules' of relationships; which behaviours will support the maintenance of friendships and which will not.

Factors that impact on choices in social behaviour include the need for approval, the desire to be part of the group, empathy for others and moral values. Being pro-social depends on the interaction of relational skills, emotional factors and contextual cues – such as prior relationships and current expectations (Wentzel et al., 2007). This suggests that actively promoting relational values, knowledge and skills, together with opportunities for developing a sense of belonging, will have an impact over time.

Students with emotional and behavioural difficulties may have negative perceptions of others and often struggle with establishing positive interactions. Other students may be rejecting and inhibit the reinforcement of any new relational skills (Frederickson, 1991). SEL is therefore more effective within the mainstream classroom so all pupils learn about positive relationships, interact with all peers and take responsibility for inclusion.

Friendly behaviour establishes a threshold for closer friendships. Students need both the opportunities and skills to approach others, communicate effectively and behave in ways that foster positive interactions. They also need to know how to deal with conflict and problem-solve relational issues. As relationships change with development (Roffey et al., 1994) these issues need to be addressed throughout each phase of education.

There is evidence that SEL programmes are making a positive difference to behavioural issues in the classroom (McCarthy, 2009; Payton et al., 2008).

It was remarkable to see the children that I had been working with since March [on Circle Time Solutions] working together as a team and creating friendships and bonds. ... No longer were they being disruptive and not talking to one another ... (university student).

RELATIONSHIPS BETWEEN COLLEAGUES

Colleagues can boost your confidence or undermine it; they can be supportive or dismissive of your approach; they can build on what you are trying to develop with students or ridicule this. One answer to this is to build relationships with those who share your views and be simply polite with those who do not.

Pupils observe the interactions between staff and learn from what they see. How well do the relationships between teachers in school model what we want students to learn? If these are visibly warm, supportive and full of good humour, this leads to higher levels of social capital and relational trust. It is easier to respond thoughtfully to challenging behaviour in such an ethos, and be more resilient when things do not go well.

The way in which teachers talk to each other about what works in relation to behaviour is both influenced by and impacts on the culture of the school. Miller (1996) found a strong reluctance to share successful strategies. The reasons given included:

- The problems (and therefore solutions) belong to the teacher concerned, no-one else would be interested
- Fear that the teacher's initial difficulties with a student would be perceived as inadequacies in the role
- Fear that strategies would be dismissed as not making a sustainable difference
- A mismatch between the teacher's enthusiasm for working on behalf of the student and a punitive school culture
- Changes in students being attributed to factors outside school rather than as an outcome of strategies employed by teachers
- No one asking or being that interested
- Having to tread carefully not to offend the sensibilities of colleagues who had not been successful with that student in the past.

〰️ Questions for reflection and discussion

How could successful interventions be shared between staff?

What would need to be taken into consideration?

Rogers (2006) defines three dimensions to collegial relationships in schools: moral support, professional support and structural support.

Moral support

This reduces the isolation that permeates so many teachers' professional lives. It gives the message that we are all in this together, we all have problems at times and need understanding and help from each other. Reciprocity is key. As Rogers says: *'accepting fallibility in oneself means acknowledging it and accepting it in others'*. It does not mean, however, not constructively addressing difficult issues. The key is *constructive*. Some colleagues may use moaning in staffroom conversations as a coping strategy but this can decrease rather than increase resilience. It does not promote responsibility for resolving problems and fosters feelings of helplessness and sometimes victimisation. In the worst scenarios negativity about students or families can permeate the ethos and become a dominant discourse, which needs to be challenged by school leaders. The trick is to show empathy for the difficulties colleagues are facing without colluding with their take on this.

The following makes school staff feel more connected. If you do this, others may follow:

- Make a point of greeting colleagues warmly.
- Sit down next to people and ask them how it's going – not just the colleagues you always sit next to.
- Find out about people outside the job – not in a nosy way but things they might want to talk about, like their family or holidays.
- Share a funny story or experience – ensuring it doesn't put anyone down. Humour promotes positive relationships, increases group cohesion and relieves tension.

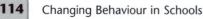 **Case study**

In one large special school everyone gets to know who has been their personal 'angel' on the last day of each term. At the beginning of term each member of staff picks the name of a colleague out of a hat. They are now the 'angel' for this person with a brief to simply watch over them. They do as much or as little in this role as they wish but actions have included organising a birthday cake, taking a playground duty when someone didn't feel well, putting positive notes or chocolate bars in their pigeon hole, sending a card home when they were off sick, offering to help out at a function, helping carry heavy loads as well as just having the occasional staffroom chat to check how things are going. Often teachers identify their 'angels' well before the end of term but not always. They love the system and feel it really helps, especially at the more stressful times of the term. Some enjoy the creativity involved in finding different ways to boost their colleague throughout the term.

Trust and respect are synonymous with healthy relationships. Respect includes courtesy and consideration. When work life is stressful these basic components of positive collegial interaction can be threatened. When the ethos of a school does not actively address negative behaviours such as rudeness, incivility or selfishness such as leaving a mess in the kitchen or talking over others in a staff meeting, everyone is affected. Positive relationships demands awareness of what is acceptable in the staffroom just as much as with student behaviour.

Respect also means acceptance of difference. People have different strengths and weaknesses and different opinions. In a healthy ethos this is acknowledged and discussed so that differences can be valued and put to good use to reach shared goals. That way lies cohesion rather than dissension. Respect means acknowledging and valuing people's efforts as well as their achievements (Roffey, 2005).

In our weekly bulletin there is always something saying thank you to someone – not for just the big things. It makes you feel really good (teacher).

I feel valued and appreciated in the department I work in, and this reflects in my enthusiasm, input and dedication to students and staff in this department (teacher).

Trust is about predictability – knowing you can rely on someone. When someone makes a point of regularly bad-mouthing their colleagues your own trust in them is dented as you wonder whether they may be doing the same to you. Trust will permeate a school if teachers have explored and agreed a shared vision. This also promotes collaboration, support and shared learning. When trust is placed in individuals alone it can disappear when those people leave (Hargreaves, 1994).

Professional support

Professional support is where colleagues share information, resources, concerns and strategies. One way of doing this is peer support. This can have many faces, from problem-solving groups, to joint ventures, mentoring and coaching and being a 'critical friend'. One of the advantages of peer support is that it is not about a power relationship in which one person is making judgments on another but working together towards agreed goals. At best it can enhance confidence and a sense of professionalism, reduce stress and increase enjoyment in the role (Rogers, 1999).

Structural support

Structural support relates to policies, practices and systems within the school. It includes things like having a manageable workload and the resources you need to be effective. Communications are part of the structure – how people get information and the opportunities they have to contribute to policy development. It also covers how people work in teams.

∿ Question for reflection and discussion

What similarities and differences are there in positive relationships with colleagues and positive relationships with students?

SUMMARY OF STRATEGIES AND APPROACHES TO PROMOTE POSITIVE BEHAVIOUR

- Show students their wellbeing matters to you.
- Build positive relationships with parents and colleagues.
- Promote universal social and emotional learning.

SUMMARY OF STRATEGIES AND APPROACHES TO DEAL WITH DIFFICULTIES

- Spend a little time and effort making positive connections with challenging students.
- Use 'I' statements rather than accusatory 'you' statements.
- Be sure the words you use promote inclusion rather than marginalisation.
- Be prepared to make the first step to repair a relationship.
- Position parents/carers as experts on their child.
- By sympathetic but do not collude with negativity in colleagues or parents.
- Share effective strategies with trusted colleagues.

Professional development activities for teachers

Power and control: paired discussion

What is the place of power in a healthy relationship?

What benefits does giving control back to students have for the teacher/for the students?

Family meeting: role play

Two people play teachers, one a class teacher and one a senior teacher. Two play parents (or a parent and supporter) and the fifth is an observer.

The scenario is as follows:

Connor is 11. He has been in the school for six months. During that time he has been seen smoking in the grounds, verbally abused female staff, made obscene gestures to some of the girls and become the leader of a small group of boys who have been bullying and intimidating others. There are suspicions he is dealing drugs but no proof of this. His parents have been asked into school to talk about concerns. Connor is currently suspended from school.

Before you begin the role play each person thinks about:

1. your expectations
2. what you are hoping to achieve.

Role play the meeting for 15 minutes then stop and de-brief with the observer.

Consider the following:

- What did people feel: about themselves, the others in the meeting and the final outcome?
- What is there to build on, if anything?
- What might be different next time?
- What else might the school do in similar situations?

Colleagues I have known

In pairs talk to each other about supportive colleagues you have come across. What did they do and say that was helpful? What have you learned from them?

Circle Solutions activities with students

These activities will support students in developing a sense of belonging and responsibility for each other.

All Circles begin with a statement of the principles:

- When one person is speaking everyone else listens.
- You may pass if you do not want to say anything.
- There are no put-downs.

Class web

All students stand together in a tight circle. The facilitator holds one end of a ball of string and throws the rest of the ball across the Circle to a student saying their name. This person does the same until a web has been made in the centre. This web represents the class and the fact that everyone is connected.

No put-downs

In small groups discuss the following:

- What is a put-down?
- Has anyone put you down?
- What did they do?
- What did you feel?
- What did you do?

How might you go about developing a proposal for the whole school to be a 'No Put-Down Zone'? Write down what might need to go into a policy document.

Sentence completions

Going around the Circle students complete the following sentences.

- Being friendly means …
- Sticking up for someone means …
- This class is a friendly place to be when …

(Continued)

(Continued)

What if this happened to you?

Ask for volunteers to role-play this scenario for the whole Circle.

Ella: You are in a new school and haven't made friends yet. You miss your mates a lot. You are pleased that Chi and Brianna are spending some time with you.

Chi and Brianna: You don't get on so well with others in your class. You are interested in Ella when she arrives and try and to find out everything you can about her.

Scene 1: Conversation between Ella, Chi and Brianna finding out about each other.

Scene 2: Chi explains to Brianna that it would be a real laugh to put Ella's picture up on Facebook and let everyone know something about her, including some really personal information. Brianna isn't so sure but goes along with Chi as her friend.

Scene 3: Ella reads what has been written about her. It isn't nice.

Scene 4: Ella comes into school and asks Chi and Brianna why they did that. Chi and Brianna attack her for not being 'fun' to be around. Ella is left stranded.

Facilitator asks the actors:

- What did you feel about being Ella?
- Did you feel comfortable being Chi or Brianna?
- How did you encourage each other?

    Facilitator asks all students (divide into smaller groups if this would be helpful):

- How would you feel if this happened to you?
- What might have stopped the cyber-bullying?
- What do you think should happen now?

RESOURCES

Peer Support has much to offer to both peer leaders and the pupils who are supported. Google YouTube and search Peer Support for videos of students talking about it. Helen Cowie and Patti Wallace, *Peer support in action* (2000, London: Sage), covers setting up Peer Support and the core skills needed.

Colin Newton and Derek Wilson provide guidelines for setting up circles of *teacher support* for responding to pupils with emotional and behavioural difficulties: www.inclusive–solutions.com/circlesofadults.asp. Gerda Hanko's book *Increasing competence through collaborative problem-solving* (1999, London: David Fulton) also has much to offer, including illustrative case studies.

Social and Emotional Learning: There are many resources for SEL including the SEAL materials published by the Department for Children, Schools and Families in the UK: http://nationalstrategies.standards.dcsf.gov.uk/primary/publications/banda/seal/

Sue Roffey's *Circle time for emotional literacy* (2006, London: Sage) has many activities for all ages addressing issues raised in this chapter.

REFERENCES

Department for Education and Skills (DfES) (2005). *The Steer Report: Learning behaviour. The report of the practitioners group on school behaviour and discipline*. London: DfES.

Ennis, C. & McCauley, M.T. (2002). Creating urban classroom communities worthy of trust. *Journal of Curriculum Studies*, 34(2), 149–72.

Frederickson, N. (1991). Children can be so cruel: Helping the rejected child. In G. Lindsay and A. Miller (Eds), *Psychological services for primary schools*. Harlow: Longman.

Glasser, W. (1998). *Choice theory*. New York: Harper Collins.

Hansberry, B. (2008) *Relationships first – relationship 1 percenters*. From the April 2008 Relationships First Community. www.hansberry.com

Hargreaves. A. (1994). Restructuring restructuring: Postmodernity and the prospects for individual change. *Journal of Education Policy*, 9(1), 47–65.

Hornby, G. & Atkinson, A. (2003). A framework for promoting mental health in school. *Pastoral Care in Education*, 21(2), 3–9.

McCarthy, F. (2009). *Circle time solutions: Creating caring school communities*. Sydney: Report for the NSW Department of Education.

Miller, A. (1996). *Pupil behaviour and teacher culture*. London: Cassell.

Ofsted (2005). *The annual report of HM's Chief Inspector of Schools 2003/2004*. London: Ofsted.

Payton, J., Weissberg, R.P., Durlak, J.A., Dymnicki, A.B., Taylor, R.D., Schellinger, K.B. & Pachan, M. (2008). *The positive impact of social and emotional learning for kindergarten to eighth-grade students. Findings from three scientific review*s. www.casel.org/sel/meta.php

Pianta, R.C. & Walsh, D.J. (1996). *High risk children in schools: Constructing sustaining relationships*. New York: Routledge.

Pomeroy, E. (1999). The teacher–student relationship in the secondary school: Insights from excluded students. *British Journal of Sociology of Education*, 20(4), 465–82.

Pomeroy, E. (2000). *Experiencing exclusion*. Stoke-on-Trent: Trentham Books.

Roffey, S. (2002). *School behaviour and families: Frameworks for working together*. London: David Fulton Publishers.

Roffey, S. (2005). *Respect in practice – the challenge of emotional literacy in education*. Australian Association for Research in Education. www.aare.edu.au/05pap/rof05356.pdf

Roffey, S., Tarrant, T. & Majors, K. (1994). *Young friends: Schools and friendship*. London: Continuum.

Rogers. B. (1999). Towards a model for colleague support: Matching support to needs and contexts. Unpublished doctoral dissertation, Melbourne University.

Rogers, B. (2006). *I get by with a little help … Colleague support in schools*. London: Paul Chapman Publishing.

Spratt, J., Shucksmith, J., Philip, K. & Watson, C. (2006). 'Part of who we are as a school should include responsibility for wellbeing': Links between the school environment, mental health and behaviour. *Pastoral Care*, September 14–21.

Wentzel, K.R., Filisetti, L. & Looney, L. (2007). Adolescent prosocial behavior: The role of self-processes and contextual cues. *Child Development*, 78(3), 895–910.

Zins, J.E., Weissberg, R.P., Wang, M.C. & Walber, H. (2004). *Building academic success on social and emotional learning: What does the research say?* New York: Teachers College Press.

PARTICIPATION, ENGAGEMENT AND AGENCY

Schools which provide mechanisms for consultation with their students and structures for listening to the collective voice of students, are those which often have lower incidences of unacceptable pupil behaviour (NUT, 2005, p. 21).

There are many ways in which student voice improves behaviour:

- Participation gives children and young people a sense of inclusion and belonging.
- Engagement in your community enhances resilience and wellbeing.
- When young people are given agency they are more likely to take responsibility for the decisions they make.
- Optimal adult–child relationships include authentic consultation.
- Seeking someone's opinion makes that person feel good about themselves and positive towards the person interested.
- Giving students opportunities to contribute increases their motivation to collaborate, encourages their creativity and thinking skills, and develops a more positive self-concept.
- Adults' views of young people may change if we provide opportunities for students to identify and demonstrate their strengths.
- Children are often marginalised in our society and in our schools: they do not have an automatic 'voice' in matters that concern them and sometimes behave in ways that are attention seeking in order to be 'heard'.
- Children have a right to be heard in matters that concern them.

The United Nations Convention on the Rights of the Child (United Nations, 1989) is signed by 194 countries in the world although not yet ratified by Somalia or the United States. The foundation principles are:

- *Non-discrimination*: all children, everywhere and in all situations should have the same rights.
- *Best interests of the child*: all decisions concerning the child should prioritise the child's best interests, not anyone else's.
- *The right to survival and development*: all children need access to basic services of health care and education to protect them from danger, ensure their wellbeing and to enable them to fulfil their potential.
- *The views of the child*: every child has the right to be involved and heard in matters that concern them. All effort must be made to promote children's active, free and meaningful participation.

〰️ **Questions for reflection and discussion**

In which ways are the rights above adhered to for students whose behaviour is causing difficulty?

What are your experiences and thoughts?

The following case study puts the rights of a child into practice across a whole local education authority and demonstrates that where schools are committed to this approach there are positive outcomes in both behaviour and student engagement.

📁 **Case study**

In the county of Hampshire, England a district-wide initiative has been undertaken to make schools consistent with the rights of the child as described in the UN convention, adopted by United Nations in 1989. The initiative, known as RRR or Rights, Respect and Responsibility, uses the rights of the UN Convention as the basis for all curricula content, pedagogy, school policies and rules. It aims to create a school climate in which all staff and students are aware of and respect the rights of others. Particular attention is paid to the child's right to participation as described in Article 12 of the Convention. In accord with the article, children play a meaningful role in school rules, policies, hiring and expenditures. These school and classroom practices are consistent with the predictors of student engagement.

Where schools had fully implemented the RRR initiative into the school ethos and into the classroom and school policies and practices, there was an increase in levels of student engagement and a decrease in teacher burnout. Compared with their peers in control schools, students showed greater respect for property, greater respect for the rights of others, increased participation and improved behaviours, and over time they showed increasingly higher levels of participation and improved positive behaviours.

(Continued)

(Continued)

   When children are behaving in a socially responsible, rights-respecting way in the classroom, and particularly when they are actively involved in their classroom and school activities, teachers have improved relationships with the students and a greater sense that their teaching is effective. In the words of one teacher: 'Teaching RRR has reminded me why I went into teaching – to make a difference'. Seeing the children's behaviour and learning improve, seeing children become more engaged in school clearly is rewarding for teachers. In fact, many teachers noted how pleased they were with the improvements they noted in their students. As one commented: 'the more you respect the kids and the more you let them participate in the classroom, the more they respect you' (Covell et al., 2009, p. 283).

GIVING STUDENTS AGENCY

'Student voice' is not merely the provision of data for others to make decisions for the student concerned, but is seen to be 'integral to encouraging young people's active participation in shared decisions and consequent action about their own present and futures'. (Holdsworth & Blanchard, 2005)

These authors identify that student voice needs to be authentic and active, not merely lip service. This means giving students agency and fully incorporating their views on decisions that affect them. It is handing over some power for action. This is the opposite of doing things for pupils or to them. It is doing *with* them. When adults take this approach the following happens:

- Young people begin to understand what is involved in taking responsibility.
- They begin to learn how to weigh up pros and cons in decision-making.
- They think through what they need and what they can do to get their needs met.
- Authentic involvement is more likely to lead to responsible actions.
- It is not so easy for a pupil to blame someone else for what is happening to them.
- Adults begin to have more faith in young people to make sensible decisions.
- Students begin to see themselves differently and more positively.

The following case study is an illustration of what can happen when you give pupils agency. As with many behavioural strategies the impact is rarely on one student alone. There is a snowball effect.

📁 Case study: on report – the alternative

Britney, aged 13, had been placed on every kind of report imaginable. She hated showing report cards to her teachers and felt that any good behaviour was ignored. 'Disruptive as usual' was the most common comment. Both the educational psychologist (EP) and deputy head had some sympathy with the teenager, knowing something of her particular situation. Britney was aware that the deputy head had her interests at heart as more than once he had rescued her from a potentially explosive crisis. After some thought and a few misgivings about staff reactions it was decided to put her on report just one more time – but this time it was to be a positive report only. Britney was involved in setting her own targets and teachers were to record only her successes – or at least her efforts. These included 'Coming into lessons quietly', and 'Working with others if asked'. The report booklet was designed using a desktop publisher and placed inside a plastic wallet. It looked a serious and valued document. Each page had a frame labelled for the day's lessons and a good-sized space for teachers' comments. Across the top of each page was written 'Britney is trying hard to complete some tasks successfully. Please write how well she is doing in your lesson'. At the end of each day the booklet had to be shown to the deputy head.

Teachers were to ask for the booklet at the beginning of every lesson and only write the good things. If they wanted to complain about behaviour or lack of work then the tutor was to be informed by other means.

Britney liked it. Though some were initially sceptical, teachers agreed to go along with the requests for positive reporting and to everyone's surprise Britney managed to get to the end of the week with the booklet intact and her behaviour somewhat improved. After two weeks, Britney, the EP, the deputy head and Britney's mother met in school. This time instead of the usual catalogue of complaints she was able to hear some praise and her mother was shown evidence of completed work, Britney was flushed with pleasure and for once able to acknowledge that improvement was possible and that she could take control of her own actions and behaviour.

Since then the booklet has been adapted for many pupils. Targets are negotiated and often there is a space for students' comments at the end of a week. Some of these are illuminating, for example, 'Thought of bunking as I got bored, thought of what we agreed and stayed put'. Sometimes discrepancies between teacher comments and self-assessments have proved a useful focus for further discussion.

Many pupils have asked if they can have a booklet, some for a second time when they felt their efforts needed a boost. They have, however, been used sparingly so as not to devalue them. They are taken seriously by staff and by students and appreciated by parents who are often requested to sign after checking them each evening.

Although it hasn't worked with every student, especially when a holiday has broken the pattern of new behaviours, for many it has made a significant difference. A genuine long-lasting improvement has begun within a few weeks of positive teacher reporting, self-assessment and a feeling by the student that perhaps after all they did have the ability to be in control of their own behaviour.

ENGAGING PEDAGOGIES

In a study in Denmark, pupils were asked about when they thought they really learnt something. Top of the list was 'debate in the classroom', and at the bottom 'when the teacher talks' (Jensen & Kostarova-Unkovska, 1998). There is surprisingly little attention paid to pedagogy in relation to children with behavioural difficulties, though engagement is becoming a buzzword in education (Field, 2004). Despite social and technological changes in the last half-century, teaching methods remain primarily didactic, particularly in high schools (Race & Powell, 2000). Common practice is for teachers to impart knowledge to students who hopefully want to learn. As we know this is not always the case. Student behaviour can be related to disengagement with the curriculum and how it is delivered. Although issues outside school impact on student motivation there is also growing evidence that student-centred rather than teacher-centred pedagogy is more effective in engaging students and by extension, reducing unwanted behaviour.

Keirsley and Shneiderman (1999) talk about the value of small teams of students being presented with 'meaningful, messy and ill-structured tasks' that they work on to find real solutions. This is sometimes referred to as problem-based learning (PBL). The teacher is coach and mentor, imparting knowledge to answer questions that evolve from the task. This takes both courage and skill on the part of the teacher who relinquishes their usual control of proceedings. Technology plays a supportive role but is not an end in itself. Three schools in low socio-economic areas who have taken on this approach have found that previously disruptive students are interested in the real-world tasks being presented to them. Teachers report greater work satisfaction (Aldred, 2008).

Cooperative learning has been advocated widely for both learning outcomes and positive behaviours. In competitive environments, some students feel they can never win or shine, so working together towards shared goals in a strengths-based framework offers a useful alternative. Cooperative learning is not having students sit at the same table talking with each other as they do their individual assignments nor one student doing all the work on behalf of the group. Although cooperation does include discussion, helping others and sharing resources it is more than this. One definition of cooperative learning (Smith et al., 2005) is that it involves three or more students working together on a common group activity with shared goals that requires them to:

- contribute to the task (positive task interdependence)
- help each other by using appropriate interpersonal and small-group skills
- ask intelligent questions
- provide detailed responses to questions
- promote each other's learning.

Positive interdependence means linking students so that success is dependent on everyone. It may be useful for each team member to have assigned roles and responsibilities. Shared findings need to be agreed by all group members and able to be explained by each. A shared mark can encourage both individual effort in the group process and enhanced interaction to reach the set goal (Johnson & Johnson, 1999).

Cooperative learning can be structured or informal. Even in teacher-led classrooms, breaking a lesson up with discussions to clarify, share understanding and add meaning can re-engage students. There is evidence that cooperative learning pedagogies enhance thinking skills, promote social and emotional learning and increase connection to school.

Gillies (2008) found that schools needed to ensure that teachers were trained in establishing cooperative learning and that students needed regular opportunities to put this into practice. When this happened they found that students were able to provide more detailed help to their peers and developed more complex thinking and problem-solving skills.

> ### 〰 **Question for reflection and discussion**
>
> Think of two learning experiences, one in which you were fully engaged and one in which you were distracted or bored.
>
> What was happening in each that gives you insight into how to increase pupil engagement with learning?
>
> Discuss your thoughts with a partner and identify what you have in common.

INCREASING CONNECTEDNESS

Without mindful processes to develop social capital, toxic environments easily develop. Where there is little sense of connectedness there is little relational trust and few shared goals. This is the atmosphere in which prejudice, intolerance and bullying thrive. One way to give students agency in a democratic forum is to ask them to collectively devise class guidelines. A framework for doing this is given in the Circle Activities at the end of this chapter.

📁 **Case studies**

One secondary school had a problem with graffiti. No sooner had it been cleaned off than it re-appeared. Staff, especially maintenance staff, were at their wits' end. The head teacher introduced a new policy. Each class in the school had responsibility for a section of the walls. When any graffiti appeared on that wall the whole class had to ensure that it was removed as quickly as possible. It wasn't long before graffiti became less visible. Now it isn't a problem at all.

In another school pupils designed and painted a large mural along the outside wall. Some of the most disaffected students were involved in this project and found a way to feel a sense of pride and identity.

In both cases students increased their sense of belonging – school became more 'theirs'.

NEGOTIATION

Adults may be concerned that young people will not make good decisions about what is best for them. When someone is not used to being given the power to make decisions they may only consider short-term consequences. It is a bit like being forbidden to eat sweets and then being handed a box of chocolates. It is tempting to scoff the lot. Negotiating decisions ensures best outcomes. A way of doing this is drawing up behavioural contracts. A contract is an agreement between two parties, not something that benefits only one signatory.

Negotiating a contract

The school writes down three things that they want to include – these should be SMART targets: Specific, Measurable, Achievable (and Agreed), Realistic and Time Limited. Keep behaviour targets positive – doing something rather than stopping something. Make behaviours observable so everyone, including the student, will know when this has been achieved. If targets are negotiated with students so they agree what is manageable for them, the chances of success will be higher.

These are examples of SMART targets:

- Mandy will bring the correct book to four out of five lessons every day for the next two weeks.
- Jack will sit with his feet and chair legs on the floor whenever he is in the classroom. This to be reviewed after one week.
- Tam will come to school by 9am and report to Ms Lang before going to class: this to be reviewed after two weeks.

The student also writes down what *they* want to include in the contract. This is potentially challenging for teachers but makes the contract a genuine two-way agreement. All staff named need to say whether or not they agree – as with students, anything imposed without genuine consultation is unlikely to be sustainable.

Some examples might be:

- Mr Patel, my science teacher, will acknowledge when I do something right at least once every lesson for the next three weeks.
- Ms Hardy, head of year, will meet with me twice a week on Tuesday and Friday lunchtime for 5 minutes to see how things are going.
- I will be allowed to leave the classroom for five minutes every lesson if I need to.
- I will be allowed into the IT room on Thursday afternoons to research my project on Leeds United Football Club for the next three weeks.

A regular review of a behavioural contract provides opportunities to identify the difference it has made for the student, acknowledge their achievements and include them in continuing conversation about progress and whether targets need to be changed. This is more motivating than telling pupils what they must do and what the consequences will be if they do not. Some students will not be willing or able to maintain contracts so having one must be their choice in the first place and all necessary support must be provided to maximise their chance of success. If schools break their side of the contract this becomes an issue for discussion with school leaders.

PUSH AND PULL FACTORS IN ATTENDANCE

Attendance may first become a concern at primary school but unauthorised absence increases as students go through school. The 'push' factors comprise what is going on at school that discourages children and young people from wanting to be there. These factors include bullying and other social issues, struggling to keep up with learning, poor relationships with teachers and getting into trouble. 'Pull' factors are outside school. These may include joining friends who are also out of school and perhaps getting paid work. Family issues often keep younger pupils at home, especially distressed parents and issues of loss. Poor attendance needs to be addressed promptly as the longer a student is away the less connected they are and the less they learn.

The most effective way of preventing unauthorised absence escalating is to make a *positive* contact with home on the first day of absence. This shows both concern for the student's welfare and vigilance on the part of the school: it conveys to families how much it matters if their child is not there. Monitoring school attendance is not only important for learning outcomes but also contributes to child protection. The quote below highlights the importance of interpersonal skills in what can be a sensitive situation.

> We trained a member of our existing support staff team to organise first day absence phone calls. We found that this person already possessed excellent negotiation skills, which we developed further with training and he soon built a rapport with many of our parents that had been considered unsupportive to the school's aims in the past. Before long he was texting some parents, emailing others as well as having regular phone contact with a number of other parents. The lines of communication improved rapidly and it had a remarkably positive impact on both attendance as well as pupil behaviour (from the Steer Report, DfES, 2005, p. 24).

RE-CONNECTING STUDENTS AFTER ABSENCE

> Children returning after a long absence cannot perform miracles – renewing or remaking friendships, catching up in the classroom, readjusting to a structured day – all take time and do not happen overnight. But throughout the process children must feel that the school is glad to see them and values their return (Cambridge County Council, 2008).

As this quote suggests, expecting students to re-integrate into school without a supportive process in place is unrealistic. Pupils who miss long periods of school through sickness, exclusion or unauthorised absence have similar needs to those who join school halfway through a year. Unlike new entrants they may already have gained a reputation that is not helpful to their re-integration. This needs to be carefully planned with all involved, especially the student concerned. The following questions need to be addressed:

- Is it better to have a phased and gradual return to school or full return from day one?
- If phased, which lessons or times of day does the student feel will bring most success and how will time in school increase? Will this be flexible, based in meeting criteria or decided at the outset?
- Who is the best person to support the student on their return and monitor how well they are doing? This person needs to be someone that has established a positive relationship with the pupil and is someone they trust.
- What will be the expectations on this person? How regularly will they meet with the student in the first week, month and term? How will this time be protected?

- Are there student peers who can support a successful re-integration? What will be the expectations on them and how will this be monitored?
- Is there a need for extra classroom support? What will be the role of support staff in this situation? What does the student say they need?
- How will information about this student's return be communicated to all staff? What are the expectations about making this student feel welcomed back. Negative or sarcastic comments can undo hours of constructive planning.
- How will parents/carers be kept informed of progress? Who is responsible for this and how will good communication be negotiated between school and home?
- What contingency provision will be made if the student feels they are having difficulty either in or out of the classroom? What would be a 'safe place' for the student?

Lown (2007) studied the experiences of students re-integrating into different schools after exclusion. Critical issues were the involvement of the pupil in decision-making and the quality of all relationships; adults with adults, adults with students and students with their peers. Peer networks were found to be one of the most important factors in both facilitating and inhibiting successful re-integration. Planning peer support, peer mentoring or similar interventions can make all the difference.

〜〜 Questions for reflection and discussion

What has been your experience of joining a group where everyone knows each other, are familiar with what happens and you are out on a limb?

What has helped you feel included?

STUDENT INFLUENCE IN THE LEARNING ENVIRONMENT

Research suggests that students who perceive they have a degree of autonomy in the learning environment are more committed and intrinsically motivated. They are more engaged in learning activities than students who regard the climate as more controlling (Ryan & Deci, 2000; Thuen & Bru, 2009). Van Merrienboer and Paas (2003) found that encouraging students to set their own goals contributed to engagement and therefore more time spent on learning activities. By engaging pupils in the planning and management of educational tasks, teachers also foster responsibility (Wang & Zollers, 1990).

SUMMARY OF STRATEGIES AND APPROACHES TO PROMOTE POSITIVE BEHAVIOUR

- Devise class guidelines with students.
- Promote an inclusive and democratic class ethos.
- Make the links between rights and responsibilities, freedoms and obligations.

- Make learning student-centred rather than teacher-centred and give students a say in setting their own learning targets.
- Develop cooperative and meaningful pedagogies.
- Teach cooperative skills.
- Encourage students to ask questions.

SUMMARY OF STRATEGIES AND APPROACHES TO DEAL WITH DIFFICULTIES

- Give students structured opportunities to have agency and develop solutions to both individual and class issues.
- Give students a say in contractual agreements.
- Plan re-integration programmes in detail and include students in decision-making.
- Make a supportive call home on the first day of absence.

Professional Development Activities for Teachers

UNCROC

In pairs, research the United Nations Convention on the Rights of the Child. Write a Charter for the Rights of the Student in School.

Contracts

In small groups draw up a contract between a student (Maddy) and school (Primrose Pond High). This student is returning to school after a suspension for verbal abuse of a science teacher (Mr Petty). Maddy was talking to her friends about the break-up with her boyfriend – she was upset. Mr Petty told Maddy to settle down to work. She continued the conversation and the situation escalated very publicly until Maddy stormed out of the classroom.

It is easy to see what the school might want in the contract – imagine what Maddy might ask for. Think of what might be negotiable and what is not.

Setting targets

Write down your own learning targets for the next few weeks. What do you want to achieve? Is this realistic? How are you going to get there? What help do you need?

Review your progress and reflect on how you were engaged in your learning. In which ways would this activity be relevant for pupils?

Circle Solutions activities with students

These activities will help foster a sense of responsibility.

All Circles begin with a statement of the principles:

(Continued)

(Continued)

- When one person is speaking everyone else listens.
- You may pass if you do not want to say anything.
- There are no put-downs.

Wants and rights

Download wants and rights cards from the Cape Breton University Children's Rights Centre. There is one set for children and another for young people: http://discovery.cbu.ca/psych/index.php?/children/resources_item/wants_and_rights_cards/

Put all the cards onto the floor in the middle of the Circle and ask students to take it in turns around the Circle to place a card that should be a basic right for all children on one side of the Circle and those that are wants on the other side of the Circle. All those they are unsure of place the middle. Ask students to talk in pairs about the decisions that they have made and what they think is the difference between a want and a right. Ask them to see if they can agree a definition for a right.

Two sides of a coin: small group activity

Present students with a 12-inch circular piece of paper to represent a coin. On one side of the 'coin' write one of the following phrases:

- Right to be safe from harm
- Right to have a say in decisions that concern you
- Right to choose your friends
- Right to be treated fairly

Groups turn over their 'coin' and discuss what responsibility comes with this right. One of the group writes what is agreed. Groups share their thoughts with the Circle.

Mix up silent statements

Stand up and change places if you agree with the following:

- Everyone should have a say in deciding guidelines for behaviour
- Once guidelines are agreed everyone has a responsibility to keep to them

Class guidelines

Explain that guidelines are agreements about how people should behave towards each other – they are not rules imposed by others but statements made by people in a group.

Pair share

How do you think people should behave in this class?
Agree two guidelines that everyone should abide by.

Small group

Pairs meet up into fours and share their guidelines.
They look at whether any are more or less the same.
Then they put them in order of importance.

All groups write up their first three guidelines. Teachers collate these to ensure there are no repeats. These are displayed in the classroom. Over the next week each person has 10 votes: he or she can give all 10 votes to one guideline, one each to 10 or any combination. The 5 guidelines with the most votes are agreed as the class guidelines.

Small group discussion

Divide the class into five groups. Each group discusses one of the guidelines and ways in which everyone can be helped to keep to them.

RESOURCES

Unicef UK have developed curriculum resources on rights and responsibilities for all phases of education: www.unicef.org.uk/tz/resources/

David and Roger Johnson are the gurus of cooperative learning. You can read more about their work on www.co-operation.org

www.jigsaw.org gives some excellent guidance on developing cooperative learning and dealing with some of the difficulties you might encounter.

How to reach hard to reach children, edited by Kathryn Pomerantz, Martin Hughes and David Thompson (2007, Chichester: John Wiley) has some excellent chapters including one by Lynn Turner on what pupils have to say about under-achieving pupils and under-achieving schools.

REFERENCES

Aldred, S. (2008). The 'silver bullet' for disengagement. *Principal Matters: Journal for Secondary School Leaders in Australia*. Autumn.

Cambridge County Council, Office of Children and Young People's Services (2008). *Attendance matters: A guide for schools and colleges*. www.teachernet.gov.uk/docbank/index.cfm?id=13973.

Cape Breton University Children's Rights Centre (2007). *Wants and rights cards*. http://discovery.cbu.ca/psych/index.php?/children/resources_item/wants_and_rights_cards/

Covell, K., McNeil, J.K. & Howe, R.B. (2009). Reducing teacher burnout by increasing student engagement. *School Psychology International*, 30(3), 282–90.

Department for Education and Skills (DfES) (2005). *The Steer report. Learning behaviour: The report of the practitioners group on school behaviour and discipline*. London: DfES.

Field, B. (2004). *Productive pedagogies & discipline: The challenge of aligning teaching and behaviour management*. Australian Association for Research in Education. www.aare.edu.au/04pap/fie04560.pdf Retrieved 29 October 2009.

Gillies, R.M. (2008). The effects of cooperative learning on junior high school students' behaviours, discourse and learning during a science-based learning activity. *School Psychology International*, 29, 328–47.

Holdsworth, R. & Blanchard, M. (2005). *Unheard voices: Student engagement research project.* Cited in Anderson, S., Kerr-Roubicek, H. & Rowling, L. (2006) Staff voices: What helps students with high mental health support needs connect to school? *Australian Journal of Guidance and Counselling,* 6(1), 1–13.

Jensen, B.B. & Kostarova-Unkovska, L. (1998). *Evaluation in collaboration with students.* Workshop on practice of evaluation at a health-promoting school: Models, experiences and perspectives, Bern/Thun, Switzerland, 19–22 November 1998. *Executive Summary,* pp. 60–71, www.schools-forhealth.eu/… FirstworkshoponpracticeofevaluationoftheHPS.pdf

Johnson, D.W. & Johnson, R.T. (1999). *Learning together and alone: Cooperative, competitive and individualistic learning, fifth edition.* Boston: Allyn & Bacon.

Keirsley, G. & Shneiderman, B. (1999). *Engagement theory: A framework for technology-based teaching and learning.* http://home.sprynet.com/~gkearsley/engage.htm Retrieved 7 December 2009.

Lown, J. (2007). What works in re-integration following exclusion: Supporting the parts only peers can reach. In K.A. Pomerantz, M. Hughes & D. Thompson (Eds), *How to reach 'hard to reach' children: Improving access, participation and outcomes.* Chichester: John Wiley.

National Union of Teachers (2005). *Learning to behave: A charter for schools.* London: NUT.

Race, K. & Powell, K. (2000). Assessing student perceptions of classroom methods and activities in the context of outcomes-based evaluation. *Evaluation Review,* 24, 635–46.

Ryan, R.M. & Deci, E.L. (2000). Self-determination theory and the facilitation of intrinsic motivation, social development, and wellbeing. *American Psychologist,* 55, 68–78.

Smith, K.A., Sheppard, S.D., Johnson, D.W. & Johnson, R.T. (2005). Pedagogies of engagement: classroom-based practices. *Journal of Engineering Education,* 94(1), 87–102.

Thuen, E. & Bru, E. (2009). Are changes in students' perceptions of the learning environment related to changes in emotional and behavioural problems? *School Psychology International,* 30(2), 115–36.

United Nations (1989). *United Nations Convention on the Rights of the Child.* www.unicef.org/crc

Van Merrienboer, J.J.G. & Paas, F. (2003). Powerful learning and the many faces of instructional design: Toward a framework for the design of powerful learning environments. In E.D. Corte, L. Verschaffel, N. Entwistle & J. Van Merrienboer (Eds), *Powerful learning environments: Unravelling basic components and dimensions.* New York: Pergamon.

Wang, M.C. & Zollers, N.J. (1990). Adaptive instruction: An alternative service delivery approach. *Remedial and Special Education,* 11, 7–21.

SECTION THREE

RESPONDING TO CHALLENGING BEHAVIOUR

There is a tendency to bundle all students who are hard to manage into the overarching category of 'social, emotional and behavioural difficulties'. With any student with a special educational need this categorisation is problematic – we may respond to the label rather than the whole child. For students with challenging behaviour this is even more of an issue.

A baby cries for many reasons but has only one way to communicate their needs. The same is true of distressed students in school. Behaviours may be similar, the root causes very different. Discriminating between students whose behaviour gives cause for concern identifies what to take into consideration in determining optimally effective responses.

There are bi-directional interactions between how students feel and the ways they interpret experiences. This cycle of thinking, feeling and behaviour can entrench negativity. Although teachers cannot make everything all right for students we can provide experiences that intervene in this spiral. Helping students feel safe, secure, successful, valued, acknowledged, included and heard will, over time, influence their constructs and the way they feel about themselves and others. This is the foundation for changing behaviour and engagement with learning.

All teachers, however, have moments when everything goes pear-shaped and they find themselves in situations that test the limits of their endurance. What do you do when this happens to you? Responses are determined by a combination of your resilience, emotional literacy and the strategies you have learnt. Paying attention to all of these helps maintain relationships with students, demonstrates self-control under fire, models self-respect and enhances your professionalism.

What happens in the aftermath of an incident is critical in maintaining high expectations throughout a school. Instead of punishments that disconnect students from school, restorative approaches focus on taking responsibility for behaviour in a meaningful way. In agreement with others involved, students take action to restore the harm they have caused to their community.

This section concludes with a focus on teacher wellbeing. Looking after yourself enables you to be the best you can be in the classroom – it is not an indulgence, it is the key to resilience and good practice in action.

THE DIVERSITY OF DIFFICULTY

Chapter objectives

- To discriminate between students whose behaviour is hard to manage
- To explore developmental and behavioural issues at different phases of education
- To discriminate between long-term and short-term difficulties
- To look more closely at the links between learning and behaviour
- To provide an assessment schedule to inform individual intervention.

Behaviour is diverse in the following ways:

- The age and developmental stage of the child/young person
- Links to other special needs
- Whether difficulties are long term or recent
- Whether they are evident in all contexts or just in some
- Contributing social issues: poverty, health, discrimination, etc.
- Personality, including emotional stability/volatility
- Personal strengths and resources of the student
- Trauma: accidents, violence, abuse, forced removal, etc.
- Contextual issues at home and at school.

Many difficulties are interactive. An optimal outcome will require a systemic intervention that addresses contributory factors. The common assessment framework has been put in place in the UK to promote the shared involvement of agencies in a child's life (DCSF, 2009).

DEVELOPMENTAL DIFFERENCES

Identifying and responding to difficulties in young children

There has been increasing concern about the behaviour of young children arriving in school. This is a crucial time for both children and families. We need to ensure that early experiences establish a positive educational pathway. Ofsted provides evidence that schools can and do make a difference and confirms that approaches suggested in this text are effective:

> *The 27 schools that had not excluded any young children shared common characteristics also evident in the schools that had managed to significantly reduce their previously high levels of exclusion. The schools were welcoming and children were made to feel valued, there were high expectations of the children and staff went out of their way to provide a model of appropriate behaviour* (*Ofsted News*, 14, October 2009).

The advantage of working with young children is that they are more open to change. You can directly teach required school behaviour and routines and reinforce positive self-concepts. You can often liaise more easily with families, though how you do this is crucial (see Chapter 7).

It is easy for young children to get a negative reputation. Without acknowledging how students are learning to behave in desired ways, their reputation as 'naughty' may determine how their school career progresses (MacLure & Jones, 2009). It is helpful to avoid this label altogether.

When young children arrive in educational settings without having learnt the basic behaviours that enable them to thrive socially or educationally, they may be unresponsive to direction and not able to settle to tasks. They may not have learnt how to share, wait, or listen. They may avoid adults or be demanding, sometimes a mixture of both. They will have learnt that certain behaviours get their needs met. This may be just for someone to take notice – regardless of whether this is positive or negative.

Observation in a supermarket

The young woman had two children with her, an infant in the shopping trolley and a young boy of about 4 walking beside her. He kept trying to engage his mother by pointing things out on the shelves. She was focused on her shopping and ignored him apart from saying 'don't touch' from time to time. Eventually he found a box of breakfast cereal he recognised and thrust it excitedly in her face showing her he knew the name. She snarled at him: 'Stop that, just put it back – NOW'. The boy responded by throwing himself on the floor screaming. His mother then gave him her undivided attention by glaring at him, yelling back and yanking him onto his feet.

∿ Question for reflection and discussion

What does this anecdote tell you about demands for attention in the classroom?

LANGUAGE ISSUES

Children arriving in their first educational placement with poor language skills do not have one of the basic tools for thinking and learning. This does not apply to those competent in a language other than English but to those who have not enjoyed many interactive conversations with adults. Children may have spent hours in front of a TV experiencing only one-way communication. When a child has limited language he may not behave in the required way because he does not clearly understand what is being asked of him. It does not help to see this behaviour as defiant, disobedient or uncooperative.

Children who struggle with expressive language get frustrated because they cannot make others understand what they mean or what they want; they have limited words to convey feelings and often have social difficulties.

Communication is not just words. You can support speech with pictures, gestures, mimes, drawing and signing. There is now a movement to help toddlers reduce frustration by giving them simple signs to help communication. It has been used with even younger infants. All children enjoy this and it does not detract from developing spoken language. Signs will be replaced by words once language skills are in place.

Hearing loss: A high percentage of young children have intermittent conductive hearing loss where they hear low frequency sounds (vowels) but not high frequency (consonants). It is as if they are underwater. Consequently they do not understand the meaning of the words being said to them. This is due to the immaturity of the Eustachian tube and is less of a problem after the age of 7. It may only occur when the child has a cold and therefore not be picked up when they enter school. Before you say a student 'hears when she wants to' get an up-to-date auditory check. In the meantime speak clearly, slowly, concisely and not in shadow so students can lip-read to aid their understanding. Support instruction with demonstrations of what is required.

Elective mutism: Occasionally young children choose not to speak in school. This usually stems from a lack of confidence, or fear of saying the wrong thing. It is not uncommon for such children to begin to speak in Circles when it is their choice to speak or 'pass'. The level of trust in the group, lack of pressure and the raising of confidence probably all contribute to this outcome. The following case study illustrates this.

📁 Case study

Selma was a 6-year-old child from an Asian family who had not spoken out loud since coming to school. She would only respond to teachers with a very quiet whisper. She was learning to read and seemed to be an able student. Other children were supportive and sometimes helped teachers work out what she was saying. She spoke English at home because her father insisted on it.

(Continued)

(Continued)

Selma was placed in a small language group of about eight children. A sequence of games was introduced in twice-weekly sessions. The first games required only non-verbal responses such as passing a smile. The second level required a vocal response such as an animal noise. The third level required a one-word response, initially with a partner. The fourth level required a short phrase and the last a sentence. Support from others was given as required and the level of games only raised when all children were participating on three consecutive occasions. By the end of the term Selma was speaking normally in school, firstly in the playground and then in the classroom.

ATTENTION AND CONCENTRATION

Children cannot learn well unless they first pay attention, and this lack of focus may lead to distracted behaviour. Some have had little practice in listening. Stories engage children's attention and help them learn to concentrate. If they have not have been read to at home, begin with very short stories, especially tales about themselves which children love. Asking questions checks they are still focused.

Strategies for developing attention skills: Children with attention difficulty work better in structured situations where it is clear what is expected, the sequence of tasks and what constitutes completion. A written or pictorial clue to support verbal instructions helps. Assignments divided into small steps that can be completed quickly provide initial success and promote motivation. It may be easier to start with non-academic tasks such as putting out equipment. There are many games and activities for increasing listening skills that can be encouraged both in the classroom and at home.

Saying the student's name helps them refocus. Ask a simple question about achievements so far. Where children are so preoccupied they become peripheral to the class, referring to their special interests may help re-integrate them. Teachers can harness the student into class discussion and whole class activities by giving them some responsibility or reporting function. They are likely to do better in pairs or small groups than in larger group work. A system that reminds teachers to give short but regular positive reinforcement can be useful.

A checklist of completed tasks and/or a simple tally encourages older students to develop greater independence and more responsibility for completing tasks. Converting this checklist into a graph gives visual evidence of improvement.

Sometimes anxiety about what to do and/or getting it right inhibits task completion. A climate of taking risks and learning from mistakes addresses this. Parental involvement provides the opportunity for teachers to discuss what conversations with students are helpful and what will raise anxiety further.

NURTURING

Young children are especially vulnerable when they have not received supportive or appropriate parenting. Much can be learnt from the approach nurture groups take (Boxall, 2002). A nurture group is a small supportive group of up to 12 children, usually located in a mainstream primary school. The focus is on social and emotional as well as academic achievement. The six principles are:

1   *Children's learning is understood developmentally.* The response to the individual child is 'as they are', underpinned by a non-judgemental and accepting attitude.
2   *The classroom offers a safe base.* The way the group is managed contains anxiety. Days are structured with predictable routines and adults are reliable and consistent in their approach.
3   *Nurture is important for the development of self-esteem.* Adults engage with the children in reciprocal shared activities, talking about what is happening and the feelings involved. As children respond to being valued and thought about as individuals, teachers notice and praise small achievements.
4   *Language is understood as a vital means of communication.* Without the vocabulary to talk about how they feel, children may act out their feelings. In nurture groups opportunities are created for extended conversations or encouraging imaginative play to understand the feelings of others.
5   *All behaviour is communication.* Understanding that a child's behaviour is a communication helps staff to resist being provoked or discouraged and helps them respond in a firm but non-punitive way. If a child senses their feelings are understood this helps diffuse difficult situations.
6   *Transitions are significant in the lives of children.* A child makes numerous transitions on a daily basis, for example between classes and between different adults. Changes in routine are invariably difficult for vulnerable children and need to be carefully managed with preparation and support.

Nurture groups have been highlighted as a successful strategy for reducing the exclusion of young children (Ofsted, 2009):

What determined a school's rate of exclusion was not its social context but the combination of its philosophy, capacity to meet challenges and, sometimes, the response received from its local authority and outside agencies when they were asked to help. Early intervention based on monitoring and evaluation helped in managing children's more complex behaviours successfully, as did strong relationships between settings, schools and parents … Nurture groups, where they were used, were highly effective in improving children's behaviour and preventing exclusion … (Ofsted, 2009, pp. 4–5).

This commentary also provides evidence for a systemic approach to behaviour.

IDENTIFYING SPECIFIC EARLY DIFFICULTIES

Autistic spectrum disorder: Occasionally the behaviour of young children confuses even experienced practitioners. It is not just confronting but also has elements of the bizarre. These children need careful monitoring as a number of related difficulties may surface. The list below outlines a number of indications that the child may be on the autistic spectrum. This realisation can cause grief and anxiety for parents who will need a great deal of support. You cannot insist parents acknowledge their child's special needs, you must wait for them to come to this understanding in their own time.

The following behaviours may be observed in children on the autistic spectrum. Seek advice if several of these are present:

- Under-developed social skills – treating others as objects
- Lack of empathy – does not tune into emotional content of communication
- Often in a world of their own
- Lack of symbolic play – lines up small toys rather than enacts scenes with them
- Repetitive, sometimes ritualistic behaviour such as hand flapping or spinning
- Strong interests, bordering on the obsessive
- Resistance to changes in routine
- Panic reactions at times
- Sensory sensitivity – may react strongly to touch, noise or smell
- Exceptionally strong preferences and dislikes – such as the way food is presented
- Unusual behaviour, such as smelling everything.

Although a few children on the autistic spectrum have a specific skill such as piano playing or recalling dates others often have learning difficulties. Children with average intelligence, showing particular difficulties in social interaction and perhaps milder indications of other difficulties are said to have Asperger's Syndrome.

Learning difficulties: When immature social behaviour appears alongside slow acquisition of new learning this may indicate a general learning difficulty, sometimes referred to as developmental delay. This term is misleading as delay suggests an eventual catching up. Although there is continual progress, learning proceeds more slowly than the norm and therefore the gap widens rather than closes over time. Often it is behaviour that alerts educators to a learning difficulty. This requires careful monitoring and sensitive interactions with families. Beware jumping to conclusions.

TEACHING EXPECTED SCHOOL BEHAVIOUR AT THE OUTSET

There is a learning component to many behaviours. Young children may not have had clear and consistent boundaries so do not know how to behave well in the school context or be considerate of others. It is useful to think about behaviour for young children in the same way as teaching other elements of the curriculum:

- It is easier for children to learn what to *do* rather than what *not* to do.
- They must be at a developmental stage where they have the ability to do what is expected. You cannot, for instance, expect all young children to sit and concentrate on a structured activity for half an hour. Some will be able to do this when they arrive in school; others need to build up their concentration span.
- It is helpful to demonstrate the desired behaviour. If you first show what is not wanted in an exaggerated way this engages children in shared laughter.
- Students may need to be shown the wanted behaviour several times.
- They need to feel they can be successful and may require help in the first instance.
- Plenty of opportunities to practice reinforces new learning.
- Children need to feel good about cooperating.
- Acknowledgement for their learning and effort will help.
- Visual support on the walls of the classroom can help reinforce expectations.

Reminders before reprimands: Young children need to know it is acceptable to not get it right first time. This applies to behaviour as much as curriculum learning.

DIFFICULTIES AT PRIMARY SCHOOL

Specific issues affect the behaviour of primary school students. If these are not actively addressed at this stage they may impact more strongly on behaviour and learning as students go through school.

Social issues

Friendships become increasingly important in how a student feels about coming to school. Children at risk may have learnt few relational values and skills. They frequently have a range of social difficulties, ranging from inappropriate interactions to active rejection and aggression. They may believe it is safer to attack others first. In some instances children take out their anger and misery on others by being bullying, domineering or just unkind. It can be hard to find something to like in these children.

Girls at this age congregate in small communication-based groups. Unfortunately some girls are 'queen bees' who dictate who can be in or out of the group. It takes whole class action to limit this relational bullying. As boys groups are usually more activity based it is helpful to provide a range of activities to maximise inclusion – some boys don't want to spend lunchtime kicking a ball and may be ostracised if they are the only one.

It is useful to check out exactly what is going on. It is not always the child in focus that is the problem.

> ### 📁 Case study
>
> Francesca was always in trouble in the playground for hitting other children. But when a teaching student in the school did some observations, she soon discovered that Francesca was trying to join groups who were actively rejecting her. It was when they told her to go away that she began to hit out and cry. Francesca's father had left the family some months before so she was experiencing rejection everywhere.

〰 Questions for reflection and discussion

How would you go about addressing the issue above?

Who would be the focus of your intervention: Francesca, other children, the family and/ or the whole class? Why?

Self-esteem and learning

Students who do not see themselves as successful learners may begin to turn off the whole idea of school, especially if they are losing status in a competitive classroom. They then begin to find other ways to maintain a positive sense of self, which can lead to disruptive behaviour. As children would usually rather be thought of as silly than stupid, work avoidance is safer than trying and failing. This is often considered to be 'attention-seeking' behaviour. When silliness raises a laugh with others this reinforces the idea that they can get kudos in ways not necessarily acceptable to teachers. Children may also be manipulated by others to do things that gain momentary attention.

Family issues

Things happening at home often affect how children behave in the classroom. These include overwhelming physical and mental health problems that inhibit supportive parenting: bereavement, domestic violence and family breakdown. A high proportion of children and young people have been affected by loss in their lives, often resulting in both grief and anger. This is not always acknowledged by adults who respond to the behavioural outcomes. Children can find themselves torn apart by parental separation – and as their parents are usually emotionally distressed and volatile themselves there may be little emotional support from home at this time. Sometimes parents do not talk to their children about what is happening and they are left with their imagination running wild. Many children, especially younger pupils, believe it is their fault when a parent leaves. They need repeated reassurance that they are not to blame.

> ### 📁 Case study
>
> One teacher of a year 6 class was astonished when a pupil admitted in a Circle session that he had been bullying other students. With a flash of insight he had said: *'My mum and dad are splitting up and I have been angry and taking it out on people'.* As the Circle concluded several other children went up to him and showed him they understood because it had happened to them too. The teacher said there had been no further incidence of bullying.

ISSUES AT TRANSITION

Starting a new school is a time when anxieties are high, behaviour difficulties may surface and students may disengage. Planning transitions well takes account of the social, organisational and academic elements of schooling. Orientation, which tells students about and sometimes gives them opportunities to visit their new school, is not the same as a planned transition that builds strong relationships between all stakeholders. An optimal transition is aware of the importance of two-way communication, learns about and focuses on student strengths and competencies, promotes an inclusive ethos and is responsive to community concerns (Perry et al., 2009).

Many students cope reasonably well in their primary school despite a high level of risk but this often breaks down with the transition to high school. The informal peer support strategies that supported their learning in primary school may be less accessible. The teacher in the quote below demonstrates awareness of how some students cope with the demands of the secondary classroom by not denying students their survival strategies.

He wanted you to do the work, but he didn't mind how you did it ... like you could talk and work at the same time ... If the teacher tells you to be quiet, you don't get the hang of it (quoted in Wise, 2000, p. 50).

ISSUES AT HIGH SCHOOL

Secondary schools are more subject-focused than student-focused. Many pupils struggle with different expectations, the diversity of subjects and staff, the level of homework, the need for organisation and the lack of security that characterised their earlier school experiences. Research by Deakin-Crick et al. (2007) shows that as schools become less learner-centred, students are less motivated, teachers become more controlling and students perceive school as a less safe place to be. Without intervention students see learning as more difficult to access.

Changes in the development of adolescents also impact on their behaviour.

Thinking: Younger children think in concrete terms and in the here and now. As they develop so does their abstract thinking. They begin to see things differently. Some students may revisit a life experience with a whole range of different feelings.

> 📂 **Case study**
>
> Jermaine was 4 when his parents split up. His father disappeared back to Jamaica and his mother set up home with another partner and soon had a baby. There was no room for Jermaine in their flat so he went to stay with his maternal grandmother. This was supposed to be a temporary arrangement but had continued. Jermaine was fine during primary school but when he became 13 his behaviour became angry, rude and defiant. He was a miserable young man getting into a lot of trouble. His grandmother put it down to him getting in with the 'wrong crowd' but Jermaine had thought about what had happened to him and was angry with everyone for having colluded in what he now saw as a rejection. He didn't know where he belonged any more so had affiliated himself with a group of older boys in the neighbourhood. He said he didn't care what trouble he got into because no one really cared about him.

Self-focus: From 11 to 14 years many young people see everything in terms of themselves. This can result in teenagers thinking in the following ways:

- *Imaginary audience*. Behaving as if they were on the stage and the focus of everyone's attention. This can lead to worrying about what 'everyone' will think of them, the way they look, how they perform and so on. This can make young teenagers sensitive to comments that may be construed as critical. It is best not to tell them they are over-reacting!
- *Personal fable*. An inflated opinion of their own uniqueness and possibly invulnerability. This may lead to risk-taking, feeling no one understands, and imagining themselves as the only ones who can reach heights or depths of experience. They may also exaggerate personal weaknesses.

Older teenagers are more realistic, more balanced in their arguments, able to see both strengths and weaknesses and be focused on events and people outside themselves.

Identity: Teenagers need to work out what their values are, what is important, what they want, and what sort of person they want to be. They need to develop confidence in themselves. Working with adolescents on this journey of discovery can be fascinating and stimulating when it is not frustrating and infuriating! According to Erikson (1959) there are healthy and unhealthy ways of developing identity. Taking on board without question the values of others such as the family or other authority figures is not healthy. It is better to try on different ways of being, ask questions and challenge the status quo. This leads to the development of an authentic adult identity. Some of the most innovative and dynamic individuals in our society were not high flyers in school and sometimes got into trouble for not conforming. One of the difficulties postulated today is that adolescents have few role models to give them alternative ways of being that promote self-respect and integrity. Boys in particular may not have an adult male figure to look up to and emulate at this important time in their lives. They might instead choose to model themselves on figures who they believe have power and status.

〰️ **Questions for reflection and discussion**

Who were your role models?
What did you learn from them and how have they influenced the person you are today?
Were any of them teachers?

Teenagers and their friends: The peer group replaces the family as the reference group for social norms and values. By the age of 13 most adolescents belong to a group consisting of both genders. Membership may be demonstrated by a dress code, greeting protocols, use of language and so on. Group loyalty legitimises and supports the move towards independence from the family and other authority figures. Trying to force a change of allegiance is bound to fail and will set up resentment, so adults need to work with rather than against teenage groups – and encourage the formation of several groups in school so one does not dominate.

Although it is the infamous young adolescents in grades 8 and 9 that give teachers sleepless nights, research shows that the majority of young people are actively and positively engaged in their communities (Trikha, 2003). Anti-social behaviours are perpetrated by a small minority. The idealism and energy of young people is a great strength and adults who recognise and acknowledge this may find themselves enjoying their company and responding effectively to inappropriate behaviour.

Conflict: Conflict between teenagers and adults is inevitable:

- Teenagers don't want to be told what to do or what is good for them.
- They want to make their own decisions (and their own mistakes).
- Teenagers want to experiment – adults want to keep them safe.
- They want to be valued for who they are, not what adults want them to be.
- Adults pull back – friends push along.
- The reference point for values, etc. is no longer familiar adults but peers.
- Age/maturity/society's norms are not congruent.

Co-regulation needs to start in middle childhood and be established by early adolescence. Rather than laying down the law adults ask respectful questions that help young people work out the pros and cons of taking certain actions, including potential consequences for different options.

Depression: Depression may present itself in school, not only as persistent sadness, but also as lack of attention and engagement, a 'don't care' attitude, irritability and self-harming. Punitive responses may very well exacerbate the difficulty whereas showing concern, giving choices where possible, suggesting alternative perspectives and modelling good social skills is more helpful (Rowe & Rowe, 2002). High schools can also provide opportunities for students to be creative, explore alternative ways to relax, create links with others and guide them to sources of individual support. Taking bullying seriously matters, including the growing phenomenon of cyber bullying. This can have a pernicious effect on the lives of young people who may become the butt of public ridicule.

Psychosis: Although onset is usually not until later, a few young people show signs of psychosis whilst still at high school. This can be both triggered and obscured by a drug habit. A psychotic episode can also be associated with extreme stress. Students may seem detached from reality and not realise others are not experiencing the same things they are. Schizophrenia has a strong genetic link so check if there is a family history.

LEARNING, ACHIEVEMENT AND BEHAVIOUR

Students rarely have problems that are exclusively learning or behaviour. Those with emotional difficulties may be distracted, poorly organised and anxious; they may not have had good relationships with adults and not see themselves as learners. Unsurprisingly, these students rarely achieve their potential in school. Those who have a learning disability may have poor self-esteem, see demands for work as a threat, seek alternative means of gaining status and may be easily influenced by peers who induce negative behaviour. Learning and behaviour are therefore frequently two sides of the same coin and need to be addressed in tandem.

SHORT-TERM AND LONGER-TERM BEHAVIOURAL CONCERNS

Sudden deterioration: The following circumstances are likely to result in acute rather than chronic behavioural difficulties. Students come to the notice of staff because their work suddenly deteriorates or they become emotionally fragile, angry or distracted. Underlying issues are often aligned with major changes in the student's life or an accumulation of risk factors:

- Moving schools
- Bereavement and loss
- Family crisis
- Re-constituted families
- Transitions between phases of school
- Personality clashes in school
- Being bullied.

A student may need understanding to help them through an adversity. If challenging behaviour is less in some situations than in others, this provides clues to factors in the environment that support positive change.

Major trauma or accumulation of adversities: You may find that an initial difficulty has become entrenched by unhelpful, inappropriate or inadequate responses in the past and a negative spiral has developed. This needs to be reversed. Students who have experienced the following may need support and help in the longer term but may also make good progress with appropriate and timely intervention:

- Trauma
- Being a refugee or asylum seeker
- Being a carer
- Chronic family ill heath
- Social difficulties, being isolated or having few interpersonal skills
- Specific learning difficulties, especially literacy
- Communication difficulties
- Family violence
- Overly permissive or authoritarian parenting
- Poor or inappropriate role models.

Entrenched difficulties: Students are likely to need longer term, more intensive intervention if the following factors are present:

- Significant learning difficulties associated with developmental delay
- Being on the autistic spectrum
- Evidence of serious physical abuse, especially on-going
- Evidence of sexual abuse
- Parental neglect due to addictions or long-term mental health problems
- Parental rejection
- Being in long-term out-of-home care.

Although promoting the positive and fostering resilience will make a difference, teachers would benefit from support, specialist advice and guidance. For some of these students this intervention will help break an intergenerational cycle of social exclusion. Werner and Smith's research (2001) found that in the lives of resilient young adults there is almost always a supportive teacher and/or positive educational experiences.

ASSESSMENT FOR CHANGE

Educators often don't know where to start when it comes to behaviour. The assessment schedule in Appendix 1 will help think through what is going on for a particular student. Good assessment is not simply using a range of standardised tests. It is asking the most relevant questions and using the answers to inform intervention. The schedule will also help identify what other information may be needed.

ACTION PLANS

Once you have identified specific difficulties the student is having you can choose a priority areas for intervention. Within this identify what the student most needs to learn. What is their current level of competence and what supports this? What is the next step? Does this require a systemic plan that involves others: peers, parents, support staff, other professionals?

Address a behaviour open to change and where you are likely to have quick success. Do not go for the most entrenched and difficult. Switch the problem to the solution. If a student is crawling under tables aim for them to sit on a chair. Changing behaviour is not just up to the student. They may need to learn about their strengths and that others value them – not just how to sit still. This also needs addressing in an action plan.

How will this plan be executed in the school? Who will do what, how often and when? Who will monitor progress? Discuss possible interventions with parents.

What support is there for the teacher with most responsibility for carrying out actions?

When will the action plan be reviewed and amended if necessary?

SUMMARY OF STRATEGIES AND APPROACHES TO PROMOTE POSITIVE BEHAVIOUR

- Know what is developmentally appropriate behaviour – young children are supposed to be very lively, adolescents are supposed to challenge authority!
- Teach and reinforce expected behaviours.
- Give young children practice with routines and extra practice to those who need it.
- Pay attention to transitions in the school day: give students warning of change, time to finish what they are doing and information about what is happening next.
- Plan for major transitions to take account of relationships, student competencies, and partnership with all stakeholders.
- Treat teenagers as responsible young people and give choices where possible.

SUMMARY OF STRATEGIES AND APPROACHES TO DEAL WITH DIFFICULTIES

- Address learning and behavioural issues together.
- Monitor carefully where this is indicated and involve parents sensitively.
- Respond to questioning and challenging authority as a strength in teenagers.
- For specific individual education plans, identify an area of concern, choose behaviours most open to change, identify targets to aim for and take into account contributing issues.

Professional development activities for teachers

For those in early years and primary settings

Observation of interactions between parents and young children

Next time you are shopping observe families with young children. Who is giving their children positive attention, conversing with them and engaging them in joint activity? What do you notice about these children's behaviour? Are other parents only giving children attention when they are being difficult? How much instruction begins with 'don't'? What expectations do parents have that their children will be helpful? What support do they have to meet these expectations?

What does this tell you about helping young children settle well into school?

Learning behaviour

With a partner make a list of all the routines children have to learn when they first come to school. Now choose one routine and divide this into small steps. How would you help a child who is struggling to do this?

For all phases of education

Loss and anger

Have you experienced a major loss or relationship breakdown? Was anger part of your response? What helped you adjust and accept the situation? Discuss with a partner what schools might do to help students in these situations and respond to the behaviour that might result.

Learning and behaviour

Identify two students, one with a behavioural difficulty and one with a learning difficulty. What do you know about the learning issues for the student with behavioural concerns? Are there any behavioural issues for the student who needs support with learning? Discuss your findings with a small group. What might this mean for your approach to each student?

For those in high school settings

Being a teenager

Think back to the time when you were a teenager. What can you remember about your relationships with adults? What was important to you then? Can you see yourself in any of the young people you come across as a teacher? Discuss with a partner.

Co-regulation

In a small group list the questions you might ask a young person to help them make a decision about:

(Continued)

(Continued)
- Going clubbing with friends
- Having a part-time job
- Revision for exams
- What they post on Facebook.

Circle Solutions activities with students

These activities will:

- Promote listening and attention skills
- Support students in thinking about their identity
- Help pupils reflect on their learning.

   All Circles begin with a statement of the principles:

- When one person is speaking everyone else listens.
- You may pass if you do not want to say anything.
- There are no put-downs.

Sentence completion

If I wasn't me I would like to be …

I know someone is listening to me when …

Paired interviews

Interview each other about why you chose the person you would like to be.

Tea with a star

Give each small group the name of a famous person – real or fictional. Ask them to imagine that they are going to have tea with this person. What would they want to know about this person and which questions would they like to ask?

Learning to learn: small group activity

Small group activity: Divide the Circle into six small groups. Each group talks about the best lesson they can remember. They then brainstorm answers to the following questions with one person writing them down:

- What things help you learn best in the classroom?
- What can a teacher do that makes a difference?
- What can friends do to support your learning?
- What can each person do to get the most out of a lesson?
- What do you think and feel when you have learnt something new and interesting?
- What gets in the way of learning?

   When one person from each group feeds back to the Circle others are asked if they have anything extra to add.

RESOURCES

Jean Robb and Hilary Letts (2002). *Creating kids who can concentrate* (2002, London: Hodder and Stoughton). Although this book has been written primarily for parents of children who have been diagnosed with attention difficulties it has many ideas relevant for the classroom. It is comprehensive, covers many of the difficulties associated with poor concentration and is full of good illustrations of practice.

Sue Roffey and Terry O'Rierdan are the authors of *Young children and classroom behaviour* (2001, London: David Fulton) and *Plans for better behaviour in the primary school* (2003, London: David Fulton). The first looks at parents, teachers and children's needs in the early days of school and how teachers might respond to the hard-to-manage child. The second provides ideas for intervention for many of the difficulties teachers face. It identifies problem and target behaviours, assessment, ideas for short-term management strategies and intervention plans for longer-term change. The original Primary Behaviour Guidelines were developed by teachers, psychologists and support staff in Haringey and cited as good practice by the DfES. Sue Roffey's book for early years practitioners is entitled *Helping with behaviour* (2006, Abingdon: Routledge).

Melanie Cross has made the link between language and behaviour in her excellent book *Children with emotional and behavioural difficulties and communication problems* (2004, London: Jessica Kingsley Publishers).

REFERENCES

Boxall, M. (2002). *Nurture groups in school: Principles and practice*. London: Sage Publications.

Department for Children, Schools and Families (DCSF) (2009). Every Child Matters: Common assessment framework. www.dcsf.gov.uk/everychildmatters/strategy/deliveringservices1/caf/cafframework/

Deakin-Crick, R., McCombs, B., Haddon, A., Broadfoot, P. & Tew, M. (2007). The ecology of learning: Factors contributing to learner-centred classroom cultures. *Research Papers in Education, Policy and Practice, 22*(3), 267–307.

Erikson, E.H. (1959). *Identity and the Life Cycle*. New York: International Universities Press.

MacLure, M. & Jones, L. (2009). *Becoming a problem: How children develop a reputation as naughty in the first years of school*. ESRC: Manchester Metropolitan University.

Ofsted (2009). *The exclusion from school of children aged four to seven*. London: Office for Standards in Education.

Ofsted News 14. (2009). Avoiding exclusion of young children. http://ofstednews.ofsted.gov.uk/article/515

Perry, B., Dockett, S., Whitton, D., Vickers, M., Johnson, C. & Sidoti, C. (2009). *Sydney transition project*. Sydney: Better Futures.

Roffey, S. (2001) *Special needs in the early years: Communication, collaboration, cooperation*, revised edition. London: David Fulton Publishers

Rowe, K.J. & Rowe, K.S. (2002). *What matters most: Evidence-based findings for key factors affecting the educational experiences and outcomes for girls and boys throughout their primary and secondary schooling.* Melbourne: ACER.

Trikha, S. (2003). *Children, young people and their communities: Summary of top-level findings from 2003 Home Office Citizenship Survey.* London: Home Office, DfES.

Werner, E. & Smith, R. (2001). *Journeys from childhood to the midlife: Risk, resilience, and recovery.* New York: Cornell University Press.

Wise, S. (2000). *Listen to me: The voices of pupils with emotional and behavioural difficulties.* Bristol: Lucky Duck Publishing.

10 BEING A CHALLENGING STUDENT – FROM SORROW TO STRENGTH

Chapter objectives

- To focus on the range of feelings resulting from negative student experiences
- To understand how the interaction of thought and emotion impact on behaviour
- To consider how to change constructs that underpin negative behaviours
- To explore how to develop strengths
- To consider how to defuse high emotions.

Students who feel valued and accepted, see themselves achieving, feel both physically and psychologically safe in school, are engaged with learning and have a say in what concerns them, are more likely to behave in pro-social and cooperative ways.

It is the expression of negative emotion that, for the most part, causes the greatest difficulties in school. Sometimes negative emotions in pupils instigated by events out of school, are met by negative adult emotions in school. Situations then escalate with a battle for control. The student may end up suspended or excluded and the teacher distressed and exhausted. It requires adults to take charge in an emotionally literate way to avoid or at least limit this scenario.

Emotion, thought, perspective, worldview (constructs) and behaviour are interactive and bi-directional. When we think about something in a certain way, these thoughts impact on how we feel. Emotions also determine how we think. When we feel confused, anxious or under threat we might see danger at every turn. If our worldview is that people are out to get us this is how we interpret the behaviour of others and feel and act accordingly.

We will not change behaviour just by challenging what students do but by supporting a different way of thinking, seeing, interpreting and understanding. Giving pupils different experiences provides a base on which to change their constructs of themselves, their school and the world in which they live. Mediating these experiences emphasises the learning that can take place. We need to build the strengths that enhance resilience, increase coping strategies and give students hope for who they might be in the future.

Early experiences, learning difficulties or specific disabilities may lead to behaviour that is volatile, impulsive and particularly hard to manage. Sometimes the best we can do is to provide a predictable and supportive environment in which students have less chance of hurting themselves and others and more chance of learning to cope with their distress. The earlier a structured intervention is in place the better. Adults need to be consistent, know that changes take time and seek support for their own resilience.

INTERVENING IN NEGATIVE SPIRALS

Students at risk do not have a sense of wellbeing unless they also have some of the protective factors in place (see Chapter 4). This lack of wellbeing extends to their sense of self, their relationships with others and often their physical and well as their psychological health. A negative spiral can ensue where one factor feeds into another.

Case study

Lee attended a pupil referral unit. He lived on his own with his mother who was an alcoholic. Lee could hold a conversation with anyone who was willing to spend the time with him although never put himself forward. He always seemed distracted and anxious. Although intelligent, his educational achievements were minimal, which was not surprising as his school attendance had been very erratic. There had been many days on which his mum had not been able to get him there. Lee was not aggressive but avoided work at all costs. Any attempt to 'make' him do anything was met with stonewalling. If anything, Lee was depressed, nothing much mattered. He came late to the unit most days, often looked like he had not slept, chain-smoked when not on school premises and admitted to smoking dope on a regular basis. He lived on junk food and was thin as a rake with fingernails bitten to the quick. Lee didn't like himself very much and resisted getting close to anyone. He always seemed to be on the margins.

Questions for reflection and discussion

In which ways might it have been possible to intervene for Lee in the past?

Who would have needed to be involved?

Lee is 15. What does he need now?

A FOCUS ON STRENGTHS

Hard to manage students, despite their bravado, rarely think well of themselves and this is confirmed by conversations focusing on their deficits and weaknesses. They therefore have little to live up to. If we want them to have the qualities that build pro-social behaviour we need to encourage pupils to identify, develop and have opportunities to demonstrate their strengths and positive qualities. If someone we respect tells us that they value our patience, helpfulness, friendliness or persistence, we begin to see ourselves in their eyes and try to meet these expectations. If we are told we are lazy, selfish or untrustworthy that is how we may think of ourselves and that is who we become. Table 10.1 lists 60 strengths for students to identify and build on. Ask pupils to think of others. The meaning of these concepts will need to be discussed.

∿ Questions for reflection and discussion

What strengths from those listed in Table 10.1 have you demonstrated in the last two weeks?

What do you feel when you are working to your strengths?

How does this enhance your wellbeing?

Table 10.1

Relationship Strengths	Resilience Strengths	Ethical Strengths	Personal Strengths	Other Strengths
friendly	thankful	responsible	creative	sporting
willing to share	optimistic	honest	adventurous	musical
warm	keeps things in perspective	trustworthy	hard-working	artistic
caring	determined	fair	neat and tidy	imaginative
good listener	cheerful	acknowledges mistakes	sense of humour	graceful
helpful	sets goals	can make amends	energetic	good with animals
supportive	adaptable	respects confidentiality	enthusiastic	relaxed
fun to be with	inclusive	reliable	thoughtful	can fix things
considerate	can change	democratic	confident	colourful
interested	positive	asks questions	courageous	independent
kind	assertive	forgiving	careful	team player
empathic	problem-solver	non-judgemental	curious	organised

FEELINGS AND BEHAVIOUR IN THE CLASSROOM

Beneath the expression of negative emotion is a longing. If we can identify this we can respond more effectively. This section explores what students might feel, how emotions and thoughts interact and what pupils may do as a result of this interaction. Some emotions drain energy, others are characterised by high levels of energy. This energy sometimes needs to be channelled in ways that do not hurt the person experiencing it or anyone else. Separating different feelings and actions here is not a reflection of reality but a way of considering intervention. Following an exploration of the negative we turn to potential solutions that meet student needs and build positive feelings, strengths and qualities.

Feeling a failure

Pupils may feel a failure for several reasons:

- Being told they can't do something, are hopeless, or will 'never learn'
- Being presented with tasks for which they do not have the prerequisite knowledge or skills
- Being constantly compared to others who are doing better
- Regularly receiving low test scores
- Being humiliated, even inadvertently
- Conversations in which their low achievements are the focus of family anxiety.

The constructs that may develop include:

- Everyone thinks I am stupid
- Teachers make me feel bad about myself
- School is not for me; I don't belong here
- I can't do it, so why should I bother
- I will never learn.

Feeling a failure is a threat to a positive sense of self so students may respond to these feelings in the following ways:

- Avoiding work by subtle means
- Outright refusal to cooperate or comply with directions
- Attempting to feel OK about themselves in other ways – this often involves disrupting others
- Being aggressive with teachers, especially those they fear will show them up
- Avoiding school by whatever means.

Although the following students give a rationale for their behaviour as fear of failure teachers are likely to interpret these actions as defiance. Their responses would not then address the root cause.

I mucked about so I could get sent out of class so I wouldn't have to do the work.

A teacher had a go at me cause I hadn't done the homework. But I didn't understand it.

(Students quoted in Wise, 2000, 57,58)

📁 **Case study**

Eight-year-old Damon's behaviour stressed his teacher out. He avoided any work that involved writing and expressed his unwillingness by taking forever to start anything, sharpening and then throwing pencils, rolling on the floor to find them and swearing under his breath at any reprimand. His teacher made him stay behind most playtimes to complete work (which he rarely did) and told him that he was just being lazy. He interfered with others' work and his disruptive behaviour led to several in-school suspensions. Discussions with Damon's mother hedged around whether or not he should be 'removed' from the school.

The following year Damon's teacher had a different approach. He told Damon he was a 'clever kid' who had a bit of a problem with reading and writing. He spent time encouraging Damon to enjoy stories and gave him opportunities to write without worrying about whether it was correct or not. He then commended Damon's creative thinking. Damon was given some support from the learning support teacher, which by then he was willing to accept. Although he was only making slow progress in literacy his behaviour that year was not a problem.

In year 6 he had another teacher who did little to stop him feeling a failure and by the end of the first term he was permanently excluded.

Students who struggle with literacy are especially vulnerable in school where so much depends on this ability. Pupils whose school life has been badly disrupted for whatever reason are particularly at risk. They may have just picked up what they could and have gaps in their learning. Students, especially in high school, sometimes deny their literacy difficulties and refuse all help as this constantly faces them with what they cannot do. They may also resist the stigma often associated with support classes. One answer to this is to have an Extension Centre where students come for extra support at both ends of the learning spectrum.

Another difficulty, which appears more prevalent with boys, is a culture where it is not seen as cool to be clever. Being interested in achievement does not always sit well with others; sometimes peers, sometimes family members. A student once told me that his uncle, having had a poor school experience himself, derided any effort he was making to learn, saying: '*What do you want to be bothered with that stuff for? No one in this family reads books*'. A wise teacher would take these cultural issues into account and make literacy links with what is relevant and meaningful to the student. Since the advent of Harry Potter, however, enthusiasm for reading has become universally more acceptable. Thanks to J.K. Rowling.

Becoming competent, persistent and successful

Some teachers hope that getting low marks will spur students on to try harder. In fact the opposite is usually true. Nothing is more motivating than success. Once you feel you have mastered something, however simple, you are much more willing to have a go at the next step. Non-resilient students give up easily. Making learning accessible and achievable therefore encourages persistence.

Students need to have tasks presented to them at the appropriate level so they are both building on prior knowledge and being challenged to go further. Vygotsky (1978) calls this the ZPD or 'zone of proximal development'. This is sometimes referred to as 'working in the tomorrow of the child'. What students can do with help today they can do independently tomorrow. Linked with the ZPD is the idea of scaffolding – a process where a teacher or more able peers, supports the student until this becomes unnecessary. The best way of getting to this 'appropriate place' according to Hattie (2009) is to build in effective feedback *from* students as well as feedback *to* students about their learning.

- Tasks need to be presented in manageable steps. Asking someone to draw a mind map – maybe in collaboration with others – is less daunting that asking them to write an essay.
- Reduce comparison with others by focusing on multiple intelligences, personal bests and learning together.
- When you have a strengths-based ethos everyone gets acknowledged, not just those who are 'academic'. This makes it more likely that pupils will strive for their 'personal bests' in diverse areas.
- Encourage all means of communication and learning, not just those based on literacy skills – discussion, debate, film, graphics, taping, peer support and reporting.

The 'Too good for violence' programme (U.S. Dept of Education, What Works Clearinghouse, 2006) used a range of pedagogies including role-play, collaborative learning games, small group activities and classroom discussions to effect changes in behaviour and knowledge, values and attitudes. In a study of 1,000 students, significant improvements were noted in behaviour and substantial changes in knowledge, values and attitudes.

Feeling no one cares

When children's experience of their family is that they do not care they may find it hard to believe that anyone does. In my experience students defend their families at all costs regardless of what they have done or not done. Saying anything directly critical may make things worse rather than better.

Feeling no one cares may lead to students not caring about themselves or others. This may be demonstrated in both a lack of empathy and risk-taking behaviours. Peer relationships may appear shallow and self-serving when young people attach themselves to others where they make demands with little reciprocity. Students need to develop understanding and skills to establish and maintain positive friendships.

Children, and especially teenagers, may say they don't care. Beware taking this at face value: often it is a defensive statement. Students who find it hard to take praise or alternatively need constant reassurance may come into this category.

The constructs aligned to feeling uncared for, rejected or lonely may be:

- I need to look after myself because no one else does.
- I do not owe anyone anything.
- Getting close to people may hurt me.
- I'm not worth caring about.
- I need everyone to pay me lots of attention before I feel OK about myself.
- People are only interested in me for what they can get.

Helping students believe they are lovable

There are many ways to demonstrate care, from smiling to showing interest to acknowledging strengths. Caring relationships can be very powerful in generating a positive learning environment – see Chapter 7.

Some of the most damaged young people you will come across will, however, resist all attempts to acknowledge you care about them. This can be for several reasons. The people they really want to care for them are their parents so you are a poor substitute. When a child has been repeatedly let down by others they will be reluctant to trust an adult. Do not aim to get close to students like this – show them respect and be accepting – but remain at a professional distance.

📁 Case study

Dawn was one of the most caring teachers I ever met. She worked in a special school and was especially motherly to the pupils in her class, who were aged 10 to 12. One summer she had bruises on her legs for weeks where Chris had kicked her on several occasions. This pupil was then living in a residential home having been rejected by both his mother and several sets of foster parents.

Chris had begun to warm towards Dawn and it seems that it was just too dangerous for him to do this. The kicking appeared to be a desperate attempt to free himself from the emotional hurt that he anticipated would follow – as it always had before.

This situation was distressing to everyone. The school gave Dawn every support and let Chris know his behaviour was absolutely unacceptable, on occasions escorting him off the premises. In consultation with others, Dawn decided the best course of action was to give Chris the space he needed. She continued to model respect but was more distant. He calmed down and although his behaviour was never easy he stopped being violent.

Showing you care means believing in the best of someone. Teachers may never know the extent to which their consistently positive approach has impacted on a student's view of themselves as someone who is worthy of being loved and cared for. The right word at the right time can make a difference for all time.

Feeling rejected

Children may feel rejected because someone walks out of the family, a new baby receives a lot of attention, there is favouritism for a sibling, a stepparent does not accept them, or because they are being bullied at school. A teacher may make a pupil feel worthless when they do not shine at their particular subject. Where students have no voice they may feel their views do not matter and this is also a form of rejection.

Students who have experienced rejection often anticipate and pre-empt this. They make assumptions about peer motivations and intentions and get in first by rejecting others: *'She looked at me funny so I told her to get lost'*. They might end up attacking others on the flimsiest of excuses.

Where children have not received much positive attention they may do things to gain attention by any means. This is particularly true of younger children.

Some children feel rejected in school because that is what they are experiencing with their peers. Teachers need to ensure that everyone takes responsibility for inclusion.

Students who are suspended from school may also experience being rejected, unless there is a careful programme of re-integration – see Chapter 8.

Feeling lonely

The social classification of children at school divides them into popular, rejected, isolated or controversial. The rejected child is most at risk but just feeling lonely can also be hard to bear. It is both a response to experience and a state of mind. Being alone is not necessarily a problem so long as the individual has the skills and confidence to interact well with others when they choose to do so. It is, however, important that children who wish to make friends are supported to do so.

 Case study

Lauren attended a reception class where the other girls had been to the same pre-school centre. They took no notice of her and she was not included in their games or invited to their birthday parties. She told her mother she felt lonely at playtimes and didn't want to go to school. When this situation did not improve after a few weeks, her mother went to speak to the teacher who said it was up to Lauren to make friends and she was not prepared to 'interfere'. When Lauren was moved to a different school the class teacher organised a buddy system to support her settling into the class. Lauren became increasingly enthusiastic about going to school.

Teenagers may feel lonely because they believe that few others understand them or they envisage everyone else as being in friendship groups and they are not.

Circles can help them realise that many people struggle with similar issues – they are not alone.

Social interaction is both complex and subtle. Children who have been diagnosed with Asperger's syndrome do not have the social understanding or skills that support the establishment of friendships. They need both a supportive environment and some specific guidance to help them learn ways of relating to others that come more naturally to other children. Social stories (Gray, 2000) help children understand more about social cues and understanding in particular contexts so they respond more appropriately.

~~~ **Question for reflection and discussion**

What responsibility do teachers have to ensure that students have a positive social experience in school?

Becoming connected

There are many ways teachers can enhance a sense of belonging which reduces feelings of rejection and isolation:

- Give instructions and reminders to whole groups rather than singling out individuals.
- Use 'we' as inclusive of everyone rather to exclude some pupils.
- Provide students with opportunities to be heard.
- Incorporate regular Circle sessions to foster a sense of belonging.
- For younger children introduce a 'play-stop' in the playground. If a student has no one to play with, they wait by the stop until someone invites them into their game. This needs preparatory work to ensure that everyone understands they have a responsibility to invite others but once established works well.
- Give students roles and responsibilities within the class group.
- Welcome new and returning members.
- Develop peer support networks and buddy systems.
- Actively address bullying as a class responsibility to ensure everyone feels safe.

Case study

Primary school students explored the values in their school and decided that their buddy system was a good way of promoting inclusion and acceptance. So if the youngest pupils could have a buddy why not everyone? With their teachers' help they set out to organise this. Year 5 students developed links with a senior citizens facility and year 6 students each had a teacher or other adult in the school as a buddy. There was someone special for everyone (Curriculum Corporation, 2008).

At the Heart of What We Do: Values Education at the Centre of Schooling. Curriculum Corporation, Commonwealth of Australia (2008). Copyright Commonwealth of Australia, reproduced by permission.

Feeling angry

Anger is usually associated with feelings of injustice or as part of the experience of loss. Students who are restricted may also react with force. The expression of anger may be repressed in school, as it is associated with aggression and sometimes violence. Students do not, however, express anger without reason. It is the inappropriate expression of this anger that causes problems. If we can locate the meaning in the anger and help the young person express this well, then the associated difficult behaviour may diminish. Anger is much easier to express in our society than hurt, especially in boys. Tears are usually brushed away in favour of punching and swearing.

Children who are angry may have constructs such as:

- Everyone is against me.
- I will be seen as weak if I cry – its better to yell.
- I can't control my feelings or actions.
- I need to let people know how I feel.
- When no one listens I have to get them to take notice.

Helping students deal with anger: becoming assertive

Students need to know that feelings themselves are not bad or unacceptable – it is how they are expressed that matters. In any difficult situation individuals have three options, do nothing, attack or be 'appropriately assertive'. This means stating what you feel and saying what you want to happen, repeating this if necessary. Sometimes it is better to walk away from an explosive situation before dealing with the issue – pupils who do this rather than lose control are to be commended.

Being able to be sad

Anger is an emotion commonly experienced in a loss situation. Grief and anger are often part of each other. It is useful for pupils to know where their anger is coming from and also that it is OK to be sad. There are ways of coping with these difficult feelings and students need to think through alternatives.

  Case study

Bishop Druitt College – an all age school – runs Seasons for Growth sessions every year with teachers who have been trained as 'Companions'. This is an educational programme for small groups of students who have experienced a major change or loss. The programme runs over eight weeks with groups of six to eight participants. Activities include talking, writing, drawing, music and movement. Not only does this promote coping strategies for difficult emotions it also promotes connection between students who have had similar experiences.

Feeling frustrated

A different sort of anger is caused by frustration. This can lead to destructive behaviour. Frustration comes about when students cannot do what is being asked of them, they perceive others as stopping them getting what they want or need or they are not being understood.

Students who are dealing with other difficulties quickly become frustrated when things do not go to plan. They can tear up work, blame others and lose control.

Some students want to get everything just right. They do not cope well when things go wrong. Many teachers will be familiar with the hard-working girl who constantly rubs out and redoes her assignments, rarely being pleased with the final result.

The constructs involved may be:

- Everything is conspiring against me.
- I never get what I want.
- No one understands what I am trying to do.
- I give up – it's all too hard.
- It has to be exactly right.
- I have to do really well to be accepted.

Helping students cope with frustration: becoming flexible

It is hard for any of us to calm down when everything seems to be going pear-shaped. The best way is to pre-empt difficulties and take evasive action. Some teachers have successfully used the traffic light system with students. This encourages them to tune into their feelings, take responsibility and take control. The student has three coloured counters/markers on their desk. When the green one is showing all is OK, when the orange one is turned over the student may need a bit of help and the teacher comes over to see what can be done, when the red one is showing the student has the right to walk out of the class and come back when they have calmed down. Teachers say that this strategy supports students' belief in their ability to be in control, and that they rarely take unfair advantage of this right.

Giving students a break from the activity or situation causing the frustration often helps. Teaching students to focus on regular breathing clears the mind and reduces heart rate. Some problem-solving with a peer may provide ideas about how to stop things getting to boiling point.

Communicate with parents the importance of learning through mistakes. It is valuable for students to learn to assess their own work to identify what they have learnt/achieved and what they need to do next. It can be a relief for anyone to know they don't have to be perfect and still be accepted as a worthwhile person.

Feeling shame

According to Nathanson (1992) shame often lies beneath anger. It is associated with failure, humiliation, feeling inferior, deficits, helplessness and/or being exposed. It is the way this shame is 'discharged' that matters. Some people withdraw from social contact, others look to create a false reality, perhaps assisted by chemical means, while some attack themselves or others. It is not uncommon for people to move between these responses as nothing makes them feel any better.

Becoming self-accepting

Feeling proud of yourself in an authentic way is not only to acknowledge your strengths and achievements but also to think well of the human being you are or are becoming. We can help students work towards being the best they can be, not by constantly pointing out their failures but by talking up their qualities and contributions. These need to be overtly valued. The students that get the accolades and prizes in school are not always the ones who most need to think well of themselves.

 Questions for reflection

Have you ever felt ashamed?

How powerful was that emotion?

Did it relate to letting yourself down or letting others down?

Now think of something you have done that has made you feel proud of yourself. Does acknowledgement make a difference to the way you feel?

Feeling confused, anxious or depressed

I can't really remember my feelings, they were just a jumble, a mess. When I got in a panic at the bus stop and phoned my Mum, my mind was in a mess (student quoted in Wise, 2000, p. 120).

This quote confirms that direct questioning of students is rarely a useful strategy when their emotions are overwhelming. Depression and anxiety is now endemic in Western society and not uncommon in both primary and secondary classrooms. Students may respond by keeping their heads down so no one pays them attention or they may continue along a continuum, from withdrawing, being actively evasive and refusing to cooperate to exploding with high levels of emotion. A pupil who is seriously depressed won't be focused on what others think they should be doing or care much about the impact their behaviour has on others. Consequently such students may be socially isolated. In a study investigating the impact on children of witnessing family violence boys whose behaviour was aggressive on the surface admitted to having very low self-worth and being anxious and depressed (Sternberg et al., 1993). Students may have lost the belief that anything will change their lives for the better.

Constructs may include:

- I just can't.
- I'm scared of what will happen.

- Nothing makes any difference.
- I am useless, hopeless, a bad person.
- I can't be bothered.
- No one understands.
- It is all too much.
- I don't feel anything, I am just numb and empty.
- Everyone else is to blame.
- I can't think straight.

Becoming courageous, optimistic and hopeful

A person's approach towards life becomes more inflexible as they get older, so it is helpful to build resilience in children throughout their formative years. This means working with them to see the positives in any situation, including developing awareness and gratitude for what they have and what goes well. Helping them get small concerns into perspective, teaching problem-solving skills and developing supportive relationships provide a slow drip feed to a more positive outlook. When children have opportunities to have agency and make a difference they do not feel so helpless (see Chapter 8).

- Making connections for students helps them learn from their experiences. Say things like 'I can see you enjoyed doing that'; 'I am sure this feels terrible now but think of a time when something felt just as bad and you were able to get over it'.
- Talk to the class about the phrase 'don't sweat the small stuff' and ask them to think what is small stuff and what isn't.
- Young children can make 'I Can' books – whole classes can make 'We Can' posters.
- Give students scenarios for which they list different possibilities for action.
- Ask students to 'blame fairly'. When something goes wrong how much was down to others, what might you have done differently and how much was due to chance?

It is often imagined fears that distress children but students may also be encouraged to use their imagination to promote coping strategies. Sayfan & Lagattuta (2009) found that children of all ages were able to identify psychological as well as behavioural strategies to overcome fears: these included *'Imagine that my mummy is there'*. Older children also have more 'reality affirming strategies' such as imagining the aspects of an ideal situation, whereas the younger early years students use more 'positive pretence' strategies such as *'I'll use a sword to fight the dragon'*.

Feeling out of control

One outcome of diagnosing children and young people with 'attention deficit hyperactivity disorder' (ADHD) is that it affirms a self-concept of not being able to have self-control. Although some individuals do have a great struggle in all contexts, they are in the minority.

> 🗁 **Case study**
>
> Rees was quick to tell me he had been diagnosed with ADHD and was therefore unable to control his behaviour in the classroom. I talked with him about the previous weekend when he had been kayaking with his family. I asked how he had managed the kayak and if he had done this by himself. 'It was great, I was good at it' he said with some pride and proceeded to tell me how his brother had turned his kayak over. We worked out that he did have quite a lot of self-control in that situation – and then we identified other situations in which he had chosen one behaviour over another. Rees began to think of himself differently.

Feeling out of control also occurs when unwanted things are happening in someone's life they cannot influence. This can be moving house, having a new stepfamily, being threatened/emotionally blackmailed/abused or being ill. Inappropriately high expectations or simply living in a household where normal mess is not tolerated can make children feel they are not accepted unless they behave in certain ways. Some students do their best to get as much control over their environment as they can to counter-balance this. Behaviours may include trying to control what goes in or out of the body (anorexia, encopresis), perfectionism, wild and reckless behaviour at school or trying to control others by bullying them.

Constructs linked with this feeling may be:

- I can't control myself.
- I am not responsible for what I do.
- I don't feel safe.
- Everything will fall apart if I lose control.
- I can let rip at school but not at home.
- Controlling others gets you what you want.

Becoming self-determined and responsible

Self-determination makes the links between freedom and responsibility. It involves supporting students in making a wide range of decisions and choices. This can include an involvement in setting their own learning targets.

Some students have difficulty holding onto more than a limited amount of information so they react to one thing before seeing the whole picture. Others just give in to temptation to what they want to do and have, regardless of the longer-term consequences or the impact on other people. This impulsive behaviour can be problematic in the school context.

Students need to practice being in control of small decisions and recognise they can be successful at this. Planning lays out a pathway to a chosen goal.

Feeling bored

Students may say they are bored when they can't do the work, or other matters in their lives make concentration on set tasks difficult. Sometimes students find it hard to link what they are learning with what they already know. For others their level of ability is beyond what they are being asked to do or they have completed similar tasks before so they disengage. Constructs linked to this feeling may be:

- I can't be bothered, this has nothing to do with me.
- I don't see the point.
- I can't focus on this now.
- I can do this already – no one values my skills.

Becoming curious, interested and engaged

Csikszentmihalyi (1990) says that 'flow' occurs when challenge and ability meet. This is being so absorbed in what you are doing time passes without noticing. You feel a deep sense of engagement, satisfaction, wellbeing.

Relevance in learning is not always easy to achieve but hooking curriculum content to something that is meaningful for students raises the chance of their engagement. Some possible links may be: animals, music, sports, family, food, TV and films, current events, cars, bikes and other transport, the local community, fashion and clothes, magazines, cartoon characters, computers, space, holidays and keeping fit.

Give able students questions and tasks that ensure they use their powers of analysis and application. Problem-solving, generalising to different contexts, opportunities to be creative and researching independently and with others can be stimulating.

Questions for reflection and discussion

When do you find yourself in 'flow'?

Are you being passive or active?

What deeply interests your students?

How can you use this information in your teaching?

SUMMARY OF STRATEGIES AND APPROACHES TO PROMOTE POSITIVE BEHAVIOUR

- Help students identify their strengths.
- Talk up their strengths rather than their deficits.
- Where possible hook curriculum content to something that is meaningful.

- Teach students about feelings; how and when they are experienced and what helps in regulating and expressing emotions well.

SUMMARY OF STRATEGIES AND APPROACHES TO DEAL WITH DIFFICULTIES

- Think about the longing being expressed in a negative emotion.
- Give students agency to make decisions and help them recognise they have control.
- Respect and build on students' own coping strategies.
- Acknowledge and accept imperfection as a step to progress.

Professional development activities for teachers

Longing for...?

With a partner identify a time when a student has expressed a negative emotion. What was this emotion? What do you think may have been the longing beneath this expression? How might this help you respond effectively? How might this help you not be overwhelmed by the situation?

Hypothetical scenarios: there is no one correct answer

In each of the scenarios below, consider the following questions:

- What constructs might these students have?
- What emotions are they expressing and what needs might these represent?
- What would it be useful to know and why?
- What three things might you do to make a difference?

Merrill

Merrill is 13 and in year 8. Her behaviour in primary school was a bit erratic but within bounds. Her transition records say that she was a popular student who was a natural leader but by the end of year 6 was beginning to use her influence in negative ways, including verbally bullying other girls. Her attainments were below average although she appeared to have strengths in dance and gymnastics. Her mother was particularly supportive of this as she was a personal trainer herself. Since being in high school Merrill's behaviour has deteriorated. She comes to school late most days and is often absent. When there she sits at the back of the class, talks to her mates about the wild time she had the night before and chews gum loudly. She rarely does homework. You need to reverse this situation before it deteriorates further.

Ricardo

Ricardo is 8. He was a polite, well-behaved and hard-working student until a few months ago. Now he hardly ever smiles and has outbursts of temper in which he destroys other peoples' work. He has punched other children and on one occasion scratched his teacher who was trying to restrain him. His parents were called into school and his mother came with her sister to say that they are just worried about how he is getting on with his reading. Ricardo is quite a popular boy and was often invited into games until he began to be aggressive. His best friend Robert has moved with his family to another town.

Using a strengths focus

Discuss in a small group how a strengths focus might change behaviour in students. In what ways could you develop this approach in everyday lessons?

Circle Solutions activities with students

These activities will:

- Demonstrate that everyone experiences both positive and negative feelings
- Help students reflect on how to regulate emotion and cope with difficult situations
- Identify and build strengths.

All Circles begin with a statement of the principles:

- When one person is speaking everyone else listens.
- You may pass if you do not want to say anything.
- There are no put-downs.

Facing fear

Explain that being courageous is not being a super-hero but facing your fear so it doesn't get the better of you. It is no big deal to be brave if you are not scared to start with. Ask students to brainstorm what might make someone scared.

Paired interview

Talk about an experience where you were a bit anxious or scared.

What helped you to face your fear and not fall apart?

Sentence completion

It helps someone to be courageous when ...

Silent statements

Stand up and change places if:

- You know someone who feels lonely sometimes
- You know someone who feels angry sometimes
- You know someone who feels depressed sometimes.

    Point out to students that everyone experiences difficult feelings at one time or another.

(Continued)

(Continued)

Feelings in our faces and bodies

Give small groups (quietly) a word for an emotion, for example pleased, disappointed, excited, proud. Ask them to think of when someone might have this feeling and what happens to their bodies when the feeling is there. Ask them to form a statue (moving or still) that represents that feeling. The rest of the Circle guesses the emotion.

Expressing anger

Anger can be useful – it tells us something is wrong. It is how anger is expressed that matters. Ask small groups to think of all the things that might make someone angry. Although this question is impersonal it may bring up situations at home which gives an insight into why students are behaving in challenging ways. It will also help students appreciate that others share their difficulties and provide some emotional support.

In the Circle ask students to think about when they are angry and what they do about it. Ask students in pairs to consider all the different ways to express anger and discuss what may be better ways to do this and why. They report their ideas to the Circle.

Sadness and depression

In groups of about six ask one person to represent sadness and another depression. Ask them to think about how they would look and stand. Are there any differences?

Ask the person who represents sad what makes people sad. Encourage others to help. Do you think sadness is something you should try and get rid of as soon as possible? Why might that not be a good idea?

Ask the person who is depressed what it feels like. What is the difference between being sad and being depressed? What can a person who is depressed do? Is it a good idea to ask for help? Who can help?

Strengths

Scatter strengths cards in the middle of the Circle. Ask students to pick a strength they have demonstrated recently. Each person says why they have chosen this. Ask students to choose a strength they would like to have or choose one for a partner. Ask students to work in groups to identify strengths that exist in the class and say how they know they are there.

RESOURCES

You can explore your own VIA (Values in Action) Strengths on www.authentichappiness.sas.upenn.edu

A wide range of strength cards for different ages are available from www.innovativeresources.org

The SOSO campaign, which stands for Smart Online, Safe Offline, is raising awareness of the dangers of cyber bullying and encouraging students to take responsibility. To see a video that students have made about the issue view www.soso.org.au/

Mark Le Mesurier's book *What's the buzz?* (2010, Abingdon: Routledge) has a number of lessons on various social issues including an excellent chapter on dealing with worries. Teachers of anxious children will find this useful for both the pupils and themselves!

More information about the Seasons for Growth programme, a group peer support programme dealing with loss and change, can be found at: http://seasonsforgrowth.co.uk/

REFERENCES

Curriculum Corporation (2008). *At the heart of what we do: Values education at the centre of schooling.* Melbourne: Commonwealth of Australia, Curriculum Corporation.

Csikszentmihalyi, M. (1990). *Flow.* New York: Harper and Row.

Gray, C. (2000). *The new social stories book.* Arlington, TX: Future Horizons Inc.

Hattie, J. (2009). *Visible learning: A synthesis of over 800 meta-analyses relating to achievement.* London and New York: Routledge.

Nathanson, D. (1992). *Shame and pride: Affect, sex and the birth of the self.* New York: Norton & Company.

Sayfan, L. & Lagattuta, K.H. (2009). Scaring the monster away: What children know about managing fears of real and imaginary creatures. *Child Development*, 80(6), 1756–74.

Sternberg, K., Lamb, M., Greenbaum, C., Cicchetti, D., Dawud, S., Cortes, M., Krispin, O. & Lorey, F. (1993). Effects of domestic violence on children's behavior problems and depression. *Developmental Psychology*, 29(1), 44–52.

U.S. Department of Education, Institute of Education Sciences, What Works Clearinghouse (2006). *Intervention report: Too good for violence.* Retrieved March 11, 2010, from www.whatworks.ed.gov

Vygotsky, L.S. (1978). *Mind and society: The development of higher psychological processes.* Cambridge, MA: Harvard University Press.

11 RESPONSES, RESTORATIVE PRACTICES AND TEACHER RESILIENCE

Chapter objectives

- To think proactively about responses in a range of challenging situations
- To maintain professional integrity and resilience when things do not go well
- To learn the basic framework for a restorative conference
- To reflect on the dimensions of teacher wellbeing.

Ewing and Smith (2003) reported that between 25 and 40 per cent of beginning teachers in the Western world are leaving teaching or are burned out. Maslach (1993, p. 20) defined burnout as a *'psychological syndrome of emotional exhaustion, depersonalization, and reduced personal accomplishment'*. Emotional exhaustion means having low resources because these have been over-extended without being replenished; depersonalisation involves a negative, detached attitude to people and reduced personal accomplishment refers to a poor self-evaluation of one's job performance. Findings from the study conducted by Brouwers and Tomic (2000) indicate that teachers' belief in their capability to maintain classroom order was a significant predictor of burnout.

This chapter therefore explores how you might conserve and restore your emotional resources, maintain positive relationships by using emotional intelligence and build confidence in yourself as professionally competent – regardless of the level of challenge.

TEACHER RESILIENCE IN THE FACE OF CHALLENGES

Highly challenging and confronting behaviour, although comparatively rare, can have a highly detrimental impact on teacher wellbeing. It is stressful and both physically and emotionally exhausting. Not only is this likely to enrage or intimidate you, it undermines confidence in general and you may doubt your competence as an educator. Even the most experienced teachers can feel at a loss. If you are implementing approaches advocated here you are already using protective strategies that will stand you in good stead. It is less likely you will experience more severe behavioural difficulties or be overwhelmed by them. But no one is immune. You may not have had time to establish a positive relationship with a student or something has happened in their life that makes them 'lose it'. Every teacher will have had a day in which they have wanted to throw in the towel.

Questions for reflection and discussion

What has been the most challenging situation you have come across in a school?

How was this dealt with?

What were the pros and cons of the approach taken?

When unacceptable behaviour occurs you have choices in responding. Not having a range of options can leave you feeling stranded and vulnerable. You may end up taking the behaviour personally, perhaps be overwhelmed by negative emotions yourself and resort to impulsive, ineffective responses. This builds up a negative spiral in your confidence and your relationship with students. Having strategies in mind raises your chances of coming out of the crisis psychologically intact – even if a little bruised.

MAINTAINING PROFESSIONAL INTEGRITY

If you are guided by professionalism you are less likely to be swayed by the emotions inherent in challenging situations. Maintaining a high level of personal and professional integrity means behaving in a way that is consistent with how you want the student to behave, even if they are currently not doing so. This means staying calm, being firm and clear in your expectations but also showing concern for the student. This is not easy to do when you are in the middle of an incident. It takes preparation and practice. We need to stand with students but also remain professional. Too much or too little engagement may prevent us from choosing the most professional response.

Challenging behaviours are invariably an outcome of negative experiences or attempts to cope with difficult situations. Despite their bluster, confrontational students lack authentic confidence, both in themselves and others. When significant adults show they can be strong without being a bully, aggressive or defiant, and despite provocation remain in control of themselves, this demonstrates alternative ways of responding when the going gets tough. It provides guidance for students in coping with adversity in ways that do not damage themselves or others further.

Questions for reflection and discussion

What does too much or too little engagement mean in practice?

What would demonstrate a professional level of engagement with a student?

DEALING WITH CHRONIC CHALLENGES

More common in schools are chronic difficulties that wear teachers down. Unacceptable behaviour is not confrontational but subtle, such as intimidation, put-downs, callousness and dishonesty. This can be especially challenging when it conflicts with your own value system. The following may be helpful:

- Be mindful that these learned behaviours are meeting or communicating the student's needs in some way. If you can identify the needs you may be able to think of other ways in which they can be met.
- Constantly reiterate acceptable behaviours and give a rationale for these in terms of equity and fairness – they are there to protect and foster everyone's wellbeing.
- Ask questions (at an appropriate moment) that gently challenge how the student wants to be seen by others and what they are doing to develop a sense of authentic pride in themselves. Do not turn this into a moral lecture – young people switch off.
- Prioritise social and emotional learning that incorporates relational values.
- Lead whole group responsibility for the development of pro-social behaviour.
- Make your classroom a 'no put-down zone' and have structured discussions with students about what that means.

The best thing about this school is the no put-down policy – if you don't have this you could get pushed, teased or bullied (student).

Irritating and annoying behaviours

Although we all have varying tolerance levels, demanding, complaining, dependent, discourteous, highly active/very passive or just loud behaviour can be very wearing. Some students may ignore or talk over teachers, others make inappropriate comments, yawn loudly or send texts. These behaviours can irritate teachers to the point of exasperation and hostility. It is thoughtless rather than malicious and particularly noticeable in students who are immature and/or struggling with learning or social relationships.

How do you resist being wound up by such behaviours? It may help if you see these students as not having yet developed the positive attitudes and behaviours that are major factors in resilience. This is a learning issue to be addressed over the longer term.

Choose the level at which you respond. Tactical ignoring for minor or secondary behaviours is useful. Secondary behaviours are the expressions, sighs or slam that signals resistance whilst complying. Don't waste your breath or time reacting. Acknowledge any move towards the appropriate behaviour – a nod or brief ' thanks' will do. Bill Rogers (2002) refers to this as 'choosing your battles wisely'. It conserves your energy for when the situation really requires it. Responding consistently at a high level will keep you in a state of permanent tension and wear you out in no time.

Non-verbal communication such as 'the look' takes little effort; a low-key comment can indicate that this is not acceptable behaviour but not a major drama. Being light and warm also promotes the relationships you want in your class:

- *OK, you lovely lot – show me your ready-to-learn faces. Who's the pair of clever clogs who can answer the first question of the lesson? Amil, when you're ready can you pair up with Kieran please?*

Give the student a moment or two to comply with a request and don't stand over them. If there is no positive response within a few minutes try the following in this sequence:

- Repeat your expectations more firmly.
- Ask if the student understands what they should be doing next.
- Ask what is possible for the student – be willing to negotiate a target.
- Give a limited choice.
- Offer consequences beginning with the positive, for example, *'if you make a start on this I will come and see how you are doing in a couple of minutes'*.
- Move onto a minor negative consequence, for example, *'if you don't have a go now you are going to end up having to do this in your own time'*.
- Do what you can to prevent minor behaviours growing into major events.

⌇⌇ Questions for reflection and discussion

Which annoying behaviours do you find especially hard to tolerate? What action can you take to (a) minimise these behaviours in your classroom and (b) keep your response in check?

Demands and dependency

When students are disruptive or just not settling, using appreciative enquiry questions may promote independence, optimism and more considerate behaviour. They will also foster cognitive and problem-solving skills. Appreciative enquiry is about discovering the best in people. Ask questions of an individual privately:

- *What have you managed to do by yourself?*
- *What would be a good thing to do now?*
- *What would help you focus better on the lesson?*
- *Do you have way of telling me this that I would find easier to hear?*
- *Tell me (or write down) what you have achieved today.*
- *What will you do next time?*
- *What can I do that will help you listen?*

To reduce dependence on the teacher and excessive demands for attention, some educators have instituted a protocol that gives students alternative strategies than immediately asking the teacher, such as: listen carefully, do as much as you can, ask a friend if you are not sure what to do next, try again. Then if you are still struggling to understand put your hand up to ask a question.

Some behaviour comes from excessive worrying and anxiety. Although some worry is normal too much leads to hyper-vigilance. As Le Mesurier (2010) says: '*For a child who is ceaselessly anxious or is continually stressed, their decision making becomes trapped in the emotional part of the brain so every new experience is perceived as a threat and dealt with as a threat'*.

To break this neurological pattern, students need reassurance they can be successful and to be reminded of their strengths.

DEFUSING AND DEALING WITH HIGHLY CHARGED INCIDENTS

Focusing on the negativity within a situation wastes valuable emotional resources and damages the possibility of relationship re-building. To maintain both self-respect and respect for the student, state clearly the behaviour expected, model this, state consequences calmly and follow through consistently. If the student is out of control, assess the situation for actual danger and ask another pupil to go for support if necessary. No teacher should feel isolated in the face of seriously threatening situations.

If aggression is directed towards you, you are likely to feel aggrieved, angry and hostile. This is entirely understandable but do not act on these feelings. Although you may have ignited the fuse, the reason for the explosion goes well beyond anything you have or have not done and going on the defensive is not helpful to you or the situation. 'Giving as good as you get', saying that you 'will not be spoken to like that', threatening retribution, or not letting the student have the last word just adds fuel to the fire. It often doesn't work and models weakness rather than strength.

So what *do* you *do*?

Physical presence

Stand tall with your hands down in front of you. Hands in pockets appears too casual, all over the place can look panicked, and raising them can be interpreted as aggressive. Do not invade space by standing too close or thrusting your fingers or face towards the student. Slouching communicates nervousness.

Acknowledge emotions first

Once feelings have been heard and validated there is less reason to escalate their expression. It also gives the message that you taking the student seriously:

- *I can see this is very upsetting for you.*
- *Something big must have happened for you to react like this.*

Often adults want to reduce the emotional content of a situation by denying the feelings inherent in it, telling students they are over-reacting, to calm down or get a grip. This can serve to exacerbate the situation. It is also natural to go into problem-solving mode but this is not effective at times of high emotion.

If you interpret the behaviour as an expression of extreme distress, a student may respond to an offer of comfort away from the class – a drink, quiet room or something to hold onto, like a cushion. This may sound strange but it can provide solace, somewhere to hide or something to punch!

Model calm confidence

Speak slowly and audibly without shouting. Speaking too fast or in a high voice communicates anxiety rather than self-assurance. Emotions are contagious so provide the model to copy rather than react to the one in front of you. Looking and sounding calm and confident helps you to feel more in charge of the situation and also gives the impression of self-respect and self-control. Pretend if you have to!

Directives

Use 'I statements' to state briefly what you want rather than what you don't want. Always refer to the behaviour as being unacceptable, not the student. Avoid getting into a public battle which risks the student losing face, so get away from an audience if you can. Use the student's name and speak quietly but repeatedly:

- *Tom, would you step outside for a moment.*
- *Tom, I need you to step outside.*
- *Tom, I cannot deal with this in here, please step outside.*
- *I'd like to see what we can do about this but not in the classroom.*

If the student is on the other side of the room, go over there and deal with the matter quietly if possible. Perhaps ask other students to do a specific piece of work while you deal with the situation:

- *You know we cannot have this behaviour in school. We will talk about it later.*
- *I am disappointed you are doing this, don't make it any worse for yourself.*

Give time and space

You cannot 'make' someone think or behave in the way you want, the only actions you have control over are yours. If the pupil is intransigent give them some space to think it over. Forcing the issue won't help. It does not hurt to tell a student that you can't make them do anything – only they have the power to do this. All you can do is let them know the outcomes their decisions will have.

Paradoxical instruction or going with the flow

So long as their behaviour is not hurting others you may consider giving students permission to do what they are already doing. It is the equivalent of allowing someone to run out of steam. You will need to make an on the spot assessment about whether this is an appropriate strategy:

- *Anything else to say while you've got my attention?*

Partial agreement can surprise and even stop them in their tracks.

- *You might have a good point there.*

These strategies undermine an attack. To others you look in control of the situation as well as yourself. Some adults are determined to have the last word – decide now that it doesn't hurt to let the student have it.

Refer to relationship

If you know the student well and have established a good relationship you can refer to this in a crisis and show your belief in the best of them:

- *Come on, this isn't like you, something must have happened to tip you over the edge.*

State how you feel

If you are emotionally distressed by the situation it may be helpful on several fronts to state your own feelings. This is not accusatory, it models good practice for emotional expression in taking ownership for what you feel and also gives you a pressure outlet:

- *I am finding this really distressing.*
- *I am feeling furious with you at the moment.*
- *I am sure you have your reasons but this makes me want to scream with frustration.*

As emotions are contagious, you may pick up feelings beneath the student's behaviour. These emotions are likely to be grief and sadness. You may want to refer to this:

- *I'm picking up that you seem really unhappy as well as angry.*

Saying to a student *'I know how you feel'* can backfire. It is better to say: *'something like that happened to me once and I felt …'*. That statement does not make presumptions. Be wary of making disclosures that risk breaching your professional relationship. Listening and responding is usually better than talking about your own experiences.

It is not usually possible, nor appropriate, to go into depth with students – you have other things to do. Perhaps ask the student if they would like to talk to you or someone else at another time or suggest they write down what is going on so you can be more aware in future or see what might be done to help.

This professional behaviour has benefits in many directions. You may feel wrung out at the end of the incident but will know you have handled yourself well. This builds both your confidence and repertoire of strategies for the future. Other students will see this and you will gain a reputation for quiet strength rather than loud confrontation. Colleagues will learn that you have these qualities and you will add to the general professionalism of the school.

GROUPS OF HARD TO MANAGE STUDENTS

Some teachers can deal with a situation when one or two students are misbehaving but find it overwhelming when a number of students are challenging. They may be oblivious to your presence or having fun at your expense. If this is fairly innocuous your best response, which requires a high level of emotional intelligence, is to take this lightly and join in with the laughter before pulling everyone back to task. Students admire teachers like this so long as they also have the confidence and ability to take charge of a classroom without it falling into chaos.

Students will do things in a group that they are unlikely to do on their own, especially teenagers. It can be very hard to be at the mercy of this 'groupthink'. Do not challenge or try and divide the group but work with the leaders to develop a more constructive focus. In a potential conflict situation it is best to address your directives at students most likely to comply.

It is easier to get the attention of young students to begin a lesson – you have more tricks up your sleeve. Simply putting one hand on your head and a finger on your lips will have everyone copying. For older students you can send a message around the class such as 'We are waiting to begin'. When you have their attention tell students briefly what the lesson will cover and engage them in the subject matter with a question that tunes into their current knowledge.

When students continue to talk over you, rather than yell, tap the desk to get their attention and ask politely if they could settle down and listen now. Some if not all students will comply. Give those who do an interesting and cooperative task and gradually approach the others and ask them when they might be ready. Stay low-key.

Valenzuela (1999) gives the example of a courageous English teacher who asked his uncooperative students to write down a criticism of the class. He then read out what had been written and encouraged a discussion of what might improve this situation. He noted that from this time on, student behaviour was much improved. He put this down to giving students the opportunity to have a say in what they needed and some control over the learning environment.

〰️ **Question for reflection and discussion**

What would you like students to learn about your strengths in a challenging situation?

FOLLOWING THROUGH

You may not be able to do much at the time a confronting situation is happening and end up feeling ineffective. But what happens afterwards is at least as important as what happens in the incident. Accountability matters. It is crucial that other students know that violations of behavioural codes will be addressed. This confirms guidelines and expectations. It is *how* this is addressed that matters. Handing out unrelated punishments to miscreants may be shameful to some and meaningless to others. Making children say sorry does not necessarily increase their remorse and can just build another level of defiance. There do, however, need to be consequences that are understood by everyone. A lecture on 'oughts' and 'shoulds' may go over the student's head, especially if this focuses on the school's reputation about which they may care little. This can disintegrate into secondary issues or simply be an interrogation that is rarely helpful. Asking 'why' may not shed light on an incident nor help resolve it. Using a restorative practices framework has much to offer. It demands that wrongdoers take meaningful responsibility for their actions.

RESTORATIVE APPROACHES

The restorative justice philosophy was introduced in Chapter 5. This approach builds on a sense of belonging to the school community and the quality of relationships there. This is what is involved in putting this approach into practice.

Conversations with students following a behavioural incident are known as 'conferences' and have a particular format, exploring what happened, what the effects were on everyone, and what needs to happen to put things right. This framework gives students opportunities to talk, listen, think and take action. It puts responsibility on wrongdoers to both acknowledge their behaviour was hurtful and do something to repair the harm. The conference also increases the confidence of students who have been hurt and lets them know this has been taken seriously. The wording of questions is amended according to the age of the students involved and the specific circumstances but the basic philosophy remains. This moves away from the language of blame and retribution to the language of relationships, hurt and healing. It emphasises our responsibility to each other. It also goes a long way beyond a simple demand to 'say sorry'.

The role of the conference facilitator

Once restorative practices have become established in a school, students know what to expect and are usually in favour. Conferences are never imposed on unwilling students or those who flatly deny any responsibility for their actions. These students face other consequences. Students need to be respectful to others and stay in the restorative conference until a resolution or agreement is reached. Conferences can be between the teacher and student, between the teacher and more than one student or between the teacher and a whole class. They require skill to handle well and training is advisable.

> *In exploring incidents of harm, the facilitator is 'gently relentless' in getting meaningful and understandable responses to the script questions. It is the facilitator's role to do their best to make sure that everyone in the conference hears and understands the different stories, feelings, thoughts and intentions of others who are present* (Hansberry, 2009, p. 51).

Conferences have a particular format, using the following questions. These may change slightly depending on the situation and the age of the student:

- What happened?
- What were you thinking (and feeling) at the time?
- What are you thinking and feeling now?
- Who has been affected by what you have done and in what ways? Who else?
- What needs to happen now?

Corridor conferences

There is a continuum to conferences, the first being an informal, 'impromptu' or 'corridor conference'. This occurs when something fairly minor has occurred but has nevertheless upset someone – like barging into a room and knocking another pupil out of the way and then ignoring them. The first statement includes an affirmation of the offender, something like:

- *Hey, Rhi, barging into Ash like that isn't exactly your more graceful self.*

If Rhi doesn't immediately acknowledge her responsibility to another student the teacher gently challenges her:

- *How do you think Ash feels right now?*

Rhi faces the fact that she has upset another student and is asked what needs to happen.

- *Just think about what you need to do.*

The teacher may not necessarily wait to see the interaction but Rhi will know that Ash may later be asked what happened. For most students it is less hassle to repair a relationship than escalate a conflict.

A three way conference

Here is an example of a conference between a teacher, an offending student and a student who has been the target of this behaviour.

The student is asked to talk with the teacher about a specific concern, not just about their behaviour. This does not happen at the time of the incident so a suitable time soon after is arranged:

- *Jed, I need to talk with you about your aggression towards Stephie in class this morning, can you come to this classroom at the end of the day?*
- *Stephie, are you willing to attend this conference?*

At the conference, all participants sit in a circle in chairs of the same height. This gives the message that all are of equal importance and that this is a serious conversation.

The first questions are about what happened, followed by what the student was thinking and feeling at the time and afterwards. This explores the difference between what happens on impulse and after reflection. Students often become aware of a discrepancy or ambivalence once they have had time to review this. Give students enough time to think through the answers to each of these questions. We often jump in much too quickly. It takes about 12 seconds to answer a searching question. Check out how long that is – it's more than you might imagine.

- *Jed, what happened, why are we here?*
- *What were you thinking/feeling when you swore and raised your fist at Stephie?*
- *What have you thought about since this morning?*

If Jed accuses Stephie of a hurtful action at this point say that you will deal with this later, at the moment the focus is on Jed's behaviour.

The next question asks about the impact of actions:

- *Who has been affected by this behaviour and in what ways?*

The answer to this extends beyond Stephie to others in the class who witnessed the behaviour and who may have been intimidated. It also includes the perpetrator. If the student does not acknowledge others the facilitator encourages this by asking:

- *And who else might have been affected? What about the people sitting next to Stephie? How has this incident affected you? What about me?*

The next question is to the person who has been most affected:

- *Stephie, how did you feel when Jed swore and raised his fist at you? What was the worst thing about it?*

Stephie is encouraged to articulate her feelings without using the language of blame.

If Jed has not already said that he did the wrong thing it may be useful to ask him at this point:

- *Jed, what do you think about your behaviour now?*

The conference moves on to questions of restoration:

- *Stephie, what do you think about this? Is there something you would like to see happen?*

Jed is asked to respond:

- *Jed, what do you think about what Stephie has said? What might be done to fix this situation/make things better?*

Finally ask both students if they have anything else to say.

Follow this up to ensure that the agreed actions have taken place.

📁 Case study

I've just been dealing with a couple of kids this morning… using the restorative approach, even though it took 35 minutes using the corridor questions. Using a punitive method, like giving them lunchtime detention, would have taken 35 seconds. But using the restorative way, the two children will be able to go out at lunch-time without continuing the fight, because the issue's been sorted out thoroughly (deputy principal quoted in Mountford, 2006, p. 49).

As this suggests, real change in behaviour is not a quick fix but saves valuable time in the longer term.

Class conference

Another restorative conference can involve a whole class or group of students. The questions are similar but everyone is involved. Usually these conferences are based on a 'no-blame' approach in which everyone takes responsibility for the resolution rather than one or two people being targeted as the perpetrators. This promotes connection within a group and enhances peer pressure for positive change in those individuals.

The facilitator introduces the issue. This could be whole class behaviour, bullying or the social exclusion of some members of the class. Each person is asked to write down what they have seen happen – without using names. This includes the teacher. These statements are then read out. Each person is then asked to say what they feel about this situation and whether or not it needs to change. The next question addresses what needs to be done to make things better. It may be advisable to split up into smaller groups. Each group then feeds back ideas for action. The whole group can then brainstorm and/or vote on which actions to take. A follow-up conference needs to take place in a few weeks to ensure that the situation has improved.

The outcomes of using a restorative justice model for behaviour

The following example is from Rozelle Public School, an inner-city primary school in Sydney. The school has 310 students comprising a diverse population of 4 per cent Aboriginal and 29 per cent with a language background other than English. Lyn Doppler is the Principal:

> *Our practice has been evaluated during the cycle of school improvement and includes qualitative and quantitative data.*
>
> - *Parents and students have indicated a positive response to the program through surveys, questionnaires and focus groups and attendance at school functions. Pre and post data indicate a change in culture has occurred. A respectful, listening climate has been cultivated. As a result personal accountability for actions has occurred and students have been empowered to 'make things right' both academically and socially.*
> - *Student achievement has increased with [results being above state and regional average].*
> - *Student suspension rates were higher at the start of the process but have now dropped dramatically to nil in the past 3 terms.*
> - *Staff and students are empowered to repair and rebuild relationships at their level negating the need for children to be referred to the office and executive.*
> - *Mistakes are viewed as opportunities for insight and there is a real 'can do' attitude.*
> - *Data on the student engagement matrix indicate a more motivated and engaged student population.*
> - *Student attendance rates are excellent and have particularly improved amongst our Indigenous students.*
> - *A higher participation rate of students in events such as swimming carnivals, where previously only the 'elite' entered.*
> - *Staff feel more confident, valued and supported as they see the positive results of this collegial approach to teaching and learning and relationship-building through circle time and firm and fair processes.*
> - *Wonderful attendance rates by parents and friends at assemblies and other school events indicate a community that feels included and valued.*

(Doppler, 2008)

∿ Question for reflection and discussion

What do restorative approaches have to offer that more traditional punitive approaches do not?

BUILDING TEACHER RESILIENCE AND AVOIDING KNEE-JERK REACTIONS

Teaching is exhausting – it is like being on stage for hours at a time, sometimes without much of a script, thinking on your feet. If you do not look after your own wellbeing you will resort to default reactions when things do not go well. It is not indulgent to take care of yourself, it is vital.

Physical wellbeing

It will be a struggle to stay on top of the demands of the job if you are sleep deprived, not taking physical exercise, hung over, ill or malnourished. Spend at least an hour before bed winding down so you sleep better. Keep active. Run up stairs rather than take a lift; get off the bus at the stop before. Exercise releases serotonin into your system which helps reduce stress and irritability. Some schools have yoga classes one lunchtime a week, others self-defence or dance – open to staff and students. This is a great way to develop both fitness and connection.

Question for reflection and discussion

What connections do you make between your physical wellbeing and that of students and the behaviours that follow for both?

Using time wisely

Teachers all say there are too many demands in school for the time available. Time is not a flexible commodity – it's a fixed quantity: the issue is using the time you have well. Much of what is advocated here means doing things mindfully and differently rather than additionally. Often this will save you time in the long run. Effective time management also includes choosing priorities congruent with your values, exploring where you can sensibly cut down, seeking ways where you might do two things at once, and being honest about how you use time. Some people spend ages telling you how much they have to do! It is also being realistic about how much you can fit in. We all want to please others but if that is at the expense of our own wellbeing or that of the students then we need to be assertive in saying no or at least 'not now'.

Plan time to relax, be with friends and family and take exercise. If you live a more balanced life you be less stressed and more able to make good decisions in challenging situations.

Social wellbeing

Social support is one of the strongest factors for resilience. A sense of belonging is as important for staff as for students. Relational quality permeates a school and what happens between teachers impacts on what happens between students and teachers. Getting to know each other breaks down barriers, fosters collaboration and promotes a sense of wellbeing in the community.

> *The social activities outside of school ... are a form of getting to know other people and introducing new people along, and just having a chance to catch up out of the school environment ... it's been terrific, wonderful, a special sort of feeling in the staff community* (teacher).

Share the load

In Miller's study (1994) a contributing factor to the emotional impact of challenging situations is the feeling of being alone. Even in a supportive school, teachers felt that they were solely responsible for what went on the classroom. An emotionally literate school in which behaviour is seen as everyone's concern can be a strongly protective factor for both teachers and pupils. It helps to feel you are in this together.

'Cause for Concern' meetings about highly challenging students have the potential to reduce feelings of isolation. They provide an opportunity to share strategies, present a consistent approach to students and maintain emotional resources. The downside is the danger they become a moan fest with everyone colluding with negativity and vitriol against the student rather than ways to identify and build effective intervention. It is important to be able to say how you feel but how you do that matters.

〰️ Question for reflection and discussion

Which of these statements is more helpful in a Cause for Concern meeting and why?

- *Jody is driving me mad, I don't know what to do. She seems to get under my skin at every opportunity; I seem to have tried everything and am at my wits' end.*
- *Jody is a lazy, foul-mouthed bully. She never does any work and is constantly disrupting my lessons. I have really had enough of her.*

Psychological wellbeing

Focus on the positive

This includes the following:

- Keep things in perspective. It is easy to let things that don't go well dominate. This can drive your spirits down: *'You maybe have 10, 15 teachers say hi to you in a day, but it's the one in the morning who walked straight past you that I will remember when I fall into bed at night.'*
- Most of us have a negative inner voice that puts the worst possible interpretation on things and gives us a hard time. Tell it to get lost! It doesn't help and often makes things worse than they need be.

- Remind yourself of your achievements, however small. Keep cards, letters and emails of appreciation to provide a boost when needed.
- Remind yourself of things you are thankful for. You have choices in your attitude, either you can ruminate on how dreadful things are or you can seek to identify and build on what is going well. This is not a Pollyanna approach to life and does not suggest you do not actively address difficulties but the more you focus on the positive the better the outcome. It's a self-fulfilling prophecy. If there is nothing good about your situation either take it in hand or go somewhere else. Don't be a victim.

Remember that however dreadful you are feeling about yourself or your day this is a powerful learning experience. It helps you understand what some of your most challenging students will feel like at times. And you are likely to have more resources at your disposal than they do.

Have fun

Just sharing a laugh with someone relieves stress, promotes a feeling of warmth and enhances collaboration. Laughing at yourself is invariably healthy, humour at the expense of others can be damaging, laughing at situations can be either.

Many teachers, however, especially in my experience male teachers, do a lot of joshing with each other – it is a mark of their friendship and allegiance. From an outsider's view the rude remarks may seem a bit harsh but when accompanied by rueful laughter on both sides the clear intention is to promote connection rather than hostility.

Compartmentalisation – leave your worry bags at the school gate

We have addressed many emotions that teachers experience in dealing with challenging students. Another powerful emotion that is not always acknowledged, however, is how deeply teachers may care about the students in their charge. They feel protective, responsible and loving towards them, recognising how much they need. It is not always easy to leave these feelings behind at the end of the school day. It can be heartbreaking to see these young people struggle, make mistakes and get into trouble.

📁 **Case study**

In my first teaching job I taught 5-year-olds and Carl was in my class. He was an unsettled, impulsive and sometimes defiant little boy who often came to school looking rumpled and tearful. I wanted to take him home with me and make everything all right! That experience taught me a lot. You can make an immense difference to what happens in your classroom and you can help that student feel better about themselves and their potential. But you cannot 'rescue' children alone. It takes a whole school, a whole of community and a long-term

(Continued)

(Continued)

plan to deliver the best outcomes – and even then some situations will never be more than 'good enough'. Spending evenings and weekends fretting will not help. You need to conserve and build your emotional energy so that you can be the best you can be in the classroom.

SUMMARY OF STRATEGIES AND APPROACHES TO PROMOTE POSITIVE BEHAVIOUR

- Maintain your own wellbeing so you can implement effective strategies.
- Follow through after an incident to reinforce to all students what is expected.

SUMMARY OF STRATEGIES AND APPROACHES TO DEAL WITH DIFFICULTIES

- Think about your professional integrity and model the behaviour you want to see.
- Use tactical ignoring or low level responses to minor or secondary behaviours.
- Tune in and respond to the emotional content of challenging situations.
- Be aware if your own emotional reactions and how to keep these in check.
- Avoid taking challenging behaviour personally.
- Practice looking and sounding confident.
- Seek support from colleagues.
- Learn to use restorative conferencing following an incident.

Professional development activities for teachers

Self-respect

In small groups discuss the following statements that define self-respect.

When you have done this add four more.

People with self-respect:

- have high expectations for themselves and for others
- do not have to constantly prove their worth to others
- do not take themselves too seriously
- are able to focus on others.

Discuss how authentic self-respect helps with behavioural issues in the classroom.

Be prepared: role-play your worst nightmare!

In groups of three take turns to role-play as a student, a teacher and an observer. Act out an incident in which the student is by turns uncooperative, defiant, offensive and then explosive. The teacher responds in ways that reflect the learning from this chapter.

Debrief afterwards with the observer. Reflect on the emotions involved and what was more and less difficult to do.

Where does the time go?

Choose a fairly normal day. Every 30 minutes from the time you wake to the time you go to bed write down how you are spending your time. Share your diary with a partner. What have you discovered? What could be different?

Be good to yourself

Write down 10 ways in which you are going to focus on your own wellbeing in the next term. Share your list with a small group and see what strategies you have in common. How easy will it be to keep to your resolutions? What will help?

When it happened to me...

Think of a time in which you felt a failure, totally confused or badly let down. Remember what those feelings were like. What were your coping strategies?

How does this help you understand students' feelings and behaviour?

Discuss with a partner.

Circle Solutions activities with students

These activities will support students in learning the basics of restorative approaches.

All Circles begin with a statement of the principles:

- When one person is speaking everyone else listens.
- You may pass if you do not want to say anything.
- There are no put-downs.

Feeling hurt

Silent statements

Stand up and change places if you have ever been hurt in an accident.

Stand up and change places if you have ever been hurt by words.

(Continued)

(Continued)

Stand up and change places if you feel better when someone shows you that they are really sorry about what happened.

Sentence completions

Being hurt might make someone feel …

Thinking twice

Sometimes when you have done something you think about it afterwards and want to make up for it. Give groups of four people four pieces of paper. The group discusses each scenario and then one of the group draws/writes.

- Paper 1: Something bad is happening – such as taking what does not belong to you or scribbling over someone's work.
- Paper 2: What the person who did that was thinking and feeling.
- Paper 3: What the person who was hurt was thinking and feeling.
- Paper 4: What might change after the person who did the bad thing had time to think about it.

Doing sorry

It is easy to say sorry but how do we 'do' sorry. Ask students in small groups to list as many ways they can think of to make amends when they have done something that has hurt someone. Share ideas with the Circle.

RESOURCES

The children's book *The huge bag of worries* by Virginia Ironside (2004, London: Hodder Children's Books), shows that some worries don't belong to you, some are best shared and some just disappear when they see the light of day. This is helpful for teachers as well as students!

More on appreciative inquiry can be found on http://appreciativeinquiry.case.edu

Hull is becoming a Restorative City with the aim of using restorative approaches with everyone who works with children, young people and families. You can purchase DVDs about restorative practices at Collingwood Primary School and Endeavour High School at http://iirpukonlineshop.org.uk/shop/article_13/Building-Our-Community.html

REFERENCES

Brouwers, A. & Tomic, W. (2000). A longitudinal study of teacher burnout and perceived self-efficacy in classroom management. *Teaching and Teacher Education*, 16, 239–53.

Doppler, L. (2008). *Restorative practices at Rozelle Public School – a way of being and learning together.* www.schools.nsw.edu.au/studentsupport/behaviourpgrms/antibullying/casestudies/

Ewing, R.A., & Smith, D.L. (2003). Retaining quality beginning teachers in the profession. *English Teaching: Practice and Critique*, 2(1), 15–32.

Hansberry, B. (2009). *Working restoratively in schools: A guidebook for developing safe and connected learning communities.* Melbourne: Inyahead Press.

Le Mesurier, M. (2010). *What's the Buzz?* London: Routledge.

Maslach, C. (1993). Burnout: A multidimensional perspective. In W.B. Schaufeli, C. Maslach & T. Marek (Eds), *Professional burnout: Recent developments in theory and research.* Washington, DC: Taylor and Francis.

Miller, A. (1994). Mainstream teachers talking about successful behaviour support. In P. Gray, A. Miller & J. Noakes. *Challenging behaviour in schools.* London and New York: Routledge.

Mountford, T. (2006) Restorative practices K-10. Developing an inclusive and sustainable approach. Masters thesis, University of Newcastle, New South Wales.

Rogers, B. (2002) *Classroom behaviour.* London: Sage Publications.

Valenzuela, A. (1999). *Subtractive schooling: U.S.-Mexican youth and the politics of caring.* Albany: State University of New York Press.

SECTION FOUR

THE ROLE OF THE WHOLE SCHOOL

School ethos is defined as the beliefs and aspirations, vision and values that underpin 'the way we do things round here' – the attitudes and behaviours that determine whole school culture. School climate is the feelings and quality of relationships that result from this and permeate all aspects of the learning environment.

You get a feel for a school when you walk in. It is seen on the faces of students, staff and parents and heard in how people talk to and about each other. It shows in the ways people are greeted, acknowledged and cared for. It is reinforced by what is on the walls and the level of buzz in the classrooms. You begin to understand the vision the school has for its students and how this is translated into priorities, policies, pedagogy and practices. In some schools the focus is on inclusion and wellbeing, ensuring that, along with high expectations, every student is supported to reach their personal potential. In others the focus is on how the school is doing in an academically competitive environment. This colours everything that happens, especially for more vulnerable and often more challenging students.

There are inspirational teachers in many classrooms doing a fine job of maximising the learning of every student in all domains of their development. Some of these teachers struggle against a school culture that does not support their endeavours and/or within an education system that overwhelms them with demands. Positive outcomes for all students are therefore not sustainable, especially for those who do not quite fit the ideal of being compliant, hard-working and able.

This last chapter is about how to embed real change for all students and what schools need to do to ensure every child matters and no child is left behind. The evidence is overwhelming from educational research across the world. When a whole school, beginning but not ending with school leaders, understands that school and student wellbeing underpins a multitude of positive outcomes, from academic achievement to student behaviour to teacher wellbeing, we begin to see sustainable change. Change that not only moves individual students forward into a more viable future, but one that can intervene in cycles of disadvantage and social exclusion, to the benefit of all our communities.

12 THE ECOLOGY OF SCHOOL WELLBEING

Chapter objectives

- To recognise that changing behaviour involves change within schools
- To understand how the ecology of schools affects behaviour
- To explore the evidence on school and student wellbeing
- To look at what is involved in building social capital
- To consider ways of being an agent of school change.

CARING AND INCLUSIVE SCHOOLS

There is overwhelming evidence that caring schools who focus on the wellbeing and participation of all, not only promote resilience and encourage more pro-social and cooperative behaviours, they are also effective learning environments (Cohen 2001, 2006; Zins et al., 2004). They have high expectations, actively build relational quality throughout the school, are inclusive and value each individual.

> The health promoting school ... emphasizes the entire organization of the school, as well as focusing upon the individual. At the heart of the model is the young person, who is viewed as a whole individual within a dynamic environment. Such an approach creates a highly supportive social setting that influences the visions, perceptions and actions of all who live, work, play and learn in the school. This generates a positive climate that influences how young people form relationships, make decisions and develop their values and attitudes. Healthy, well educated young people can help to reduce inequities in society, thus contributing to the health and wealth of the population at large (Burgher et al., 1999, p. 16).

Although individual teachers can make a significant difference in their own classrooms, the quote above shows ways in which the centrality of the whole child affects how schools organise and operate. Schools are ecologies where what happens in one part of the system affects what happens elsewhere. The values and skills of school leaders underpin policies and practices; the way students and families are discussed in the staffroom will determine how they are perceived and actions taken; teachers who feel supported will have more emotional resources to respond thoughtfully to difficulties. The following quote testifies to the systemic nature of caring schools in practical, observable actions.

> *Our senior managers recognise that, as the term goes on and we get tired, we sometimes forget to follow through agreed practices. In briefings they gently remind us about simple things like smiling at children, saying good morning and getting to classrooms on time. You can't do this once or twice a year; it has to be every two or three weeks. Then we take a shared whole staff focus for our own behaviour. We might identify a group of children whose behaviour presents problems and all make a point of saying something positive to them when we meet them in lessons, or around the school* (DfES, 2005a, p. 21).

Schools may adopt specific programmes, add-on or short-term strategies but unless these are embedded within a broader framework for wellbeing they are likely to have limited or short-lived impact (Elias et al., 2003). There is also a tendency to target 'at risk' groups rather than focus primarily on universal strategies. An integrated, inclusive, proactive approach where all teachers take responsibility for the wellbeing for all students is more likely to have sustainable outcomes (Bond et al., 2001; DfES, 2005b; Greenberg et al., 2003; Rowling, 2005; Weare, 2000). As can be seen from the following quote this message is at the heart of promoting mental health in secondary schools.

> *Through a range of strategies, the Whole Student Approach in tandem with the Whole School Approach to mental health and wellbeing constitutes a protective Continuum of Connection* (MindMatters, 2010).

FROM WELFARE FOR SOME TO WELLBEING FOR ALL

Although there will always be a need for intensive, targeted support for some individuals, putting most of the available energy and resources into the most challenging students leaves little space for universal and early provision. Where wellbeing and the quality of the learning environment are actively promoted there is far less demand for high levels of support.

The increased emphasis on whole school and student wellbeing has been stimulated by a rising concern about social exclusion and the limited effectiveness of previous practices within a new social dynamic. Several sources have provided the impetus and evidence for new approaches, including: the health promoting schools initiatives; the Delors Report on education for the 21st century (1996); the development of safe schools initiatives to limit bullying (e.g. McGrath, 2006); the importance of social and emotional issues in learning driven by CASEL in the US and Antidote in the UK; the growing influence of positive behaviour interventions (e.g. Sugai and Horner, 2002); and restorative approaches and increasing awareness of the impact of relational quality on motivation and engagement (Hattie, 2009; Martin & Dowson, 2009). Where just one approach is adopted in a school there is evidence of positive changes but not as extensively as one might have anticipated (e.g. Mooney et al., 2008; Mountford, 2006). However, where changes are being developed in a holistic way, impacting on the whole school culture, there is increasing evidence of hoped for outcomes (Hromek, 2004; Pianta & Walsh, 1996, Roffey, 2008; SHPSU, 2004; Vreeman & Carroll, 2007).

The restorative approach was most effective when a range of strategies was offered and these were linked to the core business of schools: curriculum, pedagogy and relationships (Mountford, 2006, p. 36).

Mountford makes a valid and important point. With the best will in the world, good programmes or ideas are rarely sustainable if they remain on the margins rather than central to the everyday practice within schools.

Question for reflection and discussion

In the schools in which you have had experience, where is most effort expended – in welfare or pastoral support for the most challenging students, or in promoting wellbeing all across the school?

Discuss the outcomes with a partner.

The change in focus to wellbeing requires a paradigm shift in how students and families are conceptualised, how educators perceive their role, and the ways schools go about their business. Revising long-held beliefs is not achieved by knowledge alone. This requires new experiences. In a study of change in school culture (Roffey, 2007) there were several instances of initially negative or cynical members of staff who eventually shifted their perspective as they witnessed positive outcomes in the school and experienced respectful and caring relationships themselves.

I feel valued and appreciated in the department I work in and this reflects a great deal on my enthusiasm, input and dedication to students and staff in this department (teacher).

Question for reflection and discussion

What parallels are there between changing student behaviour and change in schools?

What does it take?

There are rarely straight lines between cause and effect for human behaviour. There are many interactive, circular and accumulative factors that result in what occurs at any given time. Figure 12.1 is based on the eco-systemic theory of change and development (Bronfenbrenner, 1979) and applied to wellbeing in schools. There are bi-directional influences between each level of the system.

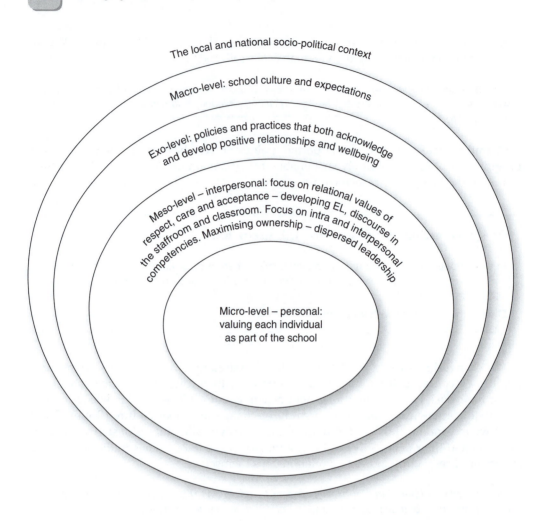

The local and national socio-political context

Macro-level: school culture and expectations

Exo-level: policies and practices that both acknowledge and develop positive relationships and wellbeing

Meso-level – interpersonal: focus on relational values of respect, care and acceptance – developing EL, discourse in the staffroom and classroom. Focus on intra and interpersonal competencies. Maximising ownership – dispersed leadership

Micro-level – personal: valuing each individual as part of the school

Figure 12.1   The ecology of school wellbeing

The most powerful determinants of any outcome are the immediate everyday experiences for individuals at the micro-level, making sure each person feels they matter. This means not only an ethic of care, but maximising opportunity and participation so that care becomes reciprocal. School leaders with a vision and passion for the potential of the whole child are the major driving force in developing wellbeing. There is also a dynamic symbiosis between teacher and student wellbeing. Fostering wellbeing for teachers enables them to support students.

If you have a happy staff, then I think that leads to you being happy in your own classroom, and leads to happy relationships with the children, and the children with each other (teacher).

At the meso-level is an awareness of the many interactions that occur each day that either build or undermine social capital. Both words and actions matter. High social capital is demonstrated by strong trust between people and commitment to shared goals and wellbeing for all. A toxic environment is fragmented; it is one where few people feel safe, valued or acknowledged.

We have a lot of professional dialogue, in terms of what makes our school a healthy place, and what makes our school a learning community. And you can't have a sense of any sort of community ... unless you're looking at how the people relate (principal).

The conversations that promote wellbeing make others feel included. The following case study shows how one school ensured that all stakeholders were involved and took ownership of the process of change.

🗁 Case study

By taking all staff, parents and students through a reflective process of what we did well, what we could do differently (we reflected on if we were happy with how we challenged children around inappropriate behaviour and commitment to learning) and what we would find to be the hardest challenges, we hoped to achieve the following via our visioning process:

- To promote a feeling of wellbeing in our school through a whole school approach to the building of respectful relationships based on accountability and repairing harm rather than focusing on blame and punishments.
- To promote values and empower individuals through a restorative practice philosophy which has at its core doing things 'with' rather than 'to' or 'for' students as the foundation for quality teaching and learning and other proactive programs.

(Doppler, 2008)

Policies and practices are at the exo-level. If wellbeing is a priority this will be reflected in the formal documentation on what happens and how it happens – especially on behaviour, bullying and social justice issues. This includes processes for consultation, how meetings are run and how support is arranged.

At the macro-level is school culture and expectations. What do stakeholders see as the aims and purpose of the school and how is that influenced by the discourse and demands at the socio-political level?

Direction of change

School culture doesn't stand still; it is a dynamic interplay between all stakeholders moving in one direction or another. Relational quality and social capital are either becoming embedded, or there is increasing tension and conflict. Congruence between all levels is hard to achieve, but where schools are led by committed teams who engage all staff in the process of development – both cognitively and emotionally – model the behaviours they are promoting, provide professional development to support change and are prepared to be there for the long haul, schools can transform. Sustainability means getting everyone on board to develop a community for wellbeing. The extract below succinctly encapsulates the social capital that facilitates this and the following quote illustrates an aspect of cultural change in practice.

> *A community is [where] members know, care about and support one another, have common goals and a sense of shared purpose, and to which they actively contribute and feel personally committed* (Solomon et al., 1996, p. 720).

> *The whole culture has changed … Kids now know how you speak to each other with respect; peers or teachers or ancillaries or cleaners. Once it's there it becomes the way things are* (principal).

 Questions for reflection and discussion

How much have your beliefs changed or deepened about education, behaviour in school and your role as an educator? What has influenced this?

BEING AN AGENT OF SCHOOL CHANGE

If you are not in a leadership position in your school you may be wondering what you can do to make any difference at the whole school level. You have more influence to promote wellbeing than you think. You begin by becoming the change you want to see and then being strategic in supporting others.

- Model good relational practice in your own classroom and around the school.
    - seek student strengths and show students you believe in the best of them
    - be primarily learner centred
    - structure opportunities to develop student agency and responsibility
    - ask questions that stimulate thinking rather than being didactic
    - use positive, strengths-based communication rather than discourses of blame and labelling
    - be emotionally intelligent, especially in challenging situations
    - re-frame difficult behaviour as an expression of need
    - have high (and appropriate) expectations of student learning and behaviour and let students know you will support them to achieve this
    - foster a sense of belonging and connection
    - encourage lightness and laughter in the classroom.

- Explore diverse pedagogies that include cooperative learning and real-life problem-solving in ways that students find meaningful, enjoyable, challenging and achievable. Be mindful of multiple intelligences.
- Welcome mistakes as an essential part of learning.
- Structure student feedback to you on their learning.
- Be enthusiastic about your role as a leading-edge educator.
- Show others you are finding enjoyment and satisfaction in your approach.
- Talk about what you are doing to others who are interested.
- Have conversations in the staffroom that put the wellbeing of the child in focus, and gently challenge negativity.
- Make alliances with colleagues who share your views.
- Identify short, stimulating articles which link wellbeing with learning and/or behavioural outcomes and leave round in the staffroom!
- Publicly celebrate student success – especially for those who have struggled.
- Explore the vision of the school leader and, with others, help them see how a wellbeing focus may help achieve this.
- Be supportive to anyone in a leadership position who is working for wellbeing.

EVERY CHILD MATTERS AND NO CHILD LEFT BEHIND

Society is changing. We cannot realistically expect an educational system that harks back to the 20th century to meet the needs of the 21st. To some extent this has been acknowledged in terms of curriculum content but less so in relation to the social, emotional and psychological needs of children and young people. Students who are vulnerable in these areas often challenge a learning environment that does not care for their wellbeing. When they don't measure up they lose out. Spratt and her colleagues (2006) suggest that where a school's focus is on discipline, conformity and high achievement, some students are punished for their circumstances and poor mental health … a double whammy.

The educational philosopher Nel Noddings says that schools have a moral obligation to care about and care for all students (Noddings, 2002). Both John Hattie (2009) and Michael Fullan (2003) come from slightly different perspectives but mirror this exhortation to schools and school leaders to ensure no child misses out on an education that meets their needs and that of a democratic and inclusive society. Beyond the ethical imperative, the evidence increasingly indicates that a focus on the values and practices of wellbeing as described here comprises the most effective way to both promote prosocial behaviour and enhance learning. There are no quick fixes – but over time this is what works.

Professional development activities for teachers

Developing school wellbeing

What makes a school a place you want to work in? Discuss in small groups.

How is your school doing? What needs to happen next? As far as you can, complete the checklist in Appendix 2 and discuss your findings with colleagues.

Being an agent for positive change

In small groups devise five actions you could take as a classroom teacher to encourage and support a whole school approach to wellbeing.

Circle Solutions activities with students

These activities will help students reflect on the support they have in the present and what they want for their future. These activities are most relevant to high school students.
   All Circles begin with a statement of the principles:

- When one person is speaking everyone else listens.
- You may pass if you do not want to say anything.
- There are no put-downs.

Support networks

Give each student a piece of paper.
   Ask them to draw themselves in the centre and then write in the names of people who they feel are supportive with the person closest to them nearest. Ask them to include family members, friends, people in school, those in their neighbourhood and any others who they think have been helpful.
   Ask them to then place lines between the people who are connected with each other: an unbroken line for a close relationship and a broken line for a weaker one.

Silent statements

Stand up and change places if you discovered:

- That your support network is stronger than you thought
- Part of your support network is in school
- Some of your supporters need supporting themselves.

Pair share

Talk to a partner about what you both do to support others.

Travelling into the future (with thanks to Tania Major)

In the centre of the Circle place a suitcase (or backpack) and a waste basket.

Ask students to think of their journey into the future. In small groups ask them to talk about and then write or draw anything that is good in their lives they want to take with them into their future. These go in the suitcase. These are not material possessions but can include, for example, good friends, a sense of humour, good health. Then ask students to think about things that are not helpful to them and they would like to leave behind, such as anxiety, conflict and arguments. These go in the waste basket. The contents of the suitcase and waste basket are shared anonymously with the Circle. This activity can focus on the future of individuals and/or the future of their communities. In later Circles students might identify and discuss what would help them hold onto the positive and change the negative.

RESOURCES

The organisation Antidote seeks to shape a more emotionally literate society through its work with schools. www.antidote.org.uk. See also Antidote (2003). *The emotional literacy handbook: Promoting whole school strategies.* London: David Fulton Publishers. *Social and emotional learning update* – published by Optimus Education in the UK – is a monthly newsletter that summarises relevant educational guidance and offers articles on good practice. See www.teachingexpertise.com
Julie Reed Kochanek (2005). *Building trust for better schools: Research-based practices.* Thousand Oaks, CA: Corwin Press.

REFERENCES

Bond, L., Glover, S., Godfrey, C., Butler, H. & Patton, G.C. (2001). Building capacity for system-level change in schools: Lessons from the Gatehouse Project. *Health Education and Behaviour,* 28, 368–83.

Bronfenbrenner, U. (1979). *The ecology of human development.* Cambridge, MA: Harvard University Press.

Burgher, M.S., Barnekow-Rasmussen, V. & Rivett, D. (1999). *The European Network of Health Promoting Schools: The alliance of education and health.* Copenhagen: WHO Regional Office for Europe.

Cohen, J. (Ed.) (2001). *Caring classrooms, intelligent schools.* New York: Teachers' College Press.

Cohen, J. (2006). Social, emotional, ethical, and academic education: Creating a climate for learning, participation in democracy, and wellbeing. *Harvard Educational Review,* 76 (2), 201–37.

Delors, J. (1996). *Learning: The treasure within.* Paris: International Commission on Education for the Twenty-First Century, UNESCO.

Department for Education and Skills (DfES) (2005a). *The Steer Report. Learning behaviour: The report of the practitioners' group on school behaviour and discipline.* London: DfES.

Department for Education and Skills (DfES) (2005b). *Developing emotional health and wellbeing – a whole school approach to improving behaviour and attendance.* http://nationalstrategies.standards. dcsf.gov.uk/node/154795

Doppler, L. (2008). *Restorative practices at Rozelle Public School – a way of being and learning together.* www.schools.nsw.edu.au/studentsupport/behaviourpgrms/antibullying/casestudies/

Elias, M.J., Zins, J.E., Graczyk, P.A. & Weissberg, R.P. (2003). Implementation, sustainability and scaling up of social-emotional and academic innovations in public schools. *School Psychology Review*, 32(3), 303–19.

Fullan, M. (2003). *The moral imperative of school leadership*. Thousand Oaks, CA: Corwin Press.

Greenberg, M., Weissber, R., O'Brien, M., Zins, J., Fredericks. L., Resnik, H. & Elias, M. (2003). Enhancing school-based prevention and youth development through co-ordinated social, emotional and academic learning. *American Psychologist*, 58, 466–74.

Hattie, J. (2009). *Visible learning: A synthesis of over 800 meta-analyses relating to achievement*. London and New York: Routledge.

Hromek, R. (2004). *Planting the peace virus: Early intervention to prevent violence in schools*. Bristol: Lucky Duck Publishing.

Martin, A.J. & Dowson, M. (2009). Interpersonal relationships, motivation, engagement, and achievement: Yields for theory, current issues, and educational practice. *Review of Educational Research*, 79(1), 327–65.

McGrath, H. (2006). What research tells us about whole-school programs for preventing bullying. In H. McGrath & T. Noble (Eds), *Bullying Solutions*. Melbourne: Pearson Education.

MindMatters (2010). *The whole school approach*. www.mindmatters.edu.au/whole-school-approach/whole-student-approach/whole-student-approach-landing-page.html

Mooney, M., Barker, K., Dobia, B., Power, A., Watson, K. & Yeung, A. (2008). *Positive behaviour for learning: Investigating the transfer of a United States system into the NSW Department of Education Western Sydney Region schools: Report*. Sydney: University of Western Sydney.

Mountford, T. (2006). Restorative practices K-10. Developing an inclusive and sustainable approach. Masters thesis, University of Newcastle, New South Wales.

Noddings, N. (2002). *Educating moral people: A caring alternative to character education*. New York: Teachers College Press.

Pianta, R.C. & Walsh, D.J. (1996). *High-risk children in schools: Constructing sustaining relationships*. London and New York: Routledge.

Roffey, S. (2007). Transformation and emotional literacy: The role of school leaders in developing a caring community. *Leading & Managing*, 13(1), 16–30.

Roffey, S. (2008). Emotional literacy and the ecology of school wellbeing. *Educational and Child Psychology*, 25(2), 29–39.

Rowling, L. (2005). Health and wellbeing and the whole school community. Presentation at MindMatters conference, Sydney.

Scottish Health Promoting Schools Unit (SHPSU) (2004). *Being well – doing well*. Dundee: SHPSU.

Solomon, D., Watson, M., Battistich, V., Schaps, E. & Delucchi, K. (1996). Creating classrooms that students experience as communities. *American Journal of Community Psychology*, 24, 719–48.

Spratt, J., Shucksmith, J., Philip, K. & Watson, C. (2006). 'Part of who we are as a school should include responsibility for wellbeing': Links between the school environment, mental health and behaviour. *Pastoral Care*, September 14–21.

Sugai, G. & Horner, R. (2002). Introduction to the special series on positive behavior support in schools. *Journal of Emotional and Behavioral Disorders*, 10(3), 130–35.

Vreeman, R.C. & Carroll, A.E. (2007). A systematic review of school-based interventions to prevent bullying. *Archives of Paediatric and Adolescent Medicine*, 161, 78–88.

Weare, K. (2000). *Promoting mental, emotional and social health: A whole school approach*. London: Routledge.

Zins, J.E., Weissberg, R.P., Wang, M.C. & Walber, H. (2004). *Building academic success on social and emotional learning: What does the research say?* New York: Teachers College Press.

APPENDIX 1

ASSESSMENT SCHEDULE

SECTION 1: Are any of the following contributing to behavioural difficulties? If so they need to be addressed in conjunction with difficulties identified in Section 2.	
Sensory and physical issues	
Ability to hear	Does the student not always understand what is being said? Do they look blank, not respond, do the wrong thing? When was the last hearing test?
Ability to see	Does the student misjudge distance, put books close to their face, trip over things? When was the last sight test?
Any known medical factors	Are these contributing to behaviour? Ask families about medical history.
Physical wellbeing Is there a need to see a medical practitioner/occupational therapist?	Tiredness/lethargy/poor sleep? Indications of malnourishment? Is the student unwell? Feeling ill is not conducive to cooperative behaviour. Difficulties with fine or gross motor skills, e.g. in using writing implements or keyboards, poor eye-hand coordination, lack of confidence in sports?
Attention skills	Is the pupil very restless and fragmented in their attention? Sometimes or all the time? When is the student most engaged?
Summary What do you now know of the student's sensory and physical wellbeing? Is this contributing to the difficulties in school? Do you need to check anything out?	
Language issues Some children are slow in speaking but can understand quite well. Occasionally it is the other way round. Disordered language includes confusing meaning or not being able to locate words.	
Receptive language	Is the student having problems understanding what is being said? Do they appear to rely on copying others?
Expressive language	Are there problems communicating with others or articulating what to say? Is the student frustrated because they cannot communicate? Do they avoid asking questions and/or having conversations with peers?

History of intervention	Have there been concerns in the past? If the student has seen a speech therapist what interventions took place? Do these need to be revisited?
Second language learners	How much exposure has the student had in the language of instruction in the school? Are expectations appropriate?

Solution-focused questions	
Can the student speak in their first language at an age appropriate level?	
In which circumstances does the student communicate most effectively?	
What communication strategies are they using? Could some be usefully developed?	
How do they respond to visual cues?	

General learning difficulties	
Indicators	Difficulties in many curriculum areas? Learning at a slower pace than their peers? Needs many opportunities to practice new skills to retain them? Difficulty generalising knowledge to new contexts? Behaviour more like that of a younger child? Choosing to interact with younger students? Developmental milestones later than expected?
Questions to consider	Are pockets of ability masking a general difficulty? Is a specific difficulty (such as reading) masking overall good ability? Is behaviour challenging in all contexts or just some?

Summary
What do you now know of the student's learning and language skills?
What has already been put in place, by whom, for how long and with what success?
What else do you need to know to plan intervention?

SECTION 2: This will help you to identify areas where students are experiencing difficulty, what is going well and how you might begin to plan an intervention.	
Settling to work	
In which contexts do difficulties appear?	With all tasks or just some? With all teachers or just some?
What are the specific difficulties?	Following/complying with instructions? Remembering what to do? Not having appropriate equipment? Begins but cannot complete tasks without support? Easily distracted by others? Anxious about work being right/perfect?
Solution-focused questions	
When and under what circumstances does the student settle to work well?	

What supports their concentration to complete a task? Small steps? Predicting outcomes? Lack of distraction?	
Does the student work better with others, independently, or being directed? Does the student have the prerequisite skills for independent or cooperative work?	
Where and when does the student feel they have self-control? What supports this?	
How does the student respond when they have achieved something? Do they take responsibility for their success?	

Summary
What do you now know about how best support to the student in settling and completing work? Is this a priority area for intervention?

General disruptive behaviour/silliness/attention seeking/self-esteem issues

Observable factors	What does the student actually do that is problematic?
Measures	How often do they do this, for how long and with what intensity?
Context	What is happening before and after the behaviour? Task expectations/peers/ teacher instructions and response?
Connections with learning areas	Does the behaviour only occur in certain situations? What are these?

Solution-focused questions

When is the student actively engaged?	
How often do they do this and for how long?	
What are the contextual factors that support this? (See above.) Does the student behave well in lessons that do not threaten their self-esteem?	

Summary
What do you now know about the student's disruptive behaviour, what might be contributing to this and how best to take action to reduce this? Is this a priority area for intervention?

Social difficulties, making and maintaining positive relationships; being collaborative	
Student behaviour	Does the student appear to want to connect with others? How do they approach them? Do they make friends but not know how to maintain a positive relationship? What happens when they are asked to work with others?
Behaviour of peers	Do peers accept or reject this student?

Context	Does the student only have difficulties in certain contexts/ with certain peers? Which is better, structured situations in the classroom or unstructured times outside?
Solution-focused questions	
What does the student understand by friendly behaviour?	
What social skills are evident and in what circumstances?	
When does the student work or play well with others? What supports this?	
Who do they get on best with?	
Summary What do you now know about this student and their relationships with peers? What skills does the student need to learn first and how can this best be supported? Is this a priority area for intervention?	

Emotional distress: anger/anxiety/depression	
Contributing factors	Are there events in the student's life that may have affected their sense of security and psychological wellbeing? Does the student's behaviour appear to stem from perceptions of themselves and/or others that are negative?
Contextual issues	Does the student appear unhappy, stressed, or anxious much of the time or only in certain circumstances? Is difficult behaviour getting worse or better?
Passivity	Is this student very blank, unresponsive? Are there indications of emotional abuse or neglect?
Depression	Is the student self-harming or talking about it? Do they appear to be disengaged with many aspects of school life? Are they behaving in a negative way in most contexts most of the time?
Solution-focused questions	
What helps the pupil to calm down/ settle/be more positive?	
Has the student learnt any emotional regulation or coping strategies?	
What support is already in place for the student/for the family?	
When does the student seem most relaxed or happy? Who and what do they find supportive in school?	
Summary What do you know now about what is contributing to this student's emotional state and what provides emotional support to them? What are the most helpful responses? Is this an area for priority intervention? Do you need to refer on?	

Unusual or highly inappropriate behaviour	
Evidence of trauma/abuse	Does the student behave in sexually inappropriate ways? Are there indications of physical or sexual harm? Is the student scared or hyper vigilant? Do they react strongly to certain stimuli?
Autistic behaviours	Are there clusters of autistic behaviours e.g. lack of social awareness, no symbolic paly, obsessive interest, need for routine, etc?
Psychosis	Does there appear to be a disconnection with reality? Does the student appear highly stressed much of the time? Do they behave in the same way regardless of audience?

Summary
If you are concerned with any of the above you need to monitor behaviour carefully and seek specialist advice. If there is evidence of abuse you need to follow mandatory reporting procedures.

APPENDIX 2

SCHOOL WELLBEING CHECKLIST

Give a rating from 1 to 5 on the following. 1 is low, 'never' or 'not at all' and 5 is high, 'always' or 'absolutely'. Sometimes the answer will be 'it depends!' This provides useful information. This checklist is for understanding where your school is at, what has been achieved and where you might go next. Look at it again in a year and see what differences have occurred.

Wellbeing vision					
There is agreement on the meaning and importance of wellbeing	1	2	3	4	5
There is a shared vision and direction for the school that reflects this	1	2	3	4	5
School leaders are driving the agenda on wellbeing	1	2	3	4	5
All stakeholders are fully consulted and feel part of the process	1	2	3	4	5
Each person is valued as a unique individual with qualities and skills to offer	1	2	3	4	5
There is a strong focus on developing positive relationships at all levels	1	2	3	4	5
A positive climate					
People enjoy working in this school	1	2	3	4	5
Students enjoy learning in this school	1	2	3	4	5
Staff feel respected and valued	1	2	3	4	5
All students feel respected and valued in all classrooms	1	2	3	4	5
The school climate is calm and purposeful	1	2	3	4	5
The overall atmosphere is warm, friendly and responsive	1	2	3	4	5
There is an inclusive ethos (we all belong here)	1	2	3	4	5
There is a strengths and solution-focused approach	1	2	3	4	5

The whole school is a 'no put-down' zone	1	2	3	4	5
Diversity is explored and celebrated through whole school and class practice	1	2	3	4	5
Everyone takes responsibility for maintaining a positive climate	1	2	3	4	5
There is a celebration of a wide range of student achievements	1	2	3	4	5
There is regular acknowledgement of a range of staff contributions	1	2	3	4	5
Communication					
Information channels are open, efficient and constructive. People know what is happening.	1	2	3	4	5
Conversations are respectful of students and families	1	2	3	4	5
Communications home are primarily positive	1	2	3	4	5
In general there are more positive than negative statements	1	2	3	4	5
Pedagogy					
Cooperative learning is well planned and happens regularly in all classrooms	1	2	3	4	5
There is bi-directional feedback between teachers and students	1	2	3	4	5
Students are encouraged to develop learning goals and aim for personal bests	1	2	3	4	5
Teaching approaches incorporate and respond to multiple intelligences	1	2	3	4	5
Tasks are differentiated to ensure all students experience progress	1	2	3	4	5
Management					
Senior management are approachable	1	2	3	4	5
Staff feel their views matter and are taken into consideration	1	2	3	4	5
Staff who are struggling are offered non judgemental support	1	2	3	4	5
Problematic issues are actively and constructively addressed	1	2	3	4	5
There are support networks for staff and mentoring for new staff	1	2	3	4	5
All students are given a voice in individual, class and school decisions	1	2	3	4	5
There are peer support networks for students	1	2	3	4	5

Collaboration is fostered throughout the school	1	2	3	4	5
Embedding social and emotional learning					
Social and emotional competencies are modelled by staff	1	2	3	4	5
Social and emotional learning is integral to the life of the school	1	2	3	4	5
Social and emotional skills are actively encouraged in students	1	2	3	4	5
The pedagogy for SEL emphasises thinking, doing and talking with others	1	2	3	4	5
Appropriate assertiveness is taught and encouraged	1	2	3	4	5
There are opportunities for all students to develop and practice leadership skills	1	2	3	4	5
Behavioural issues					
There are high expectations for pro-social behaviour across the school	1	2	3	4	5
Both difficulties and solutions are seen as the outcome of interactive factors – not just situated within the student	1	2	3	4	5
The emphasis is on promoting and reinforcing positive behaviours	1	2	3	4	5
Behavioural policies are congruent with relational and wellbeing values	1	2	3	4	5
Students are given agency for developing behavioural guidelines	1	2	3	4	5
Difficult behaviour is seen as reflective of student need	1	2	3	4	5
Staff know how to reduce conflict and confrontation	1	2	3	4	5
Staff are mutually supportive and share effective strategies	1	2	3	4	5
Students are expected to take responsibility for their behaviour by taking action to repair harm	1	2	3	4	5
Parents are positioned as experts on their child and partners with the school	1	2	3	4	5

Summarising

What are the strengths of the school?

What might be a priority for change and development?

INDEX

SUCCESSFUL TEACHING 14-19

Theory, Practice and Reflection

Warren Kidd and **Gerry Czerniawski** *both at University of East London*

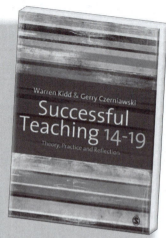

Are you looking for a complete training manual, to get you through your assignments, help you on your teaching practice and support you in your first teaching job?

For trainee teachers studying to teach the 14 to 19 age group in secondary schools and colleges, this book is a practical guide covering the essential skills that must be acquired in order to successfully complete your course. Five sections cover education policy, professional skills, theory, practice and reflection. The authors provide teaching ideas that work, and that will help trainee teachers to improve their grades and lesson observation profiles. There is a clear explanation of the theoretical underpinning that must be grasped in order to pass written assignments, and Masters level debates are addressed throughout the book, with a dedicated chapter exploring academic themes and issues. The book is also packed with ideas for classroom activities.

All the chapters contain learning objectives, discussion points, examples from practice, Masters level extensions (for those studying at that level) and suggestions for further reading. Suitable for all those studying to teach the 14 to 19 age range, this book is ideal for those on Secondary PGCE, PGDE and GTP courses leading to QTS, those studying for the post-compulsory sector PTLLS, DTLLS and CTLLS qualifications and those doing Overseas Teacher Training and Teach First courses.

 March 2010 • 320 pages
Cloth (978-1-84860-712-5)
Paper (978-1-84860-713-2)

ALSO FROM SAGE

CONTEMPORARY ISSUES IN LEARNING AND TEACHING

Edited by **Margery McMahon**, **Christine Forde** and **Margaret Martin** *all at University of Glasgow*

Contemporary Issues in Learning and Teaching looks at current issues across the three key areas of policy, learning and practice. It will help you to think critically on your Education course, and to make connections between the processes of learning and the practicalities of teaching. The book addresses key issues in primary, secondary and special education, and includes examples from all four countries of the UK.

The contributors reflect on current thinking and policy surrounding learning and teaching, and what it means to be a teacher today. Looking at the practice of teaching in a wider context allows you to explore some of the issues you will face, and the evolving expectations of your role in a policy-led environment. The book focuses on core areas of debate including:

- education across different contexts and settings
- teaching in an inclusive environment
- Continuing Professional Development (CPD) for practitioners

Each chapter follows the same accessible format. They contain case studies and vignettes providing examples and scenarios for discussion; introduction and summary boxes listing key issues and concepts explored in the chapter; key questions for discussion reflection; and further reading.

This essential text will be ideal for undergraduate and postgraduate courses, including BEd//BA degrees, initial teacher-training courses, and Masters in Education programmes.

All editors and contributors are based in the Faculty of Education at Glasgow University, UK.

November 2010 • 232 pages
Cloth (978-1-84920-127-8)
Paper (978-1-84920-128-5)

ALSO FROM SAGE

CHILDREN'S RIGHTS IN PRACTICE

Edited by **Phil Jones** *University of Leeds* and
Gary Walker *Leeds Metropolitan University*

Considering the rights of the child is now central to
good multi-agency working, and this book offers
an explanation of the theoretical issues and the
key policy developments that have impacted on
practice. It allows the reader to develop a deep
understanding of children's rights in relation to their
role in working with children and young people.
Looking at education, health, social care and
welfare, it bridges the gap between policy and
practice for children from Birth to 19.

Chapters cover:

- the child's right to play
- youth justice and children's rights
- the voice of the child
- ethical dilemmas in different contexts
- involvement, participation and decision making
- safeguarding and child protection
- social justice and exclusion

This book helps the reader understand what constitutes good practice, whilst
considering the advantages and tension of working across disciplines.

Essential reading for students on Early Years, Early Childhood Studies and
Childhood and Youth courses, it is equally relevant to professionals working across
education, health and social work.

April 2011 • 224 pages
Cloth (978-1-84920-379-1)
Paper (978-1-84920-380-7)

ALSO FROM SAGE